D0407827

Advance Praise for *The Comey Gang*

"John Ligato holds nothing back. I worked with him undercover and John is absolutely fearless whether it's with some mob guy or a bogus bureaucrat. *The Comey Gang* is the definitive book how the FBI lost its way under James Comey."

—Joe Pistone, FBI Special Agent,
Retired (aka "Donnie Brasco")

"I've supervised John Ligato and he's one of a kind. His Marine Corps experience made him a tenacious and mission-oriented FBI agent. John was one of the Bureau's best undercover operatives and I was always glad that John Ligato was part of my team."

—Anthony Daniels,
FBI Assistant Director, Retired

"I served with John Ligato in Vietnam. Lance Corporal Ligato was with the lead contingent of Marines into Hue City during the '68 Tet Offensive. Though wounded several times, John refused medical evacuation and distinguished himself on the battlefield. Believe what he says."

—Major General Ray "E-Tool" Smith,
USMC, Retired

OTHER BOOKS BY JOHN LIGATO

Lerza's Lives: Undercover Work Can Be Dangerous and Danger Can Be Seductive, St. Martin's Press, under John Danica (pseudonym), with Lucy Freeman

Dirty Boys, Post Hill Press

The Near Enemy, Post Hill Press

The Gunny, JohnCanley.com (Medal of Honor recipient)

THE
COMEY GANG

AN INSIDER'S LOOK AT
AN FBI IN CRISIS

JOHN LIGATO

Post Hill
PRESS

A POST HILL PRESS BOOK
ISBN: 978-1-64293-296-6
ISBN (eBook): 978-1-64293-297-3

The Comey Gang:
An Insider's Look at an FBI in Crisis
© 2019 by John Ligato
All Rights Reserved

Cover art by Cody Corcoran

Post Hill Press
New York • Nashville
posthillpress.com

Published in the United States of America

ACKNOWLEDGMENTS

My home was badly damaged by Hurricane Florence, but in a strange way that storm proved a blessing in disguise. The kindness shown by friends, neighbors, *and* strangers was humbling as they literally pushed the river from our home. It *somewhat* restored my faith in humanity. The Marines of Camp Lejeune were at their Semper Fi best in helping an old jarhead brother. *Once a Marine...*

The hurricane was a reminder that wood, drywall, and shingles are replaceable. Keep your friends and family close to you as the days turn into weeks, months, and years.

Thanks to the women in my life who keep me grounded—my wife Lorri; daughters, Gia and Dani; and my sister, Florence—as well as my extended family of friends who have influenced me throughout my life: Tony Daniels, James Kallstrom, Gordan Batcheller, Joe Pistone, and all the retired Marines who make fun of me while playing golf. Anthony Ziccardi and the group at Post Hill Press have been great to work with, and a shout-out to my agent Swifty Lazar. Thanks to Carey Hawkins, who keeps me grammatically tuned.

Thanks to my brother Marines of Alpha Company who served with valor at Hue City, Vietnam, during the '68 Tet Offensive. During the first week of that thirty-one-day battle, Alpha Marines received 504 Purple Hearts, and Sergeant Gonzalez and Gunny Canley were each the recipient of the Medal of Honor. And to all the Marines and military who protect us from the barbarians at our gate, thank you.

DEDICATION

This book is a testament to the men and women of law enforcement. They have a thankless job but do it despite liberal mayors who order them to stand down while rocks whiz past their heads. They protect the public no matter their color or creed *and* despite the noise made by politicians and media who rush to judge minus any facts.

To the brick agents of the FBI who ignore all the noise from inside the Beltway and do their job every day and night.

This book has been vetted by the FBI prepublication unit.

CONTENTS

Mount Olympus

"I cannot trust a man to control others
who cannot control himself."
—Robert E. Lee

Gang: *An organized group of criminals.*

Inspector General Michael Horowitz produced a five-hundred-page report regarding the actions of the FBI and Department of Justice concerning the 2016 presidential election.

It could have been reduced to just thirty words:

"An honorable FBI has been tainted by the mishandling of the Clinton investigation by former director James Comey and corrupted by the blatant political bias of officials working beneath him."

The individuals currently occupying the seventh floor of the Hoover Building have a problem. It involves a major restoration project to repair the FBI's reputation. But they seem to be painting some walls while ignoring the cracks in the foundation.

FBI headquarters and the field sometime suffer from a toxic relationship. Public-sector giants like General Motors understand the bottom line in business. Their basic mission is to sell cars at *local* dealerships, which translates into profits. The corporate office recognizes that its very survival depends on the *field's* success and therefore makes every effort to support them.

The FBI's *basic* mission is putting bad people in jail, but headquarters has an identity crisis. They've never fully accepted their role as *support* to the field. Brick agents generally consider HQ a hurdle to clear in accomplishing the mission. The Mueller-Comey era raised that bar. There's been an ongoing disconnect between the folks inside the Beltway and the field divisions. This impasse was considered a mild rash until James Comey began scratching away.

The disease could be classified as "Beltway delusion" since the symptoms include a belief that decisions made at HQ are divinely inspired.

An outbreak of this illness was Comey's decision to conduct the Hillary Clinton email "*matter*" from the throne room. Investigations are normally conducted by field divisions, so why deviate on this case? Perhaps the director wanted to *personally* select a team of highly principled investigators. Or maybe he just wanted to stack the deck.

Peter Strzok and Lisa Page were key players on both the email and Russian collusion cases. Their texts were well publicized and reveal a loathing toward candidate Donald Trump. When questioned about this bias, both insisted that they were part of a team and couldn't have influenced the *entire* group. Strzok paints an image of ten *impartial* FBI agents with diverse views sitting at a conference table and evaluating evidence. But few people are aware of the backgrounds of this supposedly unbiased unit.

Inspector General Horowitz released a few of the team's instant messages (IM).

Sally Moyer is Agent #5. She instant messaged her boyfriend, Agent #1:

"I would rather have brunch with a bunch of his [Trump's] supporters like the ones from ohio that are retarded." A later Moyer IM proclaimed, "Screw you trump. wheeeeeeeeeeeeeeeeeeeeeeeeeeeee."

Sally's boyfriend, Agent #1, replied with: "I find anyone who enjoys [supports] Trump an absolute fucking idiot."

The inspector general identified other FBI investigators on the team who harbored similar feelings toward President Trump. But all claimed that their *intense* hatred of the president had no effect on their forgone conclusion that Hillary Clinton was innocent of all criminal acts.

Ironically, it was Vladimir Putin who said, "Those who fight corruption should be clean themselves."

How did the Comey Gang evolve? What factors aligned to place this single-minded group at the same place and time in history? Whether it was a fluke, fate, or a planned coup, the result was an uppercut to the jaw of the Federal Bureau of Investigation. The Bureau is *still* staggering. The Comey Gang didn't occur overnight. The forewarnings were ignored but included the FBI's merger with the Justice Department, a change in culture, poor leadership, and other subtle shifts in the FBI's DNA.

Many will claim that the Comey Gang is no different from previous FBI leadership teams. They'd be wrong and here's an example why this group was much more destructive to our core values. Deputy Director McCabe purchased a $70,000 conference table, which seems like an expensive piece of polished mahogany. The public would've forgiven this over indulgence with a simple "*My bad,*" but the Comey Gang attempted to hide that embarrassing purchase. The Senate Judiciary Committee subpoenaed texts between Peter Strzok and Lisa Page but received a heavily redacted document under the *guise* of national security. The conference table was later discovered in *unredacted* versions. This may *seem* like the all too common occurrence of bureaucrats camouflaging their bad judgment, but the Federal Bureau of Investigation is synonymous with **F**idelity, **B**ravery, and *Integrity*. Hiding an embarrassing decision under the umbrella of our national security is cowardly and deceitful.

That black ink used to conceal a needless lie became a permanent stain on the Bureau's soul. This one incident exposes much deeper integrity issues inside *The Comey Gang*. If we deceive the public about something as trivial as a table, then it's an easy transition to conceal perjury, leaking, obstruction, and *corruption*.

CHAPTER 1:

The ABCs (Anybody but Clinton)

"It's called karma, and it's pronounced,
ah, ah…screw you!"

July 5, 2016, FBI HQ

I grab a cup of coffee and await the news conference. I'm psyched that Hillary Clinton is about to contract a heavy dose of karma. Our former secretary of state committed multiple felonies involving use of her private email server. Comey could even add perjury to her felony tab, but hey, why get greedy. The email debacle is a slam dunk, since the government need only prove two simple elements: that she stored classified stuff on a private server. Her highness has already admitted as much, so bring out the fat lady and cue up the band.

FBI director James Comey makes his entrance and begins with, "Good morning. I'm here to give you an update on the FBI's investigation of Secretary Clinton's use of a personal email system during her time as secretary of state."

I think, *Enough with updates; get the gas pellets ready.*

The FBI director stares earnestly at the camera. Jimmy Comey seems like the "all-American" guy who was probably an Eagle Scout and volunteered at a nursing home. Comey might have even passed muster with my Italian father when picking up my sister, Florence, for a date. This is the type of guy you'd want as a next-door neighbor. He'd probably lend me tools, and we'd drink beer in the backyard.

The director says, "After a tremendous amount of work over the last year, the FBI is completing its investigation, and what I would like to do today is tell you three things: what we did, what we found, and what we are recommending to the Department of Justice."

Did he just say, "*Recommending* to Justice"? The FBI never *announces* our recommendations to Justice. We are a fact-finding agency, and our job is to gather evidence, write a prosecution report, and hand it to Justice. They then review the facts and have the final say on whether to decline prosecution or convene a grand jury. That's been the official sequence since J. Edgar Hoover, and with good reason. Because if the FBI *publicly* recommends non-prosecution *prior* to Justice, they just tainted the jury pool should Justice disagree with them. In other words, the FBI becomes the *final* arbiter and essentially a branch of the Justice Department. The result is the loss of our arm's-length distance from the politically infested Justice Department *and* our independence. I rationalize in my mind, *That could never happen*, but my brain is flashing warning signals: *Danger, Will Robinson. Danger!*

Comey continues, "This will be an unusual statement in at least a couple ways. I have not coordinated or reviewed this statement in any way with the Department of Justice or any other part of the government. They do not know what I am about to say. From the group of 30,000 emails returned to the State Department, 110 emails in 52 email chains have been determined by the owning agency to contain classified information at the time they were sent or received. Eight of those chains contained information that was classified top secret. Some emails had been deleted over the years, but we found traces of them on devices."

I'm temporarily reassured since Comey is laying out a powerful case for prosecution. He just summarized Title 18, Section 793(f) of the federal code, which simply makes it unlawful to send or store classified information on personal email. Hillary also lied under oath when she repeatedly testified that she *never* sent or received classified material on her private server.

Comey explains: "Seven email chains concern matters that were classified at the Top Secret/Special Access Program level when they were sent and received. There is evidence to support a conclusion that any reasonable person in Secretary Clinton's position should have known that an unclassified system was no place for that conversation."

Comey drones on in a monotone generally reserved for NPR hosts. I nod my head in agreement as he mentions that Hillary was *extremely* careless. It never occurs to me at the time that his choice of words will put a permanent stain on the integrity of the FBI. It will have the additional consequence of further absorbing the FBI into the DNA of the Justice Department.

But for now, it appears that Lady Justice is about to whack Hillary upside her head with the scales of justice. The FBI may have given Eric Holder a perjury pass and ignored criminal charges against Lois Lerner, James Clapper, Loretta Lynch, and Bill Clinton, but all that selective prosecution crap is over. There's a new sheriff in town, and his name is James *Fu**in'* Comey.

The FBI director concludes with, "Although there is evidence of potential violations of the statutes regarding the handling of classified information, our judgment is that no reasonable prosecutor would bring such a case."

The first word that involuntarily escapes my lips is "*Bullshit!*" followed shortly by "*Asshole!*" It takes me a few seconds to realize the implication of Comey's words. His official tone, facial expression, and words all scream *guilty*! But his last eight words do not compute.

A year later it surfaces that Comey took a dive for the Clintons. He threw the fight, no different than some palooka who flops in the tenth round for cash and hookers. Memos surface that the FBI director determined Clinton's innocence prior to concluding the investigation. As a retired FBI agent, I can confirm that this investigative technique was generally frowned upon in my FBI. Comey had Peter Strzok wordsmith a May 2, 2016, memo changing his original term "gross negligence" to "extreme carelessness." Though this may be an accurate description of Lady Clinton's actions, the subtle distinction was part of an ongoing conspiracy by the highest ranking officials in the Justice Department. Those two words downgraded a felony to an image of some doddering, well-meaning old lady who accidentally hit *delete* over thirty thousand times.

Rationalizations why Comey took one for the team ring hollow on most retired agents. He knew what he was doing, and the facts are the facts. Hillary stored classified material on an unauthorized server, destroyed thousands of emails, and lied to Congress, the FBI, and the public. Those are the facts *and* a violation of law.

This verbal sleight of hand made Comey guilty of selective prosecution, which is cherry-picking on who does a five-spot at Lewisburg Federal Penitentiary. Even if we accept Comey's tortured interpretation that a person must *intend* to violate the law, the evidence is conclusive that Clinton *knew* she was committing a crime. How do we know? On January 22, 2009, Hillary Clinton signed a document titled "Classified Information Nondisclosure Agreement," which states in *very* plain language:

> I hereby accept the obligations [that in] consideration
> of my being granted access to classified information…

marked or unmarked…[it] will remain the property of, or under the control of the…Government….

…I shall return all classified materials…

…any breach of this Agreement…may constitute a violation of United States criminal laws…sections 641, 793, 794, 798, ★952 and 1924, title 18, United States Code.

This agreement, which I've also signed, leaves no doubt that Hillary violated the law, and Comey forgave her. Then, one year later, Comey violated the same law. One need not be an attorney, like Hillary and Comey, to understand the consequences of breaking a federal law—although lately that depends on your political party.

The question becomes, *why* did senior FBI officials soil their oath for their ideology? If you want the answers, then I'll tell you *how* it happened.

CHAPTER 2:

It's Just a Flesh Wound

"What the hell is going on here!"
—Vince Lombardi

My name is John Ligato, and I'm a retired FBI agent. That job title used to elicit respectful nods even when I was handcuffing some mope. But FBI headquarters recently stained my beloved institution. It wasn't just a slight blemish but rather an explosive diarrhea that will take years of legal disinfectant to sanitize. "*Clean up on aisle seven.*"

I single out the Comey Gang who occupied the seventh floor since that's where the stench emanated. The Bureau recruits from the human race, so we've had our share of bad apples. This includes killers, thieves, drug dealers, wife swappers, and even a few spies. But these were isolated cases who were *swiftly* exiled from our rolls. The public forgave us as soon as we rounded up the next drug operation.

So, what's different this time, and how did it happen? How did the core leadership of the finest law enforcement agency evolve into a bunch of banana republic goons? Fortunately, their attempt at a bloodless coup failed because they were an inept pack of amateurs who used their positions of trust to short-circuit the will of the people. That may be business as usual in Uganda, but it's unprecedented in the United States of America. They came *damn* close. A few votes here or there in Pennsylvania, Michigan, and Ohio probably saved the republic.

This book is *not* intended as a hit job on my alma mater. That would be unfair to the brick agents who are the heart and soul of the FBI. I squarely place the blame for our worst crisis on 935 Pennsylvania Avenue NW, Washington, DC. The Comey Gang abandoned their principles and traded *our* neutrality for *their* ideology.

Working agents had always tolerated these headquarters interlopers and considered them a temporary inconvenience. Field divisions learn how to maneuver through the bureaucratic minefields laid by headquarters. Initially, Comey seemed like any another footnote to our stellar 110-year history, but he was much more destructive than anyone could have imagined.

The Comey Gang could've never happened thirty years ago. It was a perfect storm of events and personalities that nearly sank the *Queen Elizabeth* of law enforcement.

The broad strokes of what went wrong include a merger with the Justice Department that blurred the lines between the two agencies. This union generated a chain reaction that undermined the Bureau's independence and neutrality. Our blended new family included the FBI hierarchy of Comey, Strzok, Page, Andrew McCabe, and James Baker, who conspired with the Justice Department honchos of Bruce Ohr, Loretta Lynch, Eric Holder, and Sally Yates.

Justice Department attorneys had no business being inside the same room with FBI agents when they interviewed Hillary. It was an active investigation, and Attorney General Loretta Lynch was a political hack with the agenda of absolving Clinton. The mixing of politics with a criminal investigation will *always* result in a polluted outcome. Think Jussie Smollett.

There were other issues contributing to a loss in reputation and honor but it all boils down to poor leadership. The Comey Gang was composed of a bunch of *managers* pretending to be *leaders.*

This malfunction was evident when James Comey chose to investigate the email case from headquarters. The FBI's own website states that headquarters provides operational and administrative *support* to its fifty-six field divisions. One of these fifty-six field divisions is located a couple of miles from FBI HQ, so *why* did Comey decide to jump the shark?

Headquarters requires a diet and should limit its menu to the budget, lab, training, policies, procedures, inspections, and running interference with all the other alphabet agencies inside the Beltway. That should be about the extent of its role, and the benefit to the public would be an additional three hundred agents transferred back to the field.

Headquarters goes through phases of mistrusting the field even though the expertise lay in operations. After every major FBI screwup, from 9/11 to the Carter Page FISA warrant, the seventh floor follows the same remedial action plan: initiate an investigation, offer a lukewarm apology, identify a martyr with a sharp sword, and then mandate corrective training for *all* the troops. But nothing ever changes since the fault lay in the building's structure and not in its curb appeal.

General George S. Patton said, "No good decision was ever made in a swivel chair."

I describe the disconnect between the field and headquarters as a case of "Beltway delusion." It's an affliction affecting bureaucrats working within the DC Beltway in which their reality is altered. They can no longer relate to individuals below their pay grade. If you doubt that Beltway delusion is real, then consider the following statement by Deputy Director McCabe following Comey's dismissal:

We are a large organization, we are 36,500 people across this country, across this globe. We have a diversity of opinions about many things. But I can confidently tell you that the majority, the *vast* majority, of FBI employees enjoyed a deep and positive connection to Director Comey.

Mr. McCabe should've picked up a phone and called some brick agent in New York City for a second opinion.

Months prior to the 9/11 attacks, Minneapolis FBI agents sent over seventy communications to HQ predicting a major terrorist attack using aircraft as weapons. FBI HQ rejected *every* request, which highlighted their lack of trust in the field and serves as an example of Beltway delusion. HQ's habit to set policy and then conduct the investigation from a distance should've been a warning to the next FBI director.

The following is an excerpt from a 2002 letter Agent Coleen Rowley penned to then FBI director Robert Mueller. It followed a major intelligence failure *by HQ* when the Minneapolis Division begged for a warrant that may have prevented the 9/11 attacks.

Dear Director Mueller,   May 21, 2002

Your plans for an FBI Headquarters' "Super Squad" simply fly in the face of an honest appraisal of the FBI's pre-September 11th failures. The Phoenix and Minneapolis office reacted remarkably well regarding the terrorist threats they uncovered or were made aware of *pre*-September 11th. [Emphasis on *pre* in the original.] The same cannot be said for the FBI Headquarters' bureaucracy and you want to expand that?! Should we put the counterterrorism unit chief and SSA who previously handled the Moussaoui matter in charge of the new "Super Squad"?! There's no denying the need for more and better intelligence but you should think carefully about how much gate keeping power should be entrusted with *any* HQ entity. If we are indeed in a "war", shouldn't the Generals be on the battlefield instead of sitting in a spot removed from the action while still attempting to call the shots?

Sincerely,
Coleen M. Rowley, Special Agent and
Minneapolis Chief Division Counsel

The Comey Gang had its seeds planted at the time of the terrorist attacks on 9/11.

There had been periodic attempts by the Justice Department to control FBI investigations going back to Bobby Kennedy. We'd always been able to repel those breaches to our perimeter, but on July 5, 2001, Bob Mueller was appointed the sixth full-time director of the FBI.

Mueller was a product of the Justice Department and gradually initiated a series of policies, procedures, and guidelines that essentially merged the FBI with Justice. It wasn't a hostile takeover but rather a subtle transformation. At the conclusion of Mueller's tenure as FBI director, agents required Justice Department approval to do their jobs. And to consolidate the takeover, James Comey became the seventh director of the Federal Bureau of Investigation.

This shotgun wedding has at times been disastrous and not without human consequences. A Justice Department civil rights attorney may have ignored evidence of an honor killing for fear of antagonizing Muslims post 9/11, and there's the curious case of Tom McHale. These and other incidents reveal the mind-set at headquarters, whose attitude at times has bordered on an arrogant omnipotence.

Hoover ran a closed shop and wouldn't tolerate outside interference, whether from a politician, attorney general, or president. This maintained our image as impartial crimefighters. Though occasionally dysfunctional, we remained proud members of the FBI family. Our squabbles remained among family members until Robert Mueller. The new FBI director, who came from the Justice Department, brought with him that culture. It was when the Bureau lost its autonomy that the family unit began to crumble.

In June 2013, President Barack Obama nominated James Comey to succeed Robert Mueller as FBI director. His ten-year appointment was confirmed the following month by a 93–1 count in the Senate.

Roman Catholic dissident John Wycliffe said, "The higher the monkey climbs, the more he shows his tail."

CHAPTER 3:

The Strzok-Page Chronicles

"Just went to a Southern Virginia Walmart.
I could SMELL the Trump support."
—text from Peter Strzok to Lisa Page

The inspector general's report answered a question inquiring minds wanted to know: Why did Lisa Page and Peter Strzok engage in hundreds of conversations vilifying Donald Trump and discussing FBI cases from their *work* cell phones?

Page explained to investigators that the reason was personal: "The predominant reason that we communicated on our work phones was because we were trying to keep our affair a secret from our spouses."

FBI director Louie Freeh addressed extramarital affairs in written guidelines two decades prior to the Strzok-Page get-together. Regarding sexual activity, Freeh stressed that an "extramarital affair that is concealed from a spouse may create a vulnerability to blackmail or coercion."

The bottom line is that sexual activity *might* be investigated and could be grounds for dismissal if an employee becomes vulnerable to coercion, espionage, or theft of documents.

Most agents are not too concerned with office romances. Special Agent Peter Strzok and FBI attorney Lisa Page were doing the happy happy, sometimes referred to the horizontal polka. This is not unusual in most workplaces, and FBI employees are not immune to infidelity. It happens. The couplings rarely result in disciplinary action since it occurs up and down the chain of command.

Many news commentators salivated whenever they'd lead with, "The two FBI lovebirds," but that was *never* the story. The Page/Strzok sexual liaison had *zero* influence on the email or Russian collusion investigations. In all likelihood their intimacy provided them freedom to express their true feelings about Trump in texts. You tend to hold nothing back with a person with whom you share bodily fluids.

It wasn't the sex so much as their occupation as FBI employees that caused a constitutional crisis. Two coworkers at General Motors can indulge in a deep hatred for their boss but do not have access to badges and subpoena power. In that regard, "the two FBI lovebirds" who vowed to uphold the Constitution went the way of Benedict Arnold. Perhaps not technically traitors, but damn close.

An investigator must view the totality of the evidence when working a case. An anonymous individual wrote, "Watch your thoughts, they become your words, and watch your words, they become your *actions*." Strzok, Page, and McCabe were in the unique position to turn their words into action, and their actions surrounding the FISA warrant and email case are highly suspicious.

Many of their private texts were made public, and a few constitute valid circumstantial evidence going to motive of a crime. They cannot logically be explained away by reasonable individuals, although Strzok gave it a go.

If the FBI agent investigating you for criminal acts called you an "enormous douche" and a "fucking idiot," would you trust them to be impartial? Those are fighting words in South Philly, but those exact words were in texts aimed at candidate Trump. Another text from FBI attorney Page to Agent Strzok stated that "maybe you're meant to stay where you are because you're meant to protect the country from that menace."

The menace the two are referring to is the president of the United States.

The definition of a menace is "a person or thing that is likely to cause harm; a *threat* or *danger*." These two FBI agents, with no evidence to the contrary, felt that the duly elected president of the United States was a threat or danger.

Put yourself in a similar situation where you could stop someone who threatened your values, home, and family. They considered Donald Trump that person. Could you remain objective if presented with the opportunity to stop him? Their feelings go directly to motive, and at that point in time any ethical FBI agent would recuse themselves from investigating someone they held in such contempt.

Judges frequently recuse themselves for having very minor or remote connections to defendants to avoid even the appearance of impropriety. Imagine a judge being assigned a case where, prior to the trial, they stated that they felt the defendant was a *fucking idiot* and a *menace*. Would it matter that he expressed these feelings in a private text?

Peter Strzok called the shots on both the Hillary exoneration and the FISA warrant leading to the bogus charge of Russian collusion. But let's give the "two FBI lovebirds" the benefit of the doubt since Strzok stated under oath, "I guess I didn't feel like I was doing anything wrong. I'm an American. We have the First Amendment. I'm entitled to an opinion."

Peter Strzok is correct, but when actions follow words, then criminal violations occur. Take the two coworkers from GM who go drinking after work and confess a deep hatred of their boss. The liquor flows and around midnight the two drunks decide that they should kill the SOB.

"We'll poison his coffee tomorrow."

"My cousin's an exterminator and has a truck filled with pesticides."

The overwhelming majority of these alcohol-induced conversations go nowhere. The drunks wake up the next morning and chuckle when they see each other at work. But what would be their criminal liability if they'd secured enough pesticide to kill their boss? In legalese, that's called an *overt* act in the furtherance of a conspiracy to commit murder. And that's a problem.

Strzok and Page had numerous electronic conversations stating their intention to stop Trump from becoming president using their position as FBI employees.

One such example is a Strzok text, "I want to believe the path u threw out 4 consideration in Andy's office-that there's no way he gets elected-but I'm afraid we *can't* take that risk. It's like an *insurance policy* in unlikely event u die be4 you're 40."

A second text exchange from Page text to Peter Strzok:

"(Trump's) not ever going to become president, right? Right?!" Strzok: "No. No he's not. We'll stop it."

These unambiguous words indicate their *intent* to violate the law but it's still not a crime. The second element required is taking *overt* acts to accomplish that intent. At that point Strzok and Page would violate several federal statutes. Did they take any actions to place legal pesticide in Trump's coffee?

Retired FBI agent Michael M. Biasello feels that "the *accommodations* afforded Clinton and her aides are unprecedented." He added, "which is another way of saying this outcome was by design." He called Comey's decision not to seek charges "cowardly." Comey has single-handedly ruined the reputation of the organization.

Fact: Comey limited the email investigation by agreeing to unheard-of ground rules and other demands by the lawyers for Clinton and her aides. A suspect's *attorney* can make demands that must be considered under due process, but some aide making demands would be politely informed to "shut the fuck up." Comey committed overt acts that negatively affected the investigation.

Dennis Hughes, the first chief of the FBI's computer investigations unit, stated that "in my twenty-five years with the Bureau, I never had any ground rules in my interviews." There's an old saying among Marines that if you're going to get into a fight, then you fight to win. Restricted rules of engagement get people killed.

Fact: Instead of going to federal prosecutors and insisting on using grand jury leverage to compel testimony and seize evidence, Comey allowed immunity for several key witnesses, including potential targets. The immunity agreements came with outrageous side deals, including preventing agents from searching for any documents on a Dell laptop owned by former Clinton chief of staff Cheryl Mills. These documents were generated *after* January 31, 2015, when she communicated with the server administrator who destroyed subpoenaed emails.

Any law enforcement agency who recommends immunity in exchange for testimony does so only if the individual has information leading to bigger fish in the case. The bargaining chip is that you will avoid legal jeopardy *if* you tell the *whole* truth.

An agent in the Washington Field Office said, "There's a perception that the FBI has been politicized and let down the country. Comey has turned a once-proud institution known for its independence into one that bows to election pressure, hands out political immunity to candidates, and effectively pardons their coconspirators. He's turned the FBI into the Federal Bureau of Immunity and lost the trust and respect of not only his agents but the country at large."

Fact: Comey cut a deal to give Clinton a "voluntary" witness interview on a major holiday weekend. The final interview in any major case is usually with the main subject, and contrary to AG Loretta "call it a matter" Lynch, Hillary Clinton was under *investigation* for violating the law. But Comey schedules the interview on a July 4 holiday weekend. And in another serious breach of protocol, he permits Cheryl

Mills, her former chief of staff, to sit in on the interview as a lawyer. But Mills was *also* under investigation, and this is *never* allowed for the most obvious of reasons.

Clinton's interview lasted three and a half hours, which is a world record given that it takes an hour and a half to meet and greet, exchange pleasantries, review the ground rules, take a potty break, and offer up some coffee and snacks. Agents had at their disposal thousands of statements that Hillary provided under oath to congressional committees in addition to television interviews and random print and media news reports. The review of these previous statements, many of which contradicted themselves, would lead to a two-day session at minimum. Mrs. Clinton also experienced over *forty* bouts of amnesia during the interview yet wasn't called back for questioning or subpoenaed before a grand jury.

Fact: Comey ordered Cheryl Mills's laptop destroyed after a very restricted search, denying Congress the chance to look at it and making the FBI an accomplice to the destruction of evidence. This action speaks volumes about Comey's intent. In a case where there is no recommended prosecution, the FBI would return Mills's laptop since it would not be evidence. If the FBI ultimately indicted Hillary, then the laptop would be considered evidence, and evidence is never destroyed until the case is fully adjudicated, and then only with a court order. This strange action by Comey has *never* been discussed or explained by the media.

Fact: Comey's immunized witnesses suddenly suffered chronic memory lapses. They also invoked unsubstantiated claims of attorney-client privilege when the questions got tougher, and at least two witnesses gave false statements. Director Comey allowed this travesty of justice, but I can assure you that any FBI agent I know would have been repeating, "Are you fucking kidding me?!"

Cheryl Mills and Heather Samuelson, two members of Clinton's legal team, as well as IT geeks Paul Combetta and Bryan Pagliano, all received immunity. Why offer anyone immunity if you receive nothing in return? Immunity is a quid pro quo for becoming a snitch to avoid prosecution. But all these individuals walked instead of talked.

There seems to be an abundant amount of *overt* acts in furtherance of words, yet the Comey Gang remains unchained with *Go Fund Me* donations, book deals, and heroes' treatment on MSNBC.

There is another and better legal option in discovering the truth with reluctant witnesses. A proffer was never utilized, yet it's the most appropriate investigative option. The FBI would give up nothing, but it would dangle the same benefits as immunity. A proffer in a criminal investigation allows individuals to give the government information about crimes with *some* assurances that they'll be protected against prosecution. The unspoken words are, "I ain't after you, but you will become collateral damage if you lie or leave out anything important."

Attorneys with clients who agree to proffer have already decided to cooperate or they wouldn't be there. I've used proffers on several occasions, and they are powerful tools in finding the truth. The individual must give up someone higher up in the food chain to avoid being prosecuted. They do so under the umbrella of civility and a gentlemen's agreement that they'll skate if truthful. But if they refuse to cooperate, then a grand jury must be convened, unless you are *not* searching for the truth.

Peter Strzok probably was the affiant or directed the affiant in the Carter Page FISA warrant that was renewed four times. The affiant appeared before a judge and under oath swore that the probable cause contained in the affidavit was the truth, the *whole*, and *nothing* but the truth. These three conditions are brilliantly worded since they cover the exact sleight of hand in the original FISA affidavit. The truth may have been massaged, but the *whole* truth and nothing but the truth was raped. The affiant omitted many facts and in all likelihood perjured themselves. But selective prosecution seems to be alive and well.

Why were many of the FBI/DOJ crew who cleared Hillary being assigned to the initial Trump investigation? Remember that there was *no* connection between the two inquiries, so we'll chalk it up to coincidence. But it gets suspicious when several of those same officials were assigned to the Mueller special counsel. This is especially questionable since FBI headquarters and Main Justice rarely involve themselves directly in investigations. That's why the field exists, and the FBI has fifty-six field offices while DOJ currently has ninety-three United States attorneys.

Contrary to the liberal line that FBI agents have diverse opinions, this particular seventh floor of headquarters had *no* diverse opinions. They assembled a group of like-minded people who were unanimous in their hatred of candidate and then President Trump. And that condition resulted in a severe case of Beltway delusion. FBI management and Justice Department attorneys existed in a whimsical world of harmony minus any naysayer who would dare declare, "Mr. Comey, Ms. Lynch, I find Hillary Clinton *incredibly* guilty."

That opposing view would result in banishment from the Beltway kingdom to a far outpost west of the Mississippi River. The problem with recruiting compatible folks is a lack of an opposing view. Many of the FBI decision makers on the seventh floor were handpicked by the director.

General George Patton said, "If everybody is thinking alike, then somebody isn't thinking!"

Another example of Beltway delusion is the Andy McCabe debacle where his wife, Jill, received a $500,000 campaign contribution from a Clinton friend while the FBI had an active investigation on Hillary. FBI attorney Lisa Page met almost daily with McCabe and had she done her job, she would have sat her boss down and said, "Are you out of your fuckin' mind? This doesn't pass any smell test. You need to recuse yourself, now!"

This conversation evidently did not happen.

The Strzok-Page role as members of the Comey Gang was antithetical to the core values of the FBI. The "lovebirds" are gone from the rolls of the FBI, but there's little chance that either will be charged with conspiracy to violate election laws. The FBI has done what it always does after a crisis: admit the wrongdoing, find someone with a sharp sword, then subject all employees to remedial training so it won't happen again.

But it always does.

CHAPTER 4:

That Magnificent Bastard

"There's something addicting about a secret."
—J. Edgar Hoover

To provide some perspective on the public's loss of confidence with the FBI, one must understand how the past has influenced the present. It may surprise you that the politicization of the FBI has *always* been a concern.

Washington, DC, 1935

Attorney General Homer Cummings had a problem. The public perceived gangsters like John Dillinger and Machine Gun Kelly as folk heroes. Cummings needed advice, so he invited columnist Drew Pearson to dine with him. Cummings argued, "If the underworld came to believe that the FBI was invincible, there would be less crime."

Pearson agreed, saying, "What you need is a top-notch public relations man." The columnist recommended Henry Suydam, the Washington correspondent for the *Brooklyn Eagle*. It proved a good choice.

On August 29, 1935, Suydam was appointed assistant to the attorney general. The newspaperman utilized his media contacts to slowly mold the image of FBI agents into steely-eyed crime fighters. This transformation was bolstered one month later when George "Machine Gun" Kelly begged FBI agents, "Don't shoot me, G-men. Don't shoot!" The agents on scene had never heard that term, but Kelly later explained it was underworld slang for "government men."

The great newspaper and radio personality Walter Winchell liked the slogan and popularized the "G-man" expression. Thus, the FBI acquired an identity of superheroes who were tough, impartial, and indestructible. That image remained intact until Robert Mueller and James Comey. We'll discuss how these two FBI directors radically altered our image, but for now let's trace the FBI's early years.

Whenever I mention that the politicization of the FBI occurred during Mueller's tenure as director, someone challenges me with, "What about Hoover?!" Okay, you've got a point that J. Edgar may have practiced the Machiavellian art of politics, but he created the FBI and its reputation as the finest law enforcement agency on earth. The director wasn't always a political opportunist. It wasn't until his power became absolute that Hoover begin dabbling in subtle blackmail. But in the Bureau's infancy, J. Edgar was a magnificent bastard.

John Edgar Hoover was born on New Year's Day, 1895, down the street from the Capitol. His dad was a printer, but it was Anna Hoover who dominated the household. Edgar, as he was known at home, never married, living with his mother until her death. Young Hoover shared a short, squat body with his mom and overcame stuttering by speaking in a quick staccato manner. Only the best Bureau stenographers could take shorthand dictation from the fast-talking Hoover.

Edgar attended law school at George Washington University while working at the Library of Congress. Although he joined ROTC,

Hoover didn't enlist when the United States entered World War I, instead reporting to work at the Justice Department in 1917. With a law degree, a brilliant mind, and a manic work ethic, Hoover's rise was rapid. This nattily dressed law clerk often worked seven days a week and could cite the most tedious federal statutes verbatim.

But it was the Red Scare that catapulted Hoover into the national limelight. After the armistice, Attorney General A. Mitchell Palmer's home was bombed by an alleged Bolshevik, which prompted the creation of the General Intelligence Division. Palmer, who survived the blast, appointed John Edgar Hoover its head. The roots of the FBI, which Hoover was to eventually lead for almost forty years, go back a decade before he joined the Justice Department. In 1908, Attorney General Charles Bonaparte had requested funds for a "small permanent detective force." Congress turned him down, citing the temptation of a permanent police force evolving into a secret police. Bonaparte's response was foretelling given the Mueller-Comey FBI era. The AG promised Congress that his force would "*never* be used for political purposes." One congressman prophetically observed that the day may come when these secret police might hide things from Congress.

Unlike his great uncle, Napoleon Bonaparte, the AG refused to accept defeat and secretly recruited nine Secret Service agents and fourteen support staff. Thus, the embryo of the FBI was created. Two years later, Bonaparte was succeeded as attorney general by George Wickersham, who christened the group the Bureau of Investigation (BI). By 1912, the BI grew to one hundred men, but one congressman referred to them as "an odd-job detective agency with fuzzy lines of authority and responsibility."

Stanley Finch, the BI's first director, was later succeeded by William Burns, a sixty-two-year-old former Secret Service chief suffering from mild senility. Intel chief John Hoover recognized an opportunity and made himself indispensable to the incompetent Burns. This proved the perfect storm for the young and ambitious Hoover, who basically became the default BI director. But BI agents were not the cream of the law enforcement crop, some with criminal records who were frequent no-shows at work. Hoover wanted to clean house, but Burns was using BI agents to moonlight at his private company, the William J. Burns International Detective Agency. These inept, lazy agents embarrassed the idealistic Hoover, who often told people that "I work for the government" rather than admit employment at the BI.

Hoover's reputation was vital to his mental well-being. He once applied for a credit account at a department store but was denied. When informed that there was another John Edgar Hoover bouncing checks around DC, he began signing all correspondence with "J. Edgar Hoover."

On April 8, 1924, Harlan Fiske Stone was sworn in as the attorney general. A month later, the AG summoned Burns into his office and fired him. Stone contacted the secretary of commerce and future president, Herbert Hoover, and said, "I need someone to replace Burns. Any ideas?" Herbert recommended his namesake, though the two were not kin. The 270-pound, 6' 1" Stone called J. Edgar to his office and scowled at the young attorney. Hoover, believing he was next on the chopping block, avoided Stone's stare.

The AG finally said, "Young man, I want you to be acting director of the Bureau of Investigation."

Hoover replied, "I'll take the job, Mr. Stone, on certain conditions."

"What are they?"

"The Bureau must be divorced from politics and not be a catchall for political hacks. Appointments must be based on merit, promotions will be made on proven ability, and the Bureau will be responsible *only* to the attorney general."

Stone glared at Hoover and announced, "I wouldn't give it to you under any other conditions. That's all. Good day."

CHAPTER 5

Is There a Deep State?

"The minute the FBI begins making recommendations on what
should be done with its information, it becomes a Gestapo."
—J. Edgar Hoover

I don't care for the term "deep state" when applied to the Comey
Gang. It elicits images of ruthless global organizations like SPECTRE
and THRUSH intent on world domination. They were led by diabol-
ical villains like Auric Goldfinger, Wolfgang Weisen, and Dr. No and
aided by guys named Oddjob. Those gents would be insulted to be
compared with the Comey Gang and their henchman, Peter Strzok.

Fifteen years ago, I would have suggested a tinfoil hat for anyone
who believed in the deep state. But recent events have made me rethink
my opinion. The term "deep state" intimates a conspiracy somewhere in
the woodshed. It's when two or more people get together and agree on
doing something bad. In the case of a shadow government, that something is to impede or overthrow the legitimate government. Evidence
indicates that the Comey Gang's goal was to prevent the presidency of

Donald Trump. But once that failed, this group of self-righteous and arrogant folks attempted to annul the will of the American people.

My friend AJ is convinced that a deep state is alive and well but is there any evidence. Let's examine the possibility through the eyes of an investigator.

Did a group of powerful individuals—that would be the Comey Gang and members of the Justice Department—gather together and attempt a bloodless government coup? Yes. Did this group operate under a *central* umbrella like SPECTRE with a hidden tattoo to signify membership? Nope. Are those two conditions required to be considered a deep state? Not really.

The deep state of the Trump era was largely a result of circumstance and timing. The Obama presidency was winding down, but there was a 91 percent chance that it would continue under Hillary Clinton. Obama had eight years of appointing liberal activists to key government positions. As his term expired, he converted many appointees to civil service positions. They call this process "burrowing." A Congressional Research Service (CRS) report found that burrowing frequently occurs during the transition period when one administration is preparing to leave office. CRS explained that appointed individuals who are converted to career positions will *likely* undermine the work of the new administration since their policies are at odds with those who appointed them. President Obama attempted to *plant* many of his political appointees inside *critical* government agencies responsible for our nation's security. The highest count includes nine in Homeland Security, eight in the Justice Department, and six in Defense. All told, the Office of Professional Management approved 78 of the 99 requests to convert Obama's political appointees to civil service jobs.

The *Washington Times* reported that seven of Mr. Obama's political appointees switched to career jobs without obtaining necessary approval from the Office of Personnel Management. Of those, four were later denied the jobs by OPM and three left their posts.

If I was tasked to investigate the record setting leaks of the Trump presidency my first 78 interviews are with the Obama burrowers.

Senator John Thune (R–SD) requested an analysis performed by the Government Accountability Office (GAO). Thune found that, "GAO determined that one out of every five attempts to move a political appointee into a career position was rejected as improper."

One example was acting Attorney General Sally Yates, who sent a memo to Justice Department employees asking them *not* to defend Trump's initial travel ban on people from seven majority-Muslim countries. Yates should've resigned upon receiving a lawful order she felt improper or immoral. By ordering her employees to join her in blatant insubordination is an indication of Yates's lack of leadership. She basically held her staff hostage on her sinking ship.

In addition to appointees who convert to permanent civil service positions, there are the outgoing cabinet and senior officials who will attempt to prevent the election of an opposing party's candidate. And if that fails, as in the case of Trump, these individuals will undermine the incoming administration. They plant bureaucratic punji sticks and IEDs, some with time-delay detonators, that are aimed at maiming and killing their political opponents.

The mind-set of the Obama inner circle is a fascinating study into that president's belief that America is *not* exceptional and the trend toward one global community. For example, his Director of National Intelligence (and James Comey's hero), James Clapper, publicly stated that the Muslim Brotherhood is a "*heterogeneous* group, largely secular, which has eschewed [avoided] violence." This curious statement was made hours after the Brotherhood claimed that sharia law was its ultimate goal. It's further contradicted by Obama's own FBI, which produced evidence that the Brotherhood had terrorist connections.

It's not likely that individuals like Susan Rice, Hillary Clinton, John Kerry, or James Clapper met with the Comey Gang and plotted *specific* deep state strategies. I doubt if Susan Rice got together with

Comey and said, "You guys write a FISA warrant so we can get a special prosecutor."

Comey nods and adds, "And then you guys unmask General Flynn and we'll get him to snitch on Trump."

But the two groups worked at an arm's-length harmony aided by another powerful institution. The *media* joined the fray to paint Trump as the crazy commie friend of Vladimir Putin who would, if elected, crash the economy, bomb North Korea, antagonize China, and piss off our European allies. Though President Trump accomplished the last two goals, the results were positive for the country.

There's also a fourth side that completes the deep state box. Once the press began bombarding the public with half-truth and false narratives, John Q. Citizen became an unwitting participant in the deep state. Citizens were whipped up into anti-Trump frenzy by social media, MSNBC, and the *New York Times*.

Donald Trump is an imperfect being, but he's a successful businessman who's been the emperor of his domain his entire adult life. If any of his employees continually screwed up, Trump would get rid of them because they hurt the bottom line. But if the employees *couldn't* be canned, then the business would eventually fail.

Trump views the government as another business that no longer functions and could eventually go belly-up. The consequences would be catastrophic, so he shook up the "business as usual" Beltway gang, who returned fire. The president has been highly successful in turning the economy around by deregulation, renegotiating trade deals, developing manufacturing, cutting taxes, and threatening Russia, China, and North Korea with the big nuclear button on his desk.

But one group that seems intent on sabotaging his agenda is the entrenched liberals in the US government. These men and women work for the president and should never permit their ideology to determine policy. Ronald Reagan once said that the midlevel bureaucrats control the government. The president can enact new policies and sign executive orders, but nothing happens unless these midlevel folks make it happen. Trump couldn't even fire some Department of Veterans Affairs directors who contributed to the deaths of veterans.

Trump doesn't accept fools lightly, but he is surrounded by fools inside the Beltway. Obama had zero experience to be the chief executive, but he's an eloquent, smooth-talking salesman who will sell you a house with a leaky roof. Trump is the New York construction guy who comes to fix your roof. He'll put the ladder up, and a few hours later you got a new roof. Somehow, the deep state media has convinced much of the public that it was Trump who *caused* the leak.

A related effect of the deep state is the recruitment of these like-minded allies. A legal term would be unindicted coconspirators. These folks share the ideology of the deep state players and act as unwitting surrogates. They're not contacted or recruited in the traditional sense but nonetheless become active participants in the shadow government. I'll provide examples of surrogates and explain how they contribute to the deep state.

James Comey reduced his alleged obstruction of justice meetings with President Trump to memos. Comey then intentionally leaked one memo to the press with the stated intent to trigger the special counsel statute. This strategy worked, and Robert Mueller was appointed by Rod Rosenstein. Comey then met with his friend Mueller and surrendered his Trump memos as evidence of a crime.

As an investigator, I would *not* consider the leaked memos to be direct evidence since they're basically written hearsay and depends on Comey's memory and veracity. The memos are no different from the observations of two drivers involved in the same traffic accident.

In my experience, if someone admits to a specific wrongdoing once—leaking, for example—it's a good bet that it wasn't his first time. A burglar never strikes *once*. There are dozens of unsolved leaks, and Director Comey was in the position to have access to the information contained in those leaks. The former FBI director would be a prime suspect if I were investigating the multiple leaks from the executive branch.

Comey hired his friend James Baker and appointed him the FBI chief legal counsel. Baker is a named suspect in leaking numerous documents to the press. My guess is that Comey used Baker in the same manner that he used his friend, Columbia Law School professor Daniel Richman, to leak documents for political purposes. The fact that Comey used shills to insulate him from directly breaking the law does not make him innocent of the crime. It does however increase his sleaze factor by ten.

Comey was asked under oath if he believed the president attempted to obstruct justice in the Flynn case. He replied that it was up to the special counsel to determine if obstruction occurred. Comey's desire for a special counsel was actually an admission that he did believe the president obstructed justice. He wouldn't wish a special counsel to prove that the president *didn't* commit a crime. Why else would he do it?

But when questioned on Loretta Lynch's orders to call the Clinton email investigation a "matter," he felt no similar compunction for an investigation. This indicates that Mr. Comey has a political and ideological agenda that affected his judgment and impartiality.

In June of 2107, Mueller met with Comey *prior* to his Senate testimony. At the time of their meeting, Mueller was recently appointed and supposedly an impartial special counsel to investigate Russian collusion. Comey had leaked investigative material to the *New York Times*, signed an unverified FISA application on three occasions, and alleged the president committed a crime based solely on his word. This should've made Comey both a witness *and* suspect in Mueller's investigation. But Mueller *always* treated Comey as a victim and never looked at his criminal exposure.

The special counsel's MO (method of operation) was to jam up folks on *any* crime even though Mueller's jurisdiction was limited to Russian collusion in the 2016 election. Rod Rosenstein allowed Mueller to freestyle minus any restrictions. Why?

James Comey was one of many satellites orbiting planet Trump who violated federal statutes. Mueller arrested Manafort, Papadopoulos, Stone, Flynn, and Cohen on lying and financial crimes, but chose to ignore Comey's perjury, public records act, and leaking investigative documents. This would be considered circumstantial evidence that Mueller had a serious conflict of interest by having a long professional and personal history with Comey.

Instead, Mueller met with Comey as his legal advocate, never asking the tough questions. You essentially had an independent prosecutor coaching a witness *and* personal friend in the court of public opinion. Though coaching a client may be proper in an attorney/client relationship, Mueller should've stayed clear of Comey and allowed him to sink or swim under oath. That is, *unless,* Mueller had *already* determined that President Trump attempted to obstruct justice.

The Special Counsel obviously didn't ask James Comey the following questions:

1. Did you sign the FISA application knowing it was based on lies, rumors, and gossip?
2. Did you leak documents that were part of an active FBI investigation?
3. Did Andrew McCabe tell you that the FISA warrant was unverified?
4. Did you know that Hillary Clinton's campaign indirectly paid for the Steele dossier?

Mueller didn't want to place Comey in a perjury trap, otherwise he would have asked these questions. They certainly were within the scope since Comey signed and *verified* a legal document filled with outright lies and half-truths.

Comey's congressional testimony was a masterful performance of evasion, double-talk, and amnesia. The substance of that Mueller-Comey chat is unknown, but let's assume they discussed obstruction of justice. These are two guys who'd worked alongside each other for years and expressed a mutual admiration for each other. Comey laid out his case that President Trump obstructed justice, and Mueller responded in *some* manner.

Since obstruction of justice can be interpreted differently by two attorneys viewing the same set of facts, any investigation can be conducted to prove a preconceived belief.

It was Edward Kennedy who said that "integrity is the lifeblood of democracy; deceit is a poison in its veins."

The number of leaks in the Trump White House was unprecedented. Mr. Comey's leak provided tacit approval and emboldened other like-minded federal employees to leak. They became surrogates and unwitting coconspirators of the deep state.

Susan Rice seemed to be an active member of the deep state after Trump was elected but before he took office. The Obama national security advisor told MSNBC that she sometimes sought the identities of Trump associates who communicated with foreigners, a request known as "*unmasking*" in the intelligence community.

Rice's admission came after she initially told PBS's Judy Woodruff that she "knew nothing" about the unmasking of Trump associates. Inconsistent statements are called clues in law enforcement. The fact that Rice has furnished other inconsistencies is called a pattern, or MO. There was the Benghazi video and the Bowe Bergdahl fib. Susan Rice described Army deserter Bergdahl as a hero and the Benghazi slaughter as a *chance* happening. Unmasking a US citizen is part of an intelligence investigation.

Supporting evidence that Rice acted outside her scope includes the fact that the White House does *not* conduct investigations. Not criminal investigations, and not intelligence investigations. Generally, it is the FBI that conducts investigations concerning American citizens suspected of acting as agents of foreign powers.

So, if unmasking was relevant to the Russia investigation, the FBI, CIA, or NSA would have done it. There would have been no need for Susan Rice to ask for identities to be unmasked. The national security advisor is not an investigator. The president's staff is a *consumer* of intelligence, not a generator or collector of it.

If Susan Rice was unmasking Americans, it was *not* to fulfill an intelligence need based on American interests; it was to fulfill a political desire based on Democratic Party interests. If it were critical to know the identities of Americans caught up in other foreign intelligence efforts, the agencies that collect the information and conduct investigations would have unmasked them.

Most Democrats are not psychologists, yet a recurring weapon of the deep state is the accusation that President Trump is mentally unbalanced. If I, as an FBI agent, ever concluded that a subject of our investigation was mentally imbalanced, the first question the defense attorney would ask is: "Well, Agent Ligato, at what medical school did you earn your degree in psychiatry?"

I would be discredited because I lacked the expertise to make a diagnosis, but many Democratic officials stare somberly at the camera with their University of Google degrees and make medical judgments. Maxine Waters and Adam Schiff are two Democratic lawmakers who have practiced medicine minus the license.

The surrogates in the media and *hate*-Trump posse repeat the diagnosis whether they believe it or not. Our media is part of the deep state. Some are active players and others are unwitting surrogates based on their ideology. In the not-too-distant past, both the FBI and the media were fact finders. We shared the standard of satisfying burden of proof by relying on multiple and reliable sources. My actions as a law enforcement officer could have a profound effect on citizens, ranging from destroying their reputation to taking away their freedom. I could not sit on the witness stand and cite gossip, rumors, or anonymous sources to convict someone.

The media share that ability to ruin reputations and lives with unfounded allegations and accusations. This power comes with the responsibility to get it right, but today's media make the most outrageous accusations, citing anonymous sources with impunity and then hiding behind a privilege that doesn't exist.

CNN has been outed for committing deep state tactics, and it is not alone. There are many journalists who are so lazy and incompetent that they merely reprint or report other people's news stories, many of which turn out to be fake news. The mainstream media act as surrogates of the deep state with the intended purpose to degrade and destroy the Trump presidency.

Conflict-of-interest charges are routinely ignored or downplayed by the media when Democrats are involved. Examples include John Podesta's financial interest in Joule Unlimited, a Russia-backed energy company partially owned by the Russian government. The allegation is that the Clinton family and Russia both benefited from an alleged "pay-to-play" scheme while Hillary Clinton was secretary of state, involving the transfer of US uranium reserves to the Russian owners of a mining operation in exchange for $145 million in donations to the Clinton Foundation.

The $500,000 speech by Bill Clinton paid for by a Russian investment bank bolsters the circumstantial evidence of an inappropriate relationship between Russia and the Clintons. The specific charges of extortion, public corruption, and bribery are difficult to prove. The investigation is tedious, but there seems to be an abundance of facts and circumstantial evidence.

The FBI was initially blocked by the Justice Department from conducting a preliminary inquiry into these allegations. The highly political office of the attorneys general Eric Holder and Loretta Lynch chose to pass.

Comey's July 5, 2016, announcement that the FBI was not recommending charges against Hillary Clinton was unprecedented. The FBI had *never* made recommendations on guilt or innocence. That is the Department of Justice's purview.

Shortly *before* Comey exonerated Hillary, the attorney general met with Bill Clinton on a tarmac in Phoenix. This get-together constituted the *appearance* of a conflict of interest. But Comey's lack of curiosity is suspicious. Wouldn't any reasonable investigator want to assure themselves that nothing improper was discussed?

Could Comey be the "insurance policy" that Strzok and Page mentioned? The tarmac meeting would make any law enforcement official suspicious, but not the director of the FBI. Comey stated under oath, and with a straight face, that he made *no* attempt to determine the details of the Clinton–Lynch airport chat. It somehow didn't interest him.

If a detective discovered that his prosecutor privately met with the husband of a suspect in his investigation, I guarantee you he'd be asking plenty of questions. Yet the FBI didn't ask the most obvious one: "Was the case discussed?"

The tarmac summit reinforces Comey's own belief of the "appearance" that Attorney General Lynch was "compromised in some fashion."

FBI agents, both past and present, were scratching their heads trying to figure out why Comey colored so far outside our lines. He later stated *on the record* that he felt that Attorney General Lynch was compromised in some fashion. Comey may be saying that Lynch was in the bag for the Clintons, but that doesn't make sense. If the FBI director believed that Lynch had already decided to exonerate Hillary, why did he do it for her?

Though the above matters merit an FBI investigation, the most blatant conflict of interest occurred with the appointment of Robert Mueller as special counsel. This statute should only be enacted when there is underlying evidence of criminal activity and not just rumors and anonymous sources. There was *no* underlying criminal activity when the special counsel statue was enacted.

The statute also spells out what constitutes a conflict of interest. The language seems to have been written for the Mueller-Comey relationship. It calls for a recusal if there is a personal or political relationship between the counsel and potential witnesses or targets. Comey fits into both categories, yet Mueller refused to recuse himself.

The fact that Mueller found no evidence of Russian collusion or obstruction of justice is a pleasant surprise. The pretend horror emanating from the Democrats that the Mueller report offered proof that the president obstructed justice is more theater of the absurd. Mueller had the authority to refer criminal charges to the attorney general, but didn't. The real purpose of the post Mueller congressional inquisition is to weaken President Trump for the 2020 election. They can procedurally huff and puff but they lack any legal avenue to lay a punch on Trump.

Robert Mueller performs well on the ideological balance beam but his tenure as the FBI director contributed to the deep state. I doubt that Mr. Mueller intended to weaken the Bureau, but his tenure did result in a significant reduction of the FBI's long-standing independence. A by-product of this loss was the politicization of the Bureau, which allowed entrée for the deep state players. The Justice Department has always had a political component. John F. Kennedy appointed his brother as attorney general, and Hillary Clinton demanded a female attorney general during her husband's presidency. But Loretta Lynch's meeting with Bill Clinton days before James Comey's announcement of Hillary's innocence was all about the deep state.

Comey's appointment as FBI director assured the Bureau's continued subservient role to the Justice Department. He was a Mueller protégé and not about to declare our independence. His decision to exonerate Hillary was clearly partisan, as was his leaking of official documents to get a special counsel.

Further evidence of the Bureau's deep state connection is Deputy Director Andrew McCabe. The wife of the number two man in the FBI received $650,000 in campaign contributions from a Democratic PAC, which would've been fine had it not come from the former chairman of Hillary Clinton's 2008 presidential campaign. McCabe failed to report the contribution, because technically, he wasn't required to do so under IRS regulations. Maybe not, but he absolutely had a duty to recuse himself even after his wife lost the election. But he didn't. If someone indirectly provided my wife a cool half million, I'd be inclined to cut them a "huss," all things being equal.

When I was undercover with the Italian Mafia, Vinny Bagodonuts would've described this accommodation as a "a fuckin' *bribe*."

CHAPTER 6:

A Lack of Leadership

"It's hard to lead a cavalry charge if you
think you look funny on a horse."

This quote may seem humorous, but it masks serious repercussions.

What makes a great leader? Experts feel that leadership involves qualities such as confidence, decisiveness, adaptability, and intelligence. *My* definition of leadership as a former combat Marine and FBI agent is identical to Supreme Court Justice Potter Stewart's definition of pornography: "I know it when I see it."

The results of poor leadership in the corporate world can cost some dough, but poor leadership in law enforcement and the military can cost a life. The FBI has a current void in leadership due to culture change, political correctness, and problems in mentoring and recruitment.

Leadership is not an acquired trait. You can attend all the leadership seminars and still be a bumbling follower. A title does not make a leader since leaders must act, knowing their decisions have consequences. I'd been spoiled in the US Marine Corps with the finest leadership imaginable.

During the 1968 Tet Offensive, I was a basic rifleman with Alpha Company, First Battalion, First Marines. We were an undersized company of 147 mud Marines who entered Hue City on 31 January 1968. Awaiting us were 10,000 NVA regulars. During a four-day period I had the honor and privilege to witness the actions of two Marines who were each the recipient of the Congressional Medal of Honor. Sergeant Al Gonzalez and Gunnery Sergeant John Canley led the Marines against these overwhelming odds.

In the first few days of the thirty-one-day battle, just four leaders of Alpha Company earned two Medals of Honor, the Navy Cross, several Silver Stars, a few Bronze Stars, and seven Purple Hearts. They *also* saved the lives of many Marines who would have perished if not for their leadership, mine included.

Their leadership didn't include decision avoidance based on careerism. These Marines made assessments under the most extreme conditions based on their character and training. They accepted the responsibilities associated with being a leader. None of these Marines would think to use a third-party shill like Comey did with his college buddy to fight their battle.

What do General Patton and James Comey have in common? Both found themselves in leadership roles during a time of war. The FBI director was tasked to lead the war against domestic terrorism, while Patton fought the Germans in World War II. Patton was surrounded by General Omar Bradley and British General Bernard "Monty" Montgomery. Comey surrounded himself with Peter Strzok and Andy McCabe.

Combat leaders don't have the luxury to engage in indecision based on the fear that a bad decision might harm their career. Soldiers, Sailors, Airmen, Coasties, and Marines depend on their leaders for their very lives. If Marine commanders employed the same leadership techniques as the Comey Gang, the result would be career ending, in the most permanent sense.

The culture of an institution directly relates to its success or failure, and that culture is determined by its leaders.

I agree that J. Edgar Hoover was controversial in many respects, but was he a good leader? If you examine his commitment, passion, and decision-making capabilities, then J. Edgar is outstanding. Other leadership qualities that Hoover had in spades were innovation, creative thinking, and futuristic ideas. He wasn't too warm and fuzzy, but leaders are allowed some quirks.

Recruitment is critical to any organization's survival. Popeye said something to the effect that "You are who you are." If you are recruiting positions for the military or law enforcement, then you may not want pacifist, antigun, tree-hugging, Green Peace, PETA-type individuals.

The new FBI may need to reevaluate its recruiting guidelines during this politically correct era. Special Agent Gamal Abdel-Hafiz refused to conduct a secret recording of a Muslim suspect. He felt that "a Muslim doesn't record another Muslim." Many of you assume that Abdel-Hafiz was canned, but you'd be wrong. His field supervisor contacted FBI headquarters and was informed by a higher-up, "Well, you have to understand where he's coming from, Bob."

Bob countered with, "I understand where *I'm* coming from. We both took the same damn oath to defend this country against all enemies foreign and domestic, and he just said no? No way in hell."

Abdel-Hafiz was not reprimanded, but he *was* promoted to one of the FBI's most important antiterrorism posts, the American Embassy in Saudi Arabia, to handle investigations for the FBI in that Muslim country.

Had there been a leader somewhere within the bowels of FBI headquarters, Abdel-Hafiz would've been gone. This is a classic example of failed leadership due to political correctness. I'm guessing that Hoover may have ordered a firing squad.

In 2018, an FBI agent accidentally dropped his gun while doing a back flip at a Denver nightclub. Retired agents may give Agent Chase Bishop kudos for the ability to perform this complex gymnastic move while drinking, in dress shoes, on a slippery dance floor and nailing the landing. But when Chase went to retrieve his handgun, he placed his finger on the trigger, discharged the weapon, and hit a bystander in the leg. FBI firearms training is the best in the world and constantly drills basic safety practices such as *when* to place your finger on the trigger. Although dancing in a bar with your sidearm is not that unusual in law enforcement (been there, done that), this new generation of G-men need a refresher course on when to engage the enemy.

Hoover's thirty-seven-year tenure as FBI director included a major improvement in the recruitment of agents. This director understood the importance of getting it right, because when he was named acting director of the Bureau of Investigation in 1924, he inherited a group of incompetent, lazy malcontents. Agents were not authorized to carry weapons and exhibited little motivation. It wasn't until 1935 that Hoover added the word "Federal" to the agency's title and it became the *Federal* Bureau of Investigation. By that time Hoover had culled out the malcontents, recruited attorneys and accountants, and provided them weapons, training, and pride.

From 1935 until his death in 1972, J. Edgar recruited many military veterans who fought in World War II, Korea, and Vietnam. These veterans brought with them a culture of discipline, brotherhood, and leadership.

When I arrived in Vietnam my lifeline to survival was the leaders with combat experience. These Marines explained how to lay claymore mines, walk point, spot ambushes, and survive monsoons, dysentery, leeches, jungle rot, and parasites. Going from the military to law enforcement is the most natural transition since both professions share common traits, and most military veterans are able to transfer a culture of leadership and mentoring to the FBI. But a few decades ago the Bureau broke that supply chain.

The FBI's current fiasco is a *direct* result of failed leadership. Plain and simple. You can get caught in the weeds analyzing the many details that produced the Comey Gang, but it begins and ends with poor leadership. Many headquarters types confuse their rank with their role. There is a *big* difference between being a leader and being a boss, since authority doesn't necessarily translate into control. Unless it's earned, it's fleeting.

Under Comey, FBI executive staff, touted as our best and brightest leaders, were linked to several DOJ Office of Professional Responsibility (OPR) investigations, including twenty-seven leaks inside HQ. Suspects included former FBI general counsel James Baker, Peter Strzok, Lisa Page, and Andy McCabe. And even our supreme leader, Director Comey, *confessed* under oath to being a leaker. The irony being that Mr. Comey was charged with identifying and arresting leakers. A mirror may have made that job easier. Other suspects under OPR's microscope included Justice Department employees Jeannie Rhee, Rod Rosenstein, and Bruce Ohr. The above *leaders* are being scrutinized with a public corruption microscope based on partisan politics. It's fortunate that the rank and file agents are discerning adults and refuse to play *follow the leader*.

***

How did the FBI mutate itself into a rudderless ship with an empty bridge? The Bureau began choosing careerists whose priorities were self-serving. Decision making was no longer based on mission but rather risk avoidance.

Good leaders recognize that things don't always go according to the operations plan. We occasionally work off script. The good leaders adapt, overcome, and improvise, while the bad leaders finger point.

I once planned a major drug takedown at a parking lot. We staged the SWAT team inside a Ryder truck, and I'd give the signal for them to run down the ramp and surround the bad guys. What could possibly go wrong?

My partner, Fred "Thumper" Snellings, was the undercover and equipped with a transmitter that I was monitoring. When Thumper observed the drugs, he'd utter the magic word that alerted me to unleash the SWAT team.

As any law enforcement officer knows, government electronic equipment thirty-five years ago was low bid. During intermittent static, Fred kept repeating the arrest code. By the time I yelled "*execute*" on the radio, the SWAT team was reduced to chasing a 1988 Buick on foot.

My tardiness resulted in the subject escaping with $88,000 in Bureau money. The getaway car began playing demolition derby with the FBI cars, alternating between sideswiping, T-boning, and rear-ending our government rides. We finally arrested the subject but somehow misplaced $10,000 of government cash.

Cars were literally smoking, roads were blocked, and the news media were flying helicopters overhead when the bosses arrived on scene. They asked me one simple question: "*What the fuck happened?*" As the case agent I was responsible for the money, cars, and drugs. The end of the story is that the subject rolled on their drug supplier, and we found the ten grand and seized more drugs hidden behind a wall. All in all, a good day since no one was *seriously* hurt, we seized drugs, we made arrests, and evidently the FBI had adequate car insurance.

But the jury was still out on my fate. Bill Brannon was the new SAC (Special Agent in Charge), and I explained to him what happened, omitting certain details. The SAC paused and smiled. "Okay, write this up," he said, "and make it good. I'll have to send a report to HQ tomorrow."

Brannon knew that we acted in good faith and that shit happens. Leaders of that era covered the honest mistakes of hard-charging agents. I suspect that things would be different in today's Bureau.

There have been countless occasions when one leader altered history for the good or bad. A lack of leadership was the major factor that contributed to the worst integrity crisis in FBI history. Had there been one individual on the seventh floor with honor and some gonads, the American public would've never heard of the term "FISA warrant."

Dwight D. Eisenhower said, "The supreme quality of leadership is integrity." Most Americans have difficulty associating the word "integrity" with Comey, McCabe, Strzok, Page, and Baker.

There was a time when the FBI had outstanding leaders. Individuals who understood that character and integrity were vital to mission. Tony Daniels and James Kallstrom, both retired assistant directors, were outstanding leaders. They took care of the troops, led from the front, and never asked you to do something that they hadn't done themselves. Kallstrom was a Marine company commander in Vietnam who became a beloved Bureau legend recognized for his outstanding leadership. Leaders inspire the troops, whether they be combat Marines or FBI agents.

Other outstanding FBI leaders that I served with included Pat Laffey, Drick Crawford, Louie Allen, John Bell, Eddie Mclaughlin, Joe Martinolich, and Lou Schilaro, to name a few. They share the common qualities associated with all good leaders, like commitment, delegation, empathy, and the ability to inspire.

The handling of the Zacarias Moussaoui case exposed three of the major weaknesses at FBI headquarters: a culture of decision avoidance, poor leadership, and a mistrust of the field.

Minnesota agents testified that the *leadership* void inside headquarters is due to a culture of decision avoidance. Their words were straightforward when they accused the Radical Fundamentalist Unit at HQ of being guilty of obstructionism, criminal negligence, and careerism, and that its opposition blocked a serious opportunity to stop the 9/11 attacks.

Sanford Ungar, director of the Free Speech Project at Georgetown University and author of a book on the FBI's history, said, "If you tear down an institution like this, you can't just build it back up next week. You have to be careful about tearing down institutions that are the bedrock of our democracy because you will cause irreparable damage to the government that maligned it."

The Mueller-Comey era could be described as the perfect storm of poor leadership, moral superiority, and culture clash. Mueller's venial sin was his unwitting merger of the FBI and Department of Justice. He had no malice in his heart, nor coconspirators. Comey's on an entirely different planet. He assembled a crew of sleazy collaborators who engaged in criminal activities. Comey also broke the hearts of most retired FBI agents. He was a temporary interloper who cracked the foundation of an agency thought indestructible.

One possible solution to the FBI leadership void may be a variation of the military's blueprint for choosing field commanders. At Officer Candidate School (OCS) and the Basic School at Quantico, Marines are evaluated by senior noncommissioned officers (NCOs) based on performance in the classroom, squad bay, and drill field, as well as on how they handle practical problems. Leaders emerge and are awarded the opportunity to lead Marines. Others receive assignments that support the mission, such as supply, admin, transportation, and intelligence.

The FBI Academy presents similar opportunities to identify leaders. The present system of selecting agents for leadership billets involves the *desire* to become a supervisory special agent and not much more. Considerations for race, gender, sexual orientation, or the *good ol' boy* network have no place in jobs where lives depend on leadership.

The Bureau makes no objective attempt to identify leaders, and the result is often leaders who can't or won't make decisions. Perhaps one size does not fit *all,* and the military option wouldn't work, but *something* must be done.

One may think that the numerous investigations and scathing reports following Waco, Ruby Ridge, 9/11, and FISA would change things. After-action documents were voluminous and discussed every aspect of what went wrong, but it *all* boiled down to a lack of leadership.

There was the usual consensus that things had to change to regain public trust. But it didn't, and probably never will due to the Bureau's failure to admit it has a leadership problem. The FBI seems stuck on the same remedial-action plan following a major scandal: admit the mistake, find a martyr, and then conduct mandatory training to prevent a recurrence.

"There is a serious problem with the culture at FBI Headquarters," said former Utah Republican senator Orrin Hatch.

Many in the media defended Comey, McCabe, Page, and Strzok as impartial investigators. They claimed that their declared hatred of Trump never influenced their objectivity. Even some individuals within the FBI leadership jumped on that bandwagon. But now that the Comey Gang has been dispersed, the leaks and negativity have calmed down. By most logical and legal standards, the Comey Gang lacked the Bureau's core values of fidelity, bravery, and integrity. When institutions keep lowering their standards, they will eventually have none.

One of the factors that judges consider when sentencing criminals is *acceptance of responsibility and remorse*. Good leaders will stare the media in the eye and say, "I screwed up." If you observe Comey, McCabe, and Strzok as they respond to questions from investigators and the media, it's clear that ain't happening. Arrogance and self-righteousness drips from their pores. They have no idea how they collectively contributed to a national crisis. "No single drop of water thinks it's responsible for the flood."

Peter Strzok was investigated by OPR, and they recommended a mild penalty of a sixty-day suspension and a demotion. But FBI deputy director David Bowdich overruled OPR and fired his butt. People called Strzok a victim and martyr of politics. Those people probably know a lot about victimhood since it seems that anyone caught in wrongdoing these days is automatically a victim of circumstance. But take a closer look at Peter Strzok's behavior and then judge if you'd still want him representing the Federal Bureau of Investigation.

Sara Carter is an investigative reporter with many sources within the FBI. Agents present a strong case that Peter Strzok should not only have been terminated but also prosecuted. "Strzok was under oath before Congress and made statements that appeared to be false and refused to answer some questions," said a former supervisory special agent from OPR adjudication, who spoke on condition of anonymity. (You *can* be fired if you refuse to answer questions during an administrative inquiry.)

He further explained that "there is absolutely no wiggle room when it comes to lack of candor in the FBI...unless you're an SES" (senior executive service).

Strzok's firing went well beyond texting about Trump. He was involved in the handling of the FISA (Foreign Intelligence Surveillance Act) application to the FISC (Foreign Intelligence Surveillance Court). The agent noted that Strzok was "well aware that he was lying by *deception* when they did not include the information on who paid for the dossier and [that] Bruce Ohr was back-channeling information from a discredited source."

"Strzok knew they were not putting the application in the right context," the former FBI supervisory special agent added. "If there was the slightest doubt that application was not 100 percent true, then that application would not go forward."

He concluded with what many former agents feel. "Unless I am mistaken, these are *felonious* actions. No wonder Strzok needs a legal defense fund."

The OPR system had always favored the senior executives, and Strzok would've been another SES type awarded the "get out of jail free" card had Bowdich not interceded.

In 1994 (seven years *before* 9/11), John Werner, FBI Supervisory Special Agent, Office of Professional Responsibility, testified before the Senate Judiciary Committee regarding OPR's investigation of Ruby Ridge. He said, "My remarks are being addressed to that vocal minority of FBI SES members, often referred to as the 'Club' by street agents, who are motivated by self-preservation and self-interest at any cost.

For the most part, these SES personnel are *not* motivated by the best interest of the FBI.

"Hiding behind a wall of arrogance, senior managers hold the belief that they always know what is best for the Bureau. These SES members are intolerant of any suggestion that their way is wrong. They use intimidation and retaliation against anyone who would be so impertinent as to challenge their interests."

Many former FBI special agents, some of whom worked with OPR for years, agreed with Bowdich's decision. They told Sara Carter that the system is broken and Bowdich had no other choice but to step in and fire Strzok.

Leaders should not be selected based on friendships or commonalities of ideology, ethnicity, religion, or politics. These dual systems of justice inside OPR have plagued how cases regarding FBI agents are handled. The OPR needs reform, as does the way we select and promote our leaders.

CHAPTER 7:

Selective Prosecution

"We find the defendant *incredibly* guilty."
—*The Producers*

My buddy A. J. Perry asked me, "Doesn't anyone go to jail these days?"

That's also been bugging me, especially when government officials commit crimes under oath, on camera, and in front of millions of witnesses. High-level bureaucrats who shred evidence, obstruct justice, perjure themselves, and accept bribes somehow fade from the news cycle, then emerge two years later on a book tour. As they plug their tell-all book on AM Pittsburgh, I ask, "Why the hell isn't that asshole in jail?"

Over the past decade the public has been regularly whipped into a frenzy after a cable news commentator cites some federal statute and concludes with, "I've never seen such overwhelming evidence, and my sources in law enforcement guarantee me that someone is going to jail this time!" No one ever does.

The public is baffled on how guilty folks *ever* end up in the gray-bar hotel. Much of the confusion lay with cable news, the internet, and my buddy A. J., who confuse opinions and gossip with facts and evidence.

Our justice system was skewed left by the Comey Gang, who ripped the blindfold off Lady Justice's eyes and placed Lois Lerner on her scales. There's always been some degree of prosecutive discretion, but it's recently evolved into a partisan art form.

The FBI that I knew dealt in facts. We targeted criminals based on evidence and not political party or ideology. But recent leadership has made a mockery of fairness by engaging in selective prosecution, the simple definition of which is that you overlook crimes committed by like-minded folks while prosecuting those who don't think like you do.

The public and media can speculate in rumors and anonymous sources, but the FBI had always been the institution that sorted it all out and put cuffs on the guilty. It now appears that senior FBI officials have amended our Constitution. The Bureau had always been the last hope for justice delivered, with the jurisdiction to go after *any* sleaze ball whether they be a mobster, US senator, or secretary of state. We were sovereign and neutral, like Switzerland. But that was several decades ago, before the Justice Department sucked us into its partisan vortex.

The public wonders when congressional committees are going to put some hides on the wall. We have witnessed numerous individuals raise their right hand and swear to tell the whole truth and then lie, lie, lie, which is a benign term for perjury. Congressional committee hearings are simply drama. They have no ability to convene a grand jury and lack the courage to refer perjury cases to Justice. Hearings are like a recurring bad movie with the same ending.

Congressional committees, the inspector general, Rachel Maddow, and Sean Hannity lack the power to cuff someone. They continually cite "sources" with "solid evidence" of criminal activity, yet none yield one significant arrest. Not even the corrupt IRS supervisor Lois Lerner who unjustly targeted conservative groups. Congressional committees have zero authority. They can embarrass witnesses, call them names, and issue reports, but it's a version of performance art. These committees are an impotent partisan waste of taxpayer's money.

FBI agents *can* arrest someone when they possess probable cause, which consists simply of facts and circumstances. There are occasional subtleties, but basically you require evidence to deprive someone of their liberty. The courts have even determined that a person is considered under arrest if they *believe* that they're under arrest. "Sit down and shut up" no longer works in today's world.

The IG can refer cases to the Justice Department, but that usually requires a duplicate investigation by FBI agents due to the limited scope of the IG. They lack the authority to operate outside their agency or interview many critical witnesses.

So, who's responsible for enforcing federal violations of law if not Congress or the inspector general? Not surprisingly, it's the Federal Bureau of Investigation, and that system had worked effectively until the Comey Gang.

Let me explain the traditional pathway from a crime to a jail cell. It involves evidence or reasonable suspicion of a crime, followed by an investigation by a law enforcement official (*not* an attorney, congressperson, or investigative reporter). The FBI agent looks at a specific federal statute that contains "elements" that must be proven. Sounds complicated, but it's actually very straightforward.

A good example is mail fraud. If you're investigating this federal violation, there are only two elements that you must prove. One is "use of the mail" and the other is a "scheme to defraud."

Put yourself in the place of the investigator. You take the envelope to a postal inspector and interview him. He confirms that the envelope markings indicate use of the US mail system. You're halfway there. You now must prove a scheme to defraud. By taking victim statements of those defrauded, both elements of mail fraud have been proven.

You write up a report and take it to the US Attorney's office. They have three choices: They can decline to prosecute, agree to prosecute, or request additional evidence. If they decide to prosecute, you obtain an arrest warrant via an affidavit or seek an indictment. Make the arrest and the defendant can either plead guilty or go to trial.

FBI agents are very familiar with this process, so why does it get complicated when dealing with public officials like a Hillary Clinton but seem straightforward with a Michael Flynn? The attorney general has discretion on the cases they select to prosecute. They'll claim that they're chosen based on evidence and priorities, but they'd be lying. They choose many of them based on politics and ideology. High-profile cases equal promotions or a move into the private sector for big bucks. If you doubt their convoluted reasoning on who gets prosecuted, then speak with General Flynn, George Papadopoulos, Martha Stewart, or the sailor who spent a year in jail for taking a photograph of his submarine.

Assistant US Attorney James Comey was instrumental in sending Stewart to jail for lying to the FBI. As you'll see later, lying to the FBI is a general sport, but very few people are ever prosecuted for it. In fact, he confessed in an interview that he almost didn't go after Stewart. He feared potential backlash prosecuting Stewart, who was rich and famous, for a comparatively *minor* securities issue. But he *did*, and that "minor" issue is an example of selective prosecution by a self-righteous prosecutor who weaponized the Justice Department.

The federal justice system files criminal charges numbering between eighty thousand and one hundred thousand cases annually. If they had unlimited attorneys and investigators, the number could easily be five million. This number includes crimes that never see the light of day—things like unreported income, bookmaking, and the little-known violations that would fill our jails *if enforced*. There are hundreds of archaic laws enacted in a different era that some prosecutor could point your way. Although you may not be the intended target, the legal shrapnel still hurts.

If you ever find yourself driving at night through rural parts of Pennsylvania, state law requires that you stop every mile to send up a rocket signal. In Salem, West Virginia, it's against the law to eat candy less than an hour and a half before church service. A city ordinance in Cleveland prohibits women from wearing patent leather shoes in public. Florida bans unmarried women from parachuting on Sundays, and Pittsburgh has a special ordinance that forbids housewives from hiding dirt under their rugs. In Memphis, women can't drive a car unless there is a man with a red flag in front of the car warning the other people on the road.

These are extreme examples, but the point is that the government can convict *anyone* of violating *some* law. This selective prosecution often ruins the lives of individuals whose only sin is being acquainted with the true target of their investigation.

Although many of these violations won't result in prison time, they can cost you time, money, and embarrassment. But some rarely used statutes can singe the legal hair off your testicles if weaponized.

For example, President Trump, for whatever reason, is reluctant to release his tax returns. Though he's not required to by law, Democrats discovered a 1924 law that gives congressional committees that set tax policy the power to examine tax returns.

Another legal threat hanging over the Trump presidency is hidden in section one, article nine of the United States Constitution. Although it has never been litigated, the so-called emoluments clause forbids officeholders from accepting compensation from foreign governments without a go-ahead from Congress. Critics of President Trump cite financial conflicts of interest due to his extensive business dealings with foreign entities, including the state-owned Bank of China.

Another rusty legal sword clutched in the hands of prosecutors is the Logan Act. It states that "any citizen who, without authority of the United States, directly or indirectly carries on any correspondence or intercourse with any foreign government or officer or agent, with intent to influence the measures or conduct of any foreign government, shall be fined under this title or imprisoned not more than three years, or both." Mueller weaponized this gem on General Flynn and others to get them to flip on the president.

A majority of federally elected officials could get "Loganized" should the opposition party choose to make their life miserable. No one has ever been prosecuted under the Logan Act, though it is used occasionally to threaten officials to snitch.

You *cannot* defeat the federal government, since it's not a living organism. It has unlimited funds, whereas a good criminal defense attorneys can charge up to $1,000 an hour, which would wipe out most savings accounts after a few meetings. The government is an unemotional freight train that will run you over and leave you financially *and* emotionally bankrupt.

Since his election in November 2016, Trump's campaign chairman, his deputy campaign manager, his national security advisor, his personal lawyer, and a foreign policy aide have pled guilty to crimes as a result of special prosecutor Robert Mueller's investigation. Would these federal felons have been targets had they'd been on Hillary Clinton's team? Well, obviously not, since *that* group went on a federal crime spree of perjury, obstruction, contempt of court, and general mopery yet they roam freely among us non-felons.

Who are these individuals committing federal crimes with impunity based on an ideology? I'll begin with the slam-dunk cases that have no legal or logical defense. You be the judge.

***

Hillary Clinton is guilty of violating Title 18, Section 793(f) of the federal code making it unlawful to send or store classified information on personal email. The FBI investigation determined that Clinton knowingly used an unsecured, private email server at her home to conduct sensitive national security business as Secretary of State. Intent is *not* a requirement, nor is the opinion that a prosecutor would not prosecute the case. In fact, it is not within the FBI's jurisdiction to offer that judgment. Prison cells are filled with people whose crimes were *not* intentional. A drunk driver who kills a family does so minus intent but breaks the law regardless.

Huma Abedin lied under oath affirming that the FBI had all her emails. Cheryl Mills *didn't* lie because she contracted a temporary case of amnesia, as did Loretta Lynch. But what did it *matter*? (Pun intended.) Which is how the AG instructed Comey to refer to the Hillary email investigation. So, let's add obstruction of justice to Lynch's felony tab.

Hillary lied to *everyone* so no need to waste words, but her coconspirators demand a mention. They include Bryan Pagliano and the guys who bleached and smashed Hillary's devices. They all received immunity, which is a legal quid pro quo for becoming a snitch. The problem is they walked instead of talked.

Lois Lerner was granted a felony pass for using the IRS as her private criminal operation.

Susan Rice illegally unmasked Trump staff and fibbed a lot on television regarding Benghazi.

Eric Holder is guilty of violating Title 18, Section 1621—Perjury, having taken an *oath* to testify truthfully, then "willfully subscribes as true any material matter which he does *not* believe to be true." Again, only two elements are required to be guilty. Attorney General Holder testified under oath before the House Judiciary Committee. When asked whether DOJ could prosecute reporters under the Espionage Act, Holder responded, "This is not something I've ever been involved in, heard of, or would think would be wise policy.

When he gave this testimony, Holder had personally signed a request to a court to authorize a wiretap on Fox News reporter James Rosen. An unnamed FBI agent falsely accused Rosen of breaking anti-espionage laws but his sin was pissing off Obama by reporting on US intelligence about North Korea. The Bureau conducted a leak investigation into Rosen's sources that included securing the reporter's telephone records and a warrant for his personal emails.

In addition, Eric Holder refused to honor congressional subpoenas for Fast and Furious. His penance was to be held in congressional contempt. This is the equivalent of being reprimanded by Mr. Rodgers.

James Comey could be prosecuted of violating Title 18, Section 641, which makes it a crime to steal, sell, or *convey "any record…*of the United States or of any department or agency thereof."* This law requires the proof of only one element (in italics). Mr. Comey leaked several confidential memos that he stated under oath were reports of conversations with President Trump. Since Comey suspected Trump of obstruction of justice, that made these documents potential evidence, and the leaking of such is a crime.

***

I can go on for quite a while with names like James "Metadata" Clapper, Bruce Ohr, Andy McCabe, and other public officials who seem immune to prosecution. And just for the record, *every* individual involved in the FISA warrant rate an indictment. That list includes those officials who signed (approved) the warrant as well as the affiant (the person swearing to the affidavit) and anyone who was aware that the PC (probable cause) was bogus. The bottom line is that the FBI and Justice Department get to choose who goes to jail but, equally important, who *doesn't*.

A recent pattern of selective prosecution and targeting appears largely directed at conservative folks. In addition to ideology, liberal prosecutors consider other factors regarding who avoids being cuffed, such as ethnicity or notoriety. Jesse Jackson kept a mistress with nonprofit funds, Al Sharpton ignored the IRS for years, the Clinton

Foundation is a continuing criminal enterprise, Black Lives Matters incites riots, and Antifa is a violent vigilante group. See anyone in jail?

In 1998–1999, the IRS audited Jesse Jackson's Citizenship Education Fund, a tax-exempt arm of his Chicago-based Rainbow/ PUSH Coalition. Jackson conceded that 1999 tax returns filed under his CEF organization failed to reflect $35,000 paid to former staff member Karin Stanford, with whom Jackson fathered a child. There seemed to be other serious problems with his tax reporting that went largely ignored.

Civil rights leader Reverend Al Sharpton owed the government some serious cash—approximately $4.5 million in state and federal taxes. According to the *New York Times*, his nonprofit advocacy organization, the National Action Network, seemed to be paying for virtually every bill incurred by Sharpton, including the clothes on his back and his daughters' private school tuition. If that's true, Reverend Sharpton blurred one of the most important lines in the tax law.

Blending personal and business is asking for trouble, but Sharpton had no problems. When the IRS brought the $4 million problem to Al's attention, the reverend cried, "It's political." This must have frightened the IRS into neglecting to arrest him or garnishing his MSNBC wages. But rest easy, Al, because Lois Lerner and President Obama assured us that the IRS does *not* target people for political reasons.

Fun fact: Sharpton is a dropout from Brooklyn College who was ordained a Baptist minister by another Baptist minister when Al was 10 years old. He never attended a seminary. Jesse Jackson graduated from North Carolina A&T and attended Chicago Theological Seminary, but dropped out. He was nonetheless ordained a Baptist minister. The title "*Reverend*" isn't an indication of education, but rather ordination by a church.

A Chicago grand jury indicted the actor Jessie Smollett on sixteen felony counts, accusing him of staging a hate crime against himself. Jessie's an African American gay actor in a TV series, which somehow entitles him to selective prosecution. A month later the prosecutor dropped all charges. It's not unusual that law enforcement and prosecutors *agree* to a plea deal. Generally, it's agreed upon by both agencies and based on new evidence or when cases are minor in nature. The Smollett case was neither. Detective Commander Edward Wodnicki said detectives uncovered "overwhelming" evidence against Smollett, yet the prosecutors ignored evidence. Why did Tina Tchen, a former top-level Obama-era official, intervene in the investigation?

If you don't believe there's two standards of American justice, then let's look how the law is applied to Peter Strzok's Walmart shoppers.

Kristian Saucier was a sailor who took photos of his submarine and was sentenced to a year in federal prison because it was technically illegal to do so. Kristian merely wanted a memento of his tour of duty *without malicious intent*.

Interpretation: no intent to profit or share the information with America's enemies.

Let's compare apples with apples: Director Comey proclaimed Hillary innocent of Title 18, Section 793, Gathering, Transmitting, or Losing Defense Information, but a year prior the FBI arrested Bryan Nishimura, a reserve naval officer, for "unauthorized removal and retention of classified materials" without malicious intent—in other words, precisely what Hillary did.

Donald Keyser earned over a year in prison for unlawfully removing classified documents from the Department of State to his residence. US Attorney Chuck Rosenberg stated that Keyser "had an absolute obligation to safeguard the classified information and utterly failed to do so." He added, "Keyser's sentence of imprisonment is a warning to others in positions of public trust." Just not Hillary Clinton.

There's Generals Petraeus and Flynn, George Papadopoulos, and Martha Stewart, all of who lied to the FBI. As a retired FBI agent, I can assure you that Title 18, Section 1001 is a *rarely* used statute, *except* on conservatives. I've conducted hundreds of official interviews with subjects, the majority of who fibbed big time.

My Marine Corps recruiter lied to me when he promised I'd go to flight school and skate Vietnam. Five months later I was a basic rifleman in Southeast Asia. The recruiter actually did me a favor, so some lies can be beneficial.

CHAPTER 8

Liar Liar Pants on Fire

"We have top men working on it right now."
"Who?"
"Top…men."
—*Raiders of the Lost Ark*

If you're branded a liar, then forget about testifying in court. If you're an FBI agent you *must* testify in court, so if you *can't* testify in court, then you really can't be an FBI agent. Deputy Director Andrew McCabe was fired for lying. After his termination, McCabe wrote a book and went on a publicity tour where he lied some more. Perhaps it's a bad habit.

During Andrew McCabe's *60 Minutes* interview with Scott Pelley, McCabe *insisted* there were meetings (plural) at the Justice Department where they discussed the possibility of invoking the Twenty-Fifth Amendment and removing the duly elected president of the United States.

Pelly, a supposedly unbiased CBS journalist, decides to put words into McCabe's mouth and declares, "The highest levels of American law enforcement were trying to figure out what do with the president." Pelly would've been better served to ask McCabe, "What was your justification to consider such a drastic action of removing a sitting president?"

The Twenty-Fifth Amendment is designed to address the physical incapacitation of a president. It guarantees a continuation of a chief executive if the president is incapacitated by a stroke or other debilitating condition. The consent of the vice president and cabinet is required.

We know one thing for certain. A meeting occurred involving the top officials of the FBI and attorney general where the Twenty-Fifth Amendment was discussed. McCabe claims that there were several meetings with *serious* discussions about removing President Trump. Rod Rosenstein alternated between denying ever discussing the matter to claiming he was being "sarcastic." After observing Rosenstein over the past few years my vote is sarcasm.

Normally one would assume that a room full of the top government attorneys would realize that the Twenty-Fifth Amendment did not apply to a president that they merely disliked. They likely made a case on a false narrative that Trump was mentally ill. That diagnosis is a slippery slope since a majority of Congress could be removed from office based on that criteria.

One example is Rep. Steve Cohen, who arrived at a House Judiciary Committee hearing with a bucket of fried chicken. He pointed to the chicken and said, "He's here." Cohen was calling Attorney General Barr a *chicken* for deciding to skip seven hours of insults by Democrats. Given the location—Congress—and position of Cohen the *stunt* was creepy and reminiscent of behavior in a psychiatric ward. An unintentional consequence of Cohen's theatrics was to poke the bear in the eye. The *chicken* is now a pissed off and motivated individual who just happens to have access to an army of investigators, attorneys, and grand juries. Thank you Chicken Little.

The day after the *60 Minutes* interview, McCabe took some heat from disclosing details of the Twenty-Fifth Amendment discussion. A spokesperson for McCabe disinfected his statement by saying, "To clarify, at no time did Mr. McCabe participate in any extended discussions about the use of the Twenty-Fifth Amendment, nor is he aware of any such discussions."

Shakespeare wrote in *Richard III*, "In thy foul throat thou liest."

AG Sessions fired the disgraced former official upon the recommendation of the FBI's Office of Professional Responsibility after it determined McCabe "lacked candor" multiple times while under oath. Trump was blamed but I'm almost certain that OPR made that decision minus any White House pressure.

Lack of candor (lying or being dishonest) is the number *one* reason why people are fired from the FBI. You can get a DUI, smoke a joint, or take your Bureau car on vacation, but *don't* lie about it. Lack of candor is usually worse than whatever you've done to hide the lie. Any brick agent would've been terminated immediately had they lied on one occasion in a substantive matter. McCabe lied repeatedly at a time the Bureau was under intense scrutiny for its past practice of holding SES staff to a lower standard.

Inspector General Horowitz's report documents McCabe's dishonesty.

He dishonestly denied knowledge of the leak he had ordered, covered his tracks by deflecting blame, and—when he finally admitted his role—falsely suggested that Comey had been aware and approving of his actions. McCabe lies to his boss, he lies to his fellow agents, and he lies—under oath—in interviews conducted by the FBI's internal investigators and the IG. Even when he changes his story, McCabe lies about the lies.

When leaks were in season, media outlets began stories with "An intelligence source stated…" It never occurred to most Americans that the FBI could be involved. McCabe's claim that he had authority to leak information to media sources was willfully misleading. He's correct that only certain individuals are approved to *speak* with the media, but I'm betting that no FBI policy allows employees to *leak* stories. Leaking can be a valuable tool for some professions, but when "leaking" is contained in the same sentence with "FBI agents," it cheapens a venerable organization. The CIA or the Agriculture Department can be sieves and maintain their image, but the FBI cannot.

Although the IG referred McCabe to the Justice Department for possible prosecution, it's unlikely he'll have to mortgage his house like General Flynn or spend time in a West Virginia prison like Martha Stewart for the *exact* same crime. The media has portrayed McCabe as a sympathetic civil servant who served the FBI with honor. Here's the problem with that image.

McCabe accused former Deputy Attorney General Rod Rosenstein of plotting to wear a wire to record President Trump. McCabe stated the topic "came up more than once, and it was so serious that he took it to the lawyers at the FBI to discuss it." Rosenstein vehemently disputes this allegation. Both men will testify under oath affirming their version, obligating one to commit perjury, which is punishable by five years in prison. It's even money on who will be the perjurer. They both have a sleazy feel to them.

It was McCabe who initiated an obstruction of justice investigation against the president of the United States. He and others within the top echelon of the FBI were deeply concerned that President Trump gained his office with the conspiratorial assistance of the Russian government and then attempted to block any investigation.

There was zero probable cause to initiate this case since it lacked evidence that President *or* candidate Trump was involved in a conspiracy with Russia. They accepted gossip and rumor as fact fueled by their ideology. This false premise eventually morphed into a FISA warrant that begat the special counsel's probe.

The Comey Gang committed many basic gaffes in conducting investigations. They took uncorroborated evidence (the Steele dossier) and gleefully made assumptions (Trump was colluding with Russia) based solely on their hatred of Trump. Once Comey and McCabe went down that dusty road, they made other blind assumptions and treated them as truth. They initiated a criminal investigation based solely on a belief that the president obstructed justice by the mere act of firing Comey. It never occurred to them that there were *other* legitimate reasons to can Comey.

Civilians have the luxury to engage in heated conversations and make wild claims all day long about politics. Wild rumors passed on as truth at the watercooler often get downright bizarre.

If the public had the authority to initiate criminal investigations based on gossip, then the American government would come to a screeching halt. (Pretty much like it has now.) As an FBI agent, I could not open cases based on my belief system. My supervisor would refer me to the ice cream factory at Quantico for observation. But McCabe and Comey were their own supervisors and had no one to stop them. The Bureau attorneys responsible for tapping their brakes were coconspirators. The FBI's General Counsel division was headed by James Baker and included Lisa Page, both of whom were non-agent attorneys who shared McCabe's belief that Trump was a criminal.

This vacuum of integrity left no rationale voice to offer, "Mr. Director, we really don't have any reliable facts to request a FISA warrant for electronic surveillance on a Trump associate. We'll have to vet Steele's information and access his reliability."

McCabe explained in his *60 Minutes* interview that he *believed* (not knew) that the president fired Comey to prevent the FBI from investigating him for Russian collusion. Probable cause is required to open a case of this significance but all McCabe had was a hunch. When pressed, McCabe concedes that FBI agents were conducting a counterintelligence investigation in which they *suspected* that Russia favored Trump in the election.

At one point he unintentionally admits that the FBI lacked any evidence to initiate an investigation on the president. He tells CBS, "So all those same *sorts* of facts cause us to *wonder* if there is an inappropriate relationship, a connection between this president and our most fearsome enemy, the government of Russia."

Two problems with McCabe's statement. Probable cause is not based on a *sort* of fact but rather a *fact* of fact. But McCabe lacked *any* facts, and secondly, the FBI wouldn't initiate a case on the president of the United States based on "wondering."

Lacking that evidence McCabe went after Trump through the back door by targeting Trump's staff—Flynn and Carter Page—and justified those investigations primarily based on their *conversations* (not collusion) with Russians.

Guilt by association has some investigative validity, but the Comey Gang set a perjury trap for Flynn, Gates, Cohen, Stone, and Papadopoulos, minus evidence of Trump's involvement. Had anyone else been the candidate or president, the FBI would've immediately briefed Trump on their suspicion. But President Trump was *always* the prime suspect based not on evidence but politics.

The case was opened on a subterfuge. McCabe reasoned that President Trump committed obstruction of justice by the mere act of firing Comey. McCabe actually posed this question during the *60 Minutes* interview: "Why would a president of the United States do that?" (i.e., fire Comey).

Gee, Andrew, maybe because your boss wasn't doing a good job. Not that the president requires a reason to terminate an employee. There was not one piece of hard evidence to connect President Trump to a Russian plot to fix the election. The midterm investigators detested Trump on a visceral level and turned rumors and false documents into evidence of a crime.

Proof of bias is their own words since, "Fuck Trump" cannot be construed as a neutral term.

McCabe walked a semantically fine line during the interview. One newspaper article reported that "former acting FBI director Andrew McCabe *hinted* at an inappropriate relationship between President Donald Trump and Russia during a wide-ranging interview on CBS *60 Minutes*."

FBI agents don't "hint." McCabe may have been reluctant to provide evidence to the media, but he seemed short on facts and long on alibis of his own wrongdoing. It would've been significantly different had McCabe said that the FBI had a *factual* basis to believe that Trump was complicit in a criminal conspiracy with the Kremlin and left it at that. He certainly had no problem leaking *other* stuff to the media.

McCabe leaked sensitive FBI information to the media. You would be right to assume that leaking secrets to the media is forbidden and illegal. When caught, McCabe stated that he had authority to leak the information to the press. This wink-and-nod sanction seems similar to James Bond's license to kill. And then to deflect blame, this stand-up guy threw his friend James Comey under the bus: "He [Comey] knew I was leaking to reporters."

When James Comey testified under oath before Senator Chuck Grassley's committee, he was asked, "Have you ever been involved or *approved* leaking."

Comey replied, "No." And then added, "Never."

Once again, it's even money on whether Comey or McCabe is lying, but one of them committed perjury, which is punishable by five years in prison.

McCabe rationalized his leak with this: "I chose to share with a reporter through my public affairs officer and a legal counselor [Lisa Page]. As deputy director, I was one of only a few people who had the authority to do that. It was not a secret; it took place over several days, and others, including the director, were aware of the interaction with the reporter."

McCabe's choice of the word "share" is a benign form of the word "leak." It's no different than interchanging the words "extinguish" and "murder." He further rationalized that since *other* people knew he was leaking, then it was all okay.

Inspector General Horowitz disputed McCabe's claim that he was "one of only a few" with authority to leak. The IG identified *numerous* FBI employees, at *all* levels of the organization, who had no official reason to be in contact with the media but were nevertheless in *frequent* contact with reporters.

The IG report stated that "a *large* number of FBI employees who were in contact with journalists during this time period impacted our ability to identify the sources of leaks. For example, during the periods we reviewed, we identified *dozens* of FBI employees that had contact with members of the media."

Bureaucratic translation: The Federal Bureau of Investigation was one big sewer of employees with access to confidential information who used it for political purposes.

FBI headquarters has been called the Puzzle Palace by the field, but it never occurred to agents of my era that it would ever be known as the *House of Leaks*.

There is an irony that the government agency responsible for *finding* leakers is the Federal Bureau of Investigation. The leaks and sham investigations served no investigative or national security purpose. It was pure agenda-driven arrogance.

Let's count up the Pinocchio's so far and assess the damage.

Rosenstein claims McCabe is lying about wearing a wire, but McCabe counters that Rosenstein is lying. McCabe claims that Comey is lying about the leaking, but Comey says "never," and the IG says that most of the executive suite at FBI HQ and the Justice Department signed, endorsed, or contributed to a FISA warrant based on lies.

"Corruption is simply crime without conscience."

—*George Richard Marek*

McCabe included his wife, Jill, in the *60 Minutes* interview. She seems like a nice lady and dedicated physician and shares no blame in her husband's legal predicament. It was Andrew who stared solemnly at the CBS camera and claimed that he and Jill *barely* knew the Clintons, then provided a spirited defense on how he couldn't have interfered in the Hillary email case.

The problem is that the facts may not support either claim.

McCabe kept many particulars close to the vest that would cause him some heartburn if known. Inspector general investigators and real estate records confirm that Andrew McCabe and his wife were long-time neighbors and likely family friends with Bill and Hillary Clinton in Chappaqua, New York, where the former president and secretary of state still reside. This revelation was uncovered by a mortgage loan McCabe secured from the Justice Department's federal credit union.

In the 1990s, Andrew McCabe worked as a supervisor in the FBI's New York Field Office. His neighbors in Chappaqua were Bill and Hillary Clinton. Is this significant? Investigators allege that the relationship between the McCabes and Clintons stretched back to 1999. The Clintons moved from the White House to Chappaqua, and records indicate that the McCabe's had just moved to Chappaqua months earlier.

Being neighbors is not a crime, but why did McCabe allegedly withhold this fact from the FBI while overseeing the email investigation? This full disclosure seems pertinent due to McCabe's claims of being unbiased and not having a relationship with the Clintons. Why not get it all out in the open rather than have the IG dropping it years later like a fifty-ton bomb?

McCabe was the assistant director of the Washington Field Office when his wife ran for Virginia state senate. His position, at that time, was *not* part of FBI HQ. McCabe *did* seek an ethics opinion from FBI attorneys regarding his wife's candidacy. The individuals who reviewed the matter supposedly had no information that McCabe's wife received several hundred thousand dollars from Clinton ally and Virginia governor Terry McAuliffe. McAuliffe himself was under an FBI investigation for campaign violations based on his time as a board member of the Clinton Global Initiative.

McCabe became FBI deputy director on February 1, 2016 (at FBI HQ), which made him the number two man in the entire FBI. At that point, McCabe assumed an active role in the supervision of the Clinton email investigation and oversight of the Clinton Foundation investigation until he recused himself from both investigations on November 1, 2016.

For nine months, Deputy Director McCabe made major decisions on the email and Russian collusion probe. During that time, McCabe was being fed a steady diet of anti-Trump rhetoric. The Strzok-Page text messages about seeing "Andy" put him at the center of discussions to damage the president while aware that the Steele dossier was garbage. The Comey Gang claimed they were "unaware of any derogatory information" about the Steele dossier and the motivation behind it. This claim was patently false.

In July of 2016, Bruce Ohr briefed Andrew McCabe, Peter Strzok, and Lisa Page on his meetings with Christopher Steele. A few weeks later Ohr briefed Andrew Weissmann (a top lawyer for then Attorney General Loretta Lynch). Months later, Weissmann joined the special counsel and starred in a one-act play that ran for two years. He nailed the role of a prosecutor who pretended to investigate high crimes and misdemeanors while aware there existed no criminal predicate acts.

Ohr—the number four attorney in the justice department—cautioned everyone that Christopher Steele's information was unverified and probably untrue. Yet his warnings about political bias were pointedly omitted weeks later from the FISA warrant that the FBI obtained from a federal court. It granted the Bureau authority to electronically spy on the Trump campaign to determine whether it was colluding with Russia to hijack the 2016 presidential election.

Ohr's activities, chronicled in handwritten notes, provide the most damning evidence to date that FBI and DOJ officials had misled federal judges in October 2016. They required that FISA warrant to prevent Donald Trump from becoming the forty-fifth president of the United States.

McCabe knew that the Steele dossier was unreliable and unverified yet after Comey's firing McCabe became acting FBI director and signed a FISA renewal affirming to the FISA court that the information *was* reliable and verified.

Ohr confirmed to investigators that Steele's credibility issue was raised with the FBI *before* the first FISA application. Ohr categorized Steele's information as "hearsay," which is defined as a statement based on rumor that is inadmissible in the court of law. There's a good reason why hearsay is inadmissible in court. It's on the same legal level as gossip spread by teenagers in the high school cafeteria.

One glaring inconsistency centers on Comey's June 8, 2017, prepared remarks before the Senate Select Committee on Intelligence, where he referred to the anti-Trump dossier as containing "salacious and unverified" material.

Yet, a memo issued by House Republicans confirmed that Comey personally signed *three* FISA court applications utilizing that same unverified dossier eight months later to obtain FISA court warrants to conduct surveillance. His target, Carter Page, briefly served as a volunteer foreign policy advisor to Trump's 2016 campaign.

This presented Comey with a major problem. The FBI director signed a FISA warrant that he *knew* was unverified. This could have led to a very dirty legal diaper, so Comey attempted to babble his way out of the mess with, "I signed off *procedurally*."

Bureaucratic translation: Comey is caught in a possible criminal act. His use of the word "procedurally" is meant to deflect his role in signing a legal document that he didn't read. Do not attempt this at home. This type of carelessness may be a defense had Comey been a homebuyer signing a twenty-page purchase agreement that a bank official slid across the desk. But James Comey was a former US attorney and FBI director, so his actions constituted possible perjury or public corruption.

Had McCabe been an unbiased, impartial public servant, he would have immediately bounced both Strzok and Page off anything dealing with Trump, Russia, FISA, or Carter Page. On November 1, 2016, Comey pressured McCabe to recuse himself from the email probe. The presidential election was one week away, and the timing smelled since McCabe and Comey had already absolved Hillary of any wrongdoing. The only reason Comey wanted McCabe at arm's length from the email investigation was an October 23 article in the *Wall Street Journal* identifying the large donations from McAuliffe's PAC to Jill McCabe. The deputy FBI director created a misconception that the general public knew all along that his wife benefited by Clinton allies while he investigated Hillary.

In the *60 Minutes* interview, McCabe made the point that his wife had already lost the election at this time, which, though true, infers that he had no reason to absolve Hillary of wrongdoing. This doesn't pass the smell test. The financial connection between the Clintons and his wife couldn't be put back in the bottle. It happened and McCabe owed Hillary for his wife's campaign contribution.

McCabe knew the Clinton email investigation was underway when his wife received the donations—September 30 through October 29,

2015—and he had to suspect that those contributions would eventually force his recusal from the investigation if they were known, but he kept mum, like any good political soldier.

The inspector general did find that McCabe rightly recused himself from the McAuliffe investigation and that there was no evidence he "participated in making or supervising substantive decisions" in the case. But the IG investigators found several instances in which McCabe did *not* fully comply with his recusals. On March 7, 2015, he and his wife met with McAuliffe at the governor's mansion prior to a political event. At the time, McCabe was running the FBI's Washington Field Office and had no business meeting McAuliffe, who was a subject in an FBI case. But McCabe kept poking the edges of noncompliance.

On February 25, 2016, the inspector general found an email that McCabe sent to senior FBI officials with instructions to schedule an interview with McAuliffe. When asked about it, McCabe said he had merely given *broad* instructions about interviews of high-profile political subjects that those below him applied to McAuliffe.

Office politics is no different anywhere, whether your office is the FBI or waste management. If the boss provides you with some "broad" instructions, there is no need for him to stipulate the desired results.

The inspector general also interviewed an FBI supervisor in DC who was probing the Clinton Foundation. He stated that the FBI's Los Angeles Field Office would not share Clinton bank records that they had subpoenaed in an unrelated case. Reluctance to share evidence with outside agencies is not unusual, but it is *very* rare among FBI field offices. The supervisor told the IG investigators that the directive not to share came from McCabe.

The IG report raises concerns if McCabe honored his recusals. But these burps are insignificant when compared to the IG's April report that alleged McCabe misled investigators exploring a media leak. Those findings ultimately led to McCabe's ouster from the FBI, and he is now facing an investigation by the US Attorney's Office into whether he committed a crime.

The *60 Minutes* interview was actually very enlightening into the mind-set of Andrew McCabe. He naturally skewed his answers to place himself as an innocent victim of a vindictive president. But McCabe conceded that he and the Comey Gang wanted to take down President Trump by constructing a solid collusion/obstruction case. They built that case on sand, and it collapsed with the Mueller findings. Minus facts and evidence, their behavior seemed like a failed coup attempt by a bunch of desperados in sombreros with rusty pistols.

CHAPTER 9

Game of (Un)-Knowns

"That's too coincidental to be a coincidence."
—Yogi Berra

Coincidences that seem too strange to be true happen all the time. In 1975, a man was accidentally struck and killed by a taxi while riding a moped in Bermuda. One year later, this man's brother was killed in the very same way while riding the very same moped. And adding to the fluke, he was struck by the very same taxi driven by the same driver, and even carrying the very same passenger. But when coincidences occur in law enforcement, they often become clues.

John Brennan. In 1976 former CIA Director John Brennan voted for the Communist candidate for president, Gus Hall. Brennan rationalized his vote by stating that he was *unhappy with the system and saw the need for change.*

Brennan forbade the use of the term "*jihadist*" to describe Islamist terrorists, both at the National Security Council and the CIA. He prefers the term "*extremists.*" One of the FBI's former top experts on Islam, John Guandolo, has repeatedly claimed that Brennan converted to Islam years ago in Saudi Arabia. Brennan decided to forgo the Bible during his swearing-in ceremony as director of the CIA and firmly believes that there's "*no link between terrorism and radical Islam.*"

A synonym is one of two or more words that have the same or nearly the same meaning. The words "*terrorism*" and "*radical,*" sound "*nearly*" close.

James Comey wrote a college thesis at William and Mary titled "The Christian in Politics." It compared the political philosophies of Reinhold Niebuhr and Jerry Falwell. Niebuhr was an avowed Marxist, claiming that communal (State) ownership of property was a requirement for social justice and capitalism was responsible for the economic imperialism.

Comey considered Niebuhr to be one of the world's greatest moral and political theologians and felt that Falwell was a huckster and inclined to "*violate the constitutional separation of Church and State.*"

Reinhold held that private ownership (corporations) of American products cause economic crises. He believed that the Ford Motor Company's vast wealth should no longer be *privately owned.* (redistribution of wealth).

Ironically, Niebuhr described his protegee, Comey, when stating that *it could be dangerous for a politician to see himself as a moral beacon.* Ouch!

Nellie Ohr, the wife of former Deputy Associate Attorney General Bruce Ohr, was hired as a Russian expert by the firm Fusion GPS. Richard L. Hauke, Nellie's dad, was a science professor who seemed interested in the "*nuclear winter.*" This nuclear theme seems to be a common thread among this group, especially *after* candidate Trump vowed to update our nuclear arsenal.

Nellie taught Russian history at Vassar College in the 1990s. Edward Baumgartner was a student during that period, majoring in Russian history. Professor Nellie seemed to be a student of Stalinism, offering Socialism as an option to capitalism.

Baumgartner *coincidentally* ends up as another Fusion GPS Russia expert. Testimony by Bruce Ohr confirms that Christopher Steele had a vile hatred toward President Trump and believed Steele fabricated the information used in the FISA warrant. Sworn testimony also corroborates that Peter Strzok, Lisa Page, and many of the FBI agents investigating the president shared that an intense animus.

So, who is Ed Baumgartner? Did Fusion GPS owner, Glenn Simpson, hire Baumgartner to assure a balanced approach to the information Steele provided? *Coincidentally not.*

White House Press Secretary Sarah Sanders tweeted a noncontroversial comment of: *"Thank God we have patriots like General John Kelly serving our country."*

Baumgartner's reply: *"Are you really the love child of Mike Huckabee and Bernie Sanders? Which ass did you crawl out of?"*

Comey, Brennan, Clapper, Nellie and Bruce Ohr, Baumgartner, and the entire legal staff of the special counsel had a deep and negative animus toward Donald Trump. This group constitute a powerful force in both the public and private sectors all in lockstep to destroy Trump. They required some fictional substance to slay their villain and they found their kryptonite in Christopher Steele. Did this former British MI6 officer offer an unbiased counterbalance to these Trump haters? Nah!

Christopher Steele attended Cambridge University and his fellow students remember him as a fierce debater and the president of the debating society. A Cambridge book called him a confirmed socialist. The future British MI6 intelligence officer supported Marxist socialism and a Campaign for Nuclear Disarmament (CND). This was a Marxist infiltrated organization investigated by British MI5. They concluded that CND was a communist and subversive since their efforts involved disarming Britain and forcing US cruise missiles off British bases.

Many Americans know that Steele was an MI6 operative but what exactly are the differences between MI5 and MI6? Both MI5 and MI6 are British intelligence entities similar to the FBI and CIA. James

Bond was an MI6 operative who was too busy saving the world to play politics. Basically, the FBI and MI5 are responsible for protecting the homeland and countering foreign intelligence at home. The CIA and MI6 are responsible for gathering intelligence on foreign soil.

MI (British **M**ilitary **I**ntelligence) once had agencies numbered up to nineteen but most were folded into MI5 and MI6 after the war. Some of the defunct ones were MI1 (codebreaking), and MI9 (under-cover operations) and conspiracy theorists will have you believe that there is still a clandestine MI7 dealing with matters extraterrestrial.

Steele was the kickstart for the dossier and former CND zealot. He supported nuclear freeze, which was at odds with candidate Trump who vowed to update and expand the US nuclear arsenal. On April 27, 2016 Trump affirmed the toughest anti-Communist stance in decades: *"Our nuclear weapons arsenal, our ultimate deterrent, has been allowed to atrophy and is desperately in need of modernization and renewal. And it has to happen immediately."*

President Trump remains suspect of colluding with Russia even *after* Mueller totally exonerated him. He's been accused of being soft on Putin and Representative Schiff has made remarks that President Trump could be a Russian spy.

But the facts paint the opposite picture. Aided by an American informant, the FBI gathered significant evidence that Russia corrupted an American uranium trucking company through bribes. The Hill reported that eyewitness accounts and documents indicating Russian fronts spent millions of dollars to *benefit* the Clinton's charitable foundation.

Why would Russian nuclear officials send money to the Clinton Foundation?

It's a sliver of distance between a conspiracy and a coincidence.

A 2010 deal allowed Rosatom, the Russian nuclear energy agency, to acquire a controlling stake in Uranium One, a Canadian-based company with mining stakes in the United States. Secretary of State Hillary

Clinton sat on the Committee on Foreign Investment in the United States (CFIUS). This panel approved strategic foreign investments such as Rosatom's Uranium One, a subsidiary of Rosatom.

The 2010 deal allowed Rosatom, the Russian nuclear energy agency, to acquire a controlling stake in Uranium One, resulting in Russia's control of a bulk of American uranium.

Peter Schweizer's book *Clinton Cash,* noted that Hillary Clinton, *not* Donald Trump, was deeply involved with the Russians on many levels. Despite the FBI's evidence of bribery, extortion, and racketeering, Hillary Clinton and then-Attorney General Eric Holder and other members of the Obama administration *approved* of Rosatom's takeover of Uranium One.

Coincidences in Bermuda traffic accidents would be suspect had someone benefited. The cab driver probably didn't benefit from mowing down mopeds driven by the same family members, *but…* In 2010 former President Bill Clinton gave a speech in Russia to the Renaissance Capital corporation for half a million dollars. *Coincidently*, in 2010 a transfer of American commercial nuclear assets was made to Russia. This could be considered a quid pro quo were the FBI currently investigating the Clinton Foundation.

Comey claimed that Putin's election interference was to benefit Donald Trump. But Trump claimed, "There's never been a president as tough on Russia as I have been." Fact or fiction?

NPR is a liberal media organization and a constant critic of Trump. An NPR July 2018 article claimed, "That might sound like hyperbole, but in this case, there's actually some basis for the president's boast. When you actually look at the substance of what this administration has done, not the rhetoric but the *substance*, this administration has been much tougher on Russia than any in the post-Cold War era," said Daniel Vajdich, senior fellow at the Atlantic Council. Take military spending: Trump sought to add $1.4 billion for fiscal year 2018 to the European Deterrence Initiative—a military effort to deter Russian aggression that was initially known as the European Reassurance Initiative. That's a 41 percent increase from the last year of the Obama administration. The president also agreed to send lethal weapons to Ukraine—a step that Obama resisted. And Trump gave US forces in Syria more leeway to engage with Russian troops."

Lily Tomlin played the precocious five-year-old Edith Ann on *Rowan and Martin's Laugh-In,* in 1969. After making some statement, Edith Ann would stare at the camera and utter, "*And that's the truth,*" followed with an emphatic raspberry.

CHAPTER 10:

Knock Knock, Who's There?
The Inspector General

"The greatest deception men suffer is from their own opinions."
—Leonardo da Vinci

Henry VIII was married six times. His brides' reigns ended by divorce, beheading, death, divorce, and beheading. But wife number six, Catherine Parr, somehow survived. The moral of this story is that certain unions will turn toxic when one has a sexual or political agenda.

Robert Mueller escorted the FBI down the aisle and gave the Bureau away to the Department of Justice. This marriage begat the Comey Gang, and the FBI can only hope to meet the same fate as Catherine Parr. The jury is still out.

On July 7, 2016, Hillary Clinton testified under oath that *no* classified material was sent or received on her private server. On the very same day, FBI director James Comey also testified under oath that emails sent or received by Clinton were "marked classified."

Perjury is willfully telling an untruth in a court after having taken an oath or affirmation.

Hillary Clinton was *never* going to be indicted. Loretta Lynch's Justice Department stacked the deck and had the motive and opportunity to make it *not* happen. The connected dots indicate that their purpose was to fix the 2016 presidential election.

Even if Comey had recommended charges, the attorney general had the final word. The FBI director may have taken the bullet for Lynch, but she wasn't taking any chances. Loretta Lynch installed a fail-safe to clear Hillary's run to the presidency. It was a poison pill that Comey swallowed. I'm sure that officials will deny any undue influence exerted by the DOJ, but consider the following facts.

Lynch was appointed by Bill Clinton, who she just *happened* to meet a few weeks before Comey waived his forgiveness wand over Hillary. They both claimed the tarmac meeting an accident. But it wasn't. The inspector general's report was five hundred–plus pages, and deep inside, on page 203, was this gem: "The Office of Public Affairs Supervisor said that he later learned that former President Clinton's Secret Service detail had contacted Lynch's FBI security detail to let them know that the former President wanted to meet with Lynch."

But Lynch's staff members maintain in the report they had no knowledge of the request and were surprised by the former president's visit. When pressed about the nature of their conversation, Clinton chuckled and said he and Lynch discussed grandkids and the golf he had played during his trip to Phoenix.

Christopher Sign, an anchor for ABC News, said there's no evidence that Clinton played golf during his visit. "Two years later and I have not found a person who can confirm that former President Clinton played golf during that trip to Phoenix," Sign remarked. Golfers may lie about their score but never about playing the game.

Why lie? Benjamin Franklin said, "Tricks and treachery are the practice of fools, that don't have brains enough to be honest."

A few days after the tarmac meeting, James Comey found that Hillary had "not intended" to violate the law. This decision can be considered prosecutorial discretion except for two problems: James Comey is *not* a prosecutor, and Loretta Lynch set a legal hurdle that couldn't be cleared.

Very early in the Hillary email case, the attorney general *required* the FBI to establish evidence of *intent*—even though the gross negligence statute explicitly does *not* require this element. It was also Lynch who'd previously ordered Comey to refer to the investigation as a "matter." This semantic illusion was a smoke screen to confuse the voting public into believing that Hillary had no legal problems. Or as Mrs. Clinton so eloquently stated at the Benghazi hearings, "What difference, at this point, does it matter!"

The intent prerequisite required the FBI to find a smoking gun, such as the confession, "I intended to violate a federal law by using an unsecure server for transmitting classified information." That, obviously, was never going to happen.

The FBI and Justice Department attorneys assigned to the Clinton email case spent days discussing exactly what legally constitutes *intent*. I won't bore you with the details, but it was basically a ton of esoteric bullshit similar to college freshmen debating if consciousness proves that immaterial entities exist.

This precondition of intent is a prime example that the FBI and Justice Department are joined at the hip. Their roles and function are blurred like a Jackson Pollock abstract painting. The Justice Department should *never* set preconditions on an FBI investigation, and the FBI should *never* announce guilt or innocence of the subject of an investigation. It should also be noted that the FBI has never been known as the Federal Bureau of *Matters*.

If you still doubt that the FBI has lost all independence and become a political weapon of the Justice Department, then here's an excerpt from FBI attorney Lisa Page's testimony to a Congressional committee.

Rep. Ratcliffe: Okay…I think, when you talk about intent…it sounds like you all just blew over gross negligence.

Ms. Page: We did not blow over gross negligence…And we had multiple conversations, multiple conversations with the Justice Department about charging gross negligence.

Rep. Ratcliffe: Okay…but when you say advice you got from the department, you're making it sound like it was the department that told you: you're not going to charge gross negligence because we're the prosecutors and we're telling you we're not going to—

Ms. Page: That is correct.

This admission by Page confirms that the FBI had surrendered its soul to the Justice Department. Some FBI agent should've politely requested that the Justice attorneys remove themselves from the interview.

"This is *our* investigation and when we conclude, we'll submit a prosecutive report. Thank you and good-bye."

Loretta Lynch was a politician masquerading as an impartial arbiter. The Comey Gang caved to ridiculous and unfair conditions by Lynch rather than politely explaining to butt out until their investigation was concluded.

The FBI director's ten-year appointment was specifically designed to eliminate politics from the position. Even if a president wins two terms (eight years), the FBI director continues in office.

During my career, I've had several assistant United States attorneys ask if they could accompany me on an interview or while executing a warrant. I'd refuse and explain that if they participated in an active investigation, they then become a witness and could not prosecute the case. The Bureau must return to the time when it "did its thing" (investigate cases) minus any interference from the Justice Department.

The president should remove the FBI from the attorney general's umbrella and place the FBI director on an even plane with the attorney general. The administrative precedent for such a chain of command is already in place. Most of the public wrongly assume that the Marine Corps is under the control of the Navy. In fact, they are coequal branches of the Department of the Navy. The commandant of the Marine Corps has equal status with the Chief of Naval Operations on the Joint Chiefs of Staff. *Both* answer to the Secretary of the Navy.

The Justice Department should adopt this coequal branch model with the FBI and US Attorney division.

The issue at the heart of the Clinton email investigation was summarized by Ryan Breitenbach, who was the House majority counsel. He said that "the Department of Justice made a decision that intent was required, even though we have a statute on the books that does not require intent [but only] requires gross negligence."

When the Justice Department required evidence of intent in order to prosecute, it managed to castrate the entire FBI investigation from the outset. Snip, snip.

When Hillary arrived for her July 2 interview, her innocence was already predetermined. The interview was theater—part comedy, part tragedy—but a show nonetheless. Comey was criticized for drafting his exoneration statement months *before* the investigation concluded. He never offered a logical explanation, but I believe that he penned the absolution because he knew that Justice had already made their decision. There was an attempt to justify Comey's pre-absolution memo by a member of the gang with something to the effect of "It's not unusual to draft different versions of an investigation prior to its outcome." Career agents can only shake their heads at this pathetic attempt at Beltway delusion. Even the general public can smell the seventh-floor poop.

Here's the sequence that should have occurred in July of 2016 had the FBI been apolitical and independent.

Director Comey sends the prosecutive report to the Justice Department with evidence of Hillary Clinton violating several federal statutes. The Lynch Justice Department would have declined prosecution using a *lack of intent* to violate the law as their standard. Comey would meet privately with AG Lynch and strongly disagree with the decision and ask them to reconsider. Justice refuses and then Comey holds his press conference and lays out the facts to the public. He cites the Justice Department's interference with the FBI's investigation. Comey may have taken a hit from the liberal media, but he would have declared our independence and impartiality. Instead he caved.

Hillary Clinton was effectively in the clear from the beginning of the FBI investigation, and that is not justice served in the America I know.

What happens next is critical to the survival of the FBI as an American institution. The Bureau can withstand this dark period, but only if we cut the umbilical cord with the Justice Department.

The fact that Comey permitted Justice Department attorneys to monitor the FBI interviews with key witnesses is telling. We know the identity of some of the FBI players inside that room when Hillary was interviewed, but there are a few surprises. The inspector general's report identified *other* FBI agents with political agendas who influenced the Bureau's history.

The IG's report detailed a series of instant messages between some unknown but crucial players in the Clinton investigation. The IG prefaced them with "We do not question that the FBI employees who sent these messages are entitled to their own political views." Indeed, federal statutes and regulations explicitly protect the right of federal employees to "express…opinion[s] on political subjects and candidates" and to "exercise fully, freely, and without fear of penalty or reprisal."

As an FBI agent, I had opinions on sports, food, and politics. We would be robots absent these feelings, so the critical and simple question is, Did the political views of the agents investigating Russian collusion, Hillary's email, and the many spin-off investigations allow their feelings to influence their impartiality?

If Strzok and Page had been alone in their hatred of Trump, then perhaps these other impartial FBI agents involved would've thrown a penalty flag. Strzok emphasized under oath that he was not the sole decision maker in the email and Russian collusion investigation. But Strzok is an arrogant manipulator of the truth. Just ask any Walmart customer in southern Virginia.

(A Peter Strzok text to Lisa Page, *"Just went to a Southern Virginia Walmart. I could smell the Trump support."*

When confronted with his Walmart observation, Strzok babbled this explanation to Congress. *"I clearly wasn't smelling one thing or the other. What I meant by that was, living in Northern Virginia, having traveled 100, 150 miles south within the same state, I was struck by the extraordinary difference in the expression of political opinion and belief amongst the community there and from where I live."*)

* * *

Let's look at a few of these unbiased, impartial members of the team. The inspector general's report identified the two FBI agents who worked with Strzok and Page as FBI Agents #1 and #5. Sally Moyer was identified as Agent #5 by Representative Mark Meadows in congressional hearings. Agent #1 has not yet been identified.

According to the IG, Sally texted "f★★★ Trump" to Agent #1, then called Trump voters "retarded." She promised to quit the FBI "on the spot" if Trump was elected. Sally sadly reneged on that promise. Moyer, an attorney and registered Democrat, previously worked for the law firm Crowell & Moring after graduating from Allegheny College in 1996 with a degree in political science." (Moyer was dating Agent #1 at the time of the texts. She later married Agent #1.)

Keep in mind that according to the IG report, "Agent #1 was one of four agents responsible for the day-to-day activities of the investigation. Agent 1's duties included conducting witness interviews and

Agent 1 was one of several agents who interviewed former Secretary Clinton on July 2."

> **Agent #1:** future pres. Trump cant win, demographics dont line up, America has changed
> **Agent #5:** go baby, go! let's give her Virginia
> **Agent #1:** not to my country. You just cant get up and try to appeal to all the worst things in humans and fool my country…" [He's referencing Trump voters.]

On October 28, Comey sent the first letter to Congress about finding the Clinton emails on Anthony Weiner's laptop. After a very brief investigation, Comey advised Congress that the Weiner emails contained nothing of new significance. Agent #5, aka Sally Moyer, IM'd her boyfriend.

> **Agent #5:** jesus christ…Trump: Glad FBI is fixing "horrible mistake" on clinton emails…for fuck's sake…the fuck's sake part was me, the rest was trump.
> **Agent #1:** Not sure if Trump or the fifth floor is worse…
> **Agent #5:** I'm so sick of both… "+o TRUMP" +o Average American public" [Sally awarded 0 grades for Trump and the "average American public." Her comment infers that she and her FBI HQ posse are above-average Americans. It's also an honest snapshot into the smug elitism of the Comey Gang.]

On August 29, 2016, Agent #1 and Agent #5 exchanged the following instant messages as part of a discussion about their jobs.

> **Agent #1:** I find anyone who enjoys [supports Trump] an absolute fucking idiot. If you dont think so, ask them one more

question. Who are you voting for? I guarantee you it will be Donald Drumpf.

Agent #5: i forgot about drumpf...that's so sad and pathetic if they want to vote for him. someone who can't answer a question [That'd be the American public.]

Agent #5 continued: someone who can't be professional for even a second [What the heck is the reference to "can't be a professional"? It implies that Hillary voters are professionals but Trump folks are camel dung.]

On September 9, 2016, Agent #1 and Agent #5 exchanged the following instant messages.

Agent #5: i'm trying to think of a "would i rather" instead of spending time with those people

Agent #1: stick your tongue in a fan??

Agent #5: i would rather have brunch with trump

Agent #1: ha...french toast with drumpf

Agent #5: i would rather have brunch with trump and a bunch of his supporters like the ones from ohio that are retarded. [This was personally offensive since I spent twenty-plus years in the great state of Ohio.]

Sally Moyer told the inspector general that these instant messages "referenced TV programming and commentary that Agent 1 and Agent 5 had recently viewed together." She unconvincingly stated under oath that "the reference was not a general statement about a particular part of the country [Ohio]; rather it was in jest and pertained to individuals' inability to articulate any reason why they so strongly favored one candidate over another."

(Sally's alibi makes no sense and really peg one's BS meter.)

These class and intelligence insults by liberal FBI agents are a fascinating view into the culture at FBI HQ. Hillary called Trump supporters "deplorables," and now we have FBI Agent Moyer calling them "retards." And don't forget Peter Strzok smelling the Walmart customers in Virginia.

On Election Day, November 8, 2016, Agent #1 and Agent #5 exchanged the following instant messages.

Agent #1: You think HRC is gonna win right? You think we should get nails and some boards in case she doesnt

Agent #5: she better win…otherwise i'm gonna be walking around with both of my guns, and likely quitting on the spot.

Agent #1: You should know;…that I'm…with her. Oooooo ooooooooooooo.show me the money

Agent #5: screw you trump.wheeeeeeeeeeeeeeeeeeeeeeeeee! go baby, go! let's give her Virginia

Sally later claimed that she didn't treat Hillary (at the July 2 interview) any differently despite her political viewpoint. Yep, sounds like it. In a December 6, 2016, exchange, Sally complained to Agent #1 about being required to be on call on the day of the presidential inauguration and concluded with a "fuck trump."

Evidently Agent #1 didn't believe that Hillary should be interviewed on July 2 regarding her emails. He was insulted that her highness was subjected to silly questions and texted Sally that "My god…I'm actually starting to have embarrassment sprinkled on my disappointment…Ever been forced to do something you adamantly opposed."

Asked by the IG about his comments, Agent #1 insisted he hadn't meant to say what he *actually* said: "I don't want to make it sound like there was no reason to interview her." When attempting to explain his "adamantly opposed" comments, Agent #1's memory went south. My daughter Dani may respond with a "Duh."

Now, after reading the above exchanges, some may give the benefit of the doubt and accept the fact that a human being can be totally
unbiased and not take sides. But humans *cannot* totally detach themselves from their emotions and prevent them from seeping into their
objectivity. Mr. Spock even had his human emotions override the
Vulcan blood at times.

The fact is that Agents #1 and #2 were totally infatuated with
Hillary Clinton. After interviewing Clinton (while she was still a suspect
in a criminal case), Agent #5 informed Agent #1 that she was "done
interviewing the *President*." (She is referring to *candidate* Clinton.)

Further proof that the fix was in are some highlights of Agent
#1's comments about his work on the "Midyear" investigation, as the
Clinton case was code-named:

> "…the most meaningless thing I've ever done with
> people acting like f---ing 9/11."

> "…I dont care about it. I think its continued waste of
> resources and time and focus…"

> "…Its just so obvious how pointless this exercise is…"

When the IG questioned Agent #1, he provided an absurd excuse
that his indiscreet comments "are just the nature of using instant messaging." (This makes no sense since he is blaming a *thing* [IM] for putting words in his mouth. It's also a classic non-answer.)

According to Agent #1, he succumbed to a "watercooler" style of
"jocularity" because he thought IMs "were not retained by the FBI and
therefore used less caution with those communications than he would
have with other types of communications." (More BS since Agent #1
is actually admitting that he would've used different—meaning less-in-
criminating—words had he known his IM was a matter of record.)

It got worse. Agent #1 then began spewing gobbledygook. He told the IG investigators, "You know, guys, I just, I think this was primarily used as a personal conversation venting mode for me. I'm embarrassed for it, [but] I don't think that it affected my actions. The Midyear investigation team was crammed into a sensitive compartmented information facility at headquarters, and I was unable to use personal electronic devices at work and was also in a small space with his coworkers and supervisors, thereby preventing phone communication."

Agent #1's long-winded description of office space and electronic devices does *not* include an explanation for his stated intentions. The lack of substance is telling, but perhaps more to the point are his stated words on February 9, 2016. In response to Agent #5 complaining about her working conditions, Agent #1 sent a reply to her.

> Yeah, I hear you. You guys have a shitty task, in a shitty environment. To look for something conjured in a place where you can't find it, for a case that doesn't matter and is *predestined*.

It's bad enough that a lead agent on the Clinton case was convinced the outcome was "predestined." (Another word for "fixed.")

Agent #1 described the politics involved during this supposedly impartial active investigation: "DOJ comes in there every once in a while and takes a wishy-washy, political, cowardice stance."

This may sound like the usual work complaints had it not involved a silent coup. But when asked about that message, Agent #1 had another take altogether for the IG: "I have no information that [the Clinton investigation] was a predetermined outcome by anyone." (Interpretation: Ignore what I previously said even though that was the truth, but now I'm backtracking because this whole IM thing became public.)

But Agent #1 continued to speak with forked tongue concerning the Hillary fix. His January 2016 message to Agent #4 (another unknown agent) proclaimed, "What we want to do and what we're going to be allowed to do are two different things."

Asked about this quote by the IG, Agent #1 suffered a temporary bout of amnesia, unable to remember what he had been talking about. What he *did* know was that he had merely been "venting." Jack the Ripper also vented, but it didn't excuse his criminal activity. It seems the fix was in not just for Hillary but her enablers too. In February 2016, right after Agent #1 interviewed Hillary's personal IT guy, he had this exchange with a fellow FBI employee:

FBI employee: boom…how did the [witness] go

Agent #1: Awesome. Lied his ass off. Went from never inside the scif [sensitive compartmented information facility] at res, to looked in when it was being constructed, to remove the trash twice, to troubleshoot the secure fax with HRC a couple times, every time there was a secure fax i did it with HRC. Ridic,

FBI employee: would be funny if he was the only guy charged n this deal

Agent #1: I know. For 1001. [Lying to the FBI.] Even if he said the truth and didnt have a clearance when handling the secure fax—aint no one gonna do s--t

Though Agent #1 was being cynical, he was also right. Had the IT guy been a Republican, he'd join General Flynn, George Papadopoulous, Roger Stone, and Paul Manafort in the lying wing at the federal pen. It pays to be a friend of Bill and Hillary.

The IG concluded that the "conduct of these employees cast a cloud over the entire FBI investigation and sowed doubt about the FBI's work on, and its handling of, the Midyear investigation. The damage caused by these employees' actions extends far beyond the scope of the Midyear investigation and goes to the heart of the FBI's reputation for neutral fact-finding and political independence."

The FBI hierarchy seems to be following its ineffective remedial action plan to correct problems: investigate, apologize, and mandate training. This remedy constitutes placing a Band-Aid on a gushing wound.

The above written interactions indicate that the conspiracy wasn't limited to a few bureaucrats with a political grudge. It wasn't just Page and Strzok and their prejudicial beliefs but a *culture* that permeated FBI headquarters. These facts and circumstances make a case that the FBI requires an engine overhaul. How could individuals collectively rise to senior levels within the FBI if their views and language indicate ongoing public corruption? Is this behavior a temporary glitch in the FBI DNA or something more permanent?

The inspector general report stated, "The conduct of these FBI employees has brought discredit to themselves, sowed doubt about the FBI's handling of the Midyear investigation and impacted the reputation of the FBI. The conduct by these individuals sowed doubt the FBI's work on, and its handling of, the Midyear investigation. Moreover, the damage caused by their actions goes to the heart of the FBI's reputation for neutral fact-finding and political independence."

Let's recap this chapter with Special Agent Sally Moyer's IM messages. Sally seems to be a hardworking FBI agent who should've recused herself from this investigation, *but* she does have a way with words. She joked that Donald Trump's supporters in Ohio were "retarded." She sneered that she didn't know who was worse: Trump, the FBI, or the average American public. Come Election Day she proclaimed that, should Hillary lose, "I'm gonna be walking around with both of my guns, and likely quitting on the spot."

And who can forget Sally's witty discourse of "Screw you Trump," followed by her closing argument of "wheeeeeeeeeeeeeeeeeeeeeeeeeeeeeeee!"

CHAPTER 11

The Art of Decision Avoidance

"Some live in a state of passionate indecision."
—Mason Cooley

Minneapolis FBI Office, August 2001, one month
prior **to the terror attacks**

"That ain't ever gonna happen."

The Minnesota brick agents had been hearing this crap for several months. They sent seventy communications to FBI HQ warning of an "imminent" terrorist attack. Alternate warnings of looming, forthcoming, and pending generated a similar arrogant response from Mike Maltbie. This was the latest conference call imploring HQ for a FISA warrant to search Zacarias Moussaoui's computer and personal effects. A criminal warrant didn't require HQ approval, but a FISA warrant went through a secret court in DC and required approval from an HQ supervisor.

The Radical Fundamentalist Unit (RFU) at FBI headquarters was headed by Dave Frasca along with supervisors Mike Maltbie and Rita

Flack. The Minnesota agents couldn't figure out Maltbie's hesitancy since FISA warrants were usually slam dunks. They generally require less probable cause than traditional criminal warrants. Prior to this Minnesota request, Maltbie had rejected only one other FISA request.

Minnesota agent Harry Samit rationalizes that Maltbie's reluctance was standard operating procedure for HQ types who have perfected the art of risk avoidance. It's a faulty strategy similar to a football team's "prevent" defense. FBI HQ's decision-making process includes second-guessing, overanalyzing, criticizing things to death, offering impracticable options, and *always* rejecting the initial request.

It seems that Maltbie has a history of obstructionism with the FBI Minneapolis Field Office. Samit had a previous case when a man planned to travel from the US to Afghanistan to train militants. The agent identified one of his relatives who applied to join the Minnesota National Guard and wanted to run a check on him and notify the National Guard since guardsmen have access to local airports. Inexplicably, Maltbie blocked this routine request and flew into a hissy fit, lecturing Samit that it was "just the sort of thing that would get the FBI into trouble."

Did the Minnesota agents have sufficient probable cause for a FISA warrant on Moussaoui? Let's examine an abbreviated sequence of events that typify dealings with FBI HQ. Keep in mind that after the second plane struck the south tower (WTC 2), the FISA warrant was approved and discovered credible evidence linking Moussaoui to the September 11, 2001, attacks.

1. In July 2001, Phoenix FBI agent Ken Williams sends a memo to Dave Frasca of the RFU theorizing that Osama bin Laden was sending agents to the US to train in flight schools.
2. Zacarias Moussaoui enrolls in a Minnesota flight school and is unable to give agents a convincing explanation why he is paying $8,300 in cash for 747 flight training.

3. Minnesota agent Harry Samit arrests Moussaoui.

4. RFU supervisor Rita Flack reads the Phoenix memo regarding terrorist pilots but apparently does not tell her colleagues about it, nor does she share the information with the Minnesota agents.

5. French authorities advise Minnesota agents that Moussaoui is connected to Chechen rebels. They add that he is preparing to "fight."

6. Minnesota agents send a request for a FISA warrant to Maltbie, who rejects it.

7. Minnesota agents learn Moussaoui wants to go on jihad, but Frasca is not concerned and says jihad does not necessarily mean holy war.

8. Frustrated, Minnesota agents attempt to secure a *criminal* search warrant. This would overcome the RFU's opposition, but Maltbie stops them from contacting the Justice Department. He says, "You will not question the unit chief and you will not question me. We've been through a lot. We know what's going on. You will not question us."

9. On August 24, 2001, the CIA issues a warning that Moussaoui might be "involved in a larger plot to target airlines traveling from Europe to the US."

10. On August 29, 2001, Samit drafts a memo to the Federal Aviation Administration summarizing the facts of the Zacarias Moussaoui case. In it, he writes, "FBI Minneapolis believes that Moussaoui, and his roommate, Hussein al-Attas, and others yet unknown are preparing to seize a Boeing 747-400 in commission of a terrorist act."

11. Maltbie blocks Samit from sending the memo.

12. On August 27, 2001, Samit's boss, Greg Jones, calls Maltbie at HQ and states that Moussaoui might be part of a plot "to get control of an airplane and crash it into the World Trade Center or something like that."

(A Wednesday May 8, 2019, *Newsweek* article by Philip Shenon confirms this conversation.)

Supervisory Special Agent Jones's notes from that August 27 conversation follow:

Maltbie: What you have done is couched [the request] in such a way that people get spun up.

Jones: Good. We want to make sure he [Moussaoui] doesn't get control of an airplane and crash it into the World Trade Center or something like that.

Maltbie: That's *not* going to happen. We don't know he's a terrorist. You don't have enough to show he's a terrorist. You have a guy interested in this type of aircraft—that's it!

General Patton said, "A good plan…executed now is better than a perfect plan next week." At this point, rational human beings would connect the terrorist dots and assist the Minnesota agents in any way possible. But not Mike Maltbie.

Phoenix FBI agent Williams was not the first FBI agent in Phoenix to complain about interference and obstruction by FBI headquarters. In 1994 Special Agent James Hauswirth complained about it after retiring and wrote a letter of complaint to FBI Director Mueller in December 2001. Hauswirth wrote, "The [international anti-terrorism] program ground to a halt a couple of years ago because of the micromanaging, constant indecision, and stonewalling."

FBI agent Coleen Rowley later sums up how the Minneapolis agents feel at this point, when she says FBI headquarters "almost inexplicably, throw up roadblocks" and undermine their efforts. Headquarters personnel bring up "almost *ridiculous* questions in their apparent efforts to undermine the probable cause." One of Jones' emails to FBI headquarters says they are "setting this up for failure."

In August 2001, Harry Samit contacts Maltbie one more time, expressing his frustration with RFU's position that Minnesota lacks evidence for a FISA warrant. In a later interview with the Justice Department's Office of Inspector General, he recalls telling Maltbie "if you're not going to advance this the FISA route, or if you don't believe we have enough for a FISA, I shudder to think—[pause]…and…"

Maltbie interrupts and abruptly ends the discussion.

Not all conversations were tense. There were occasions when Maltbie offered some "fatherly" advice, counseling Samit that "getting an intelligence warrant can be bad for an agent's career if it gets fouled up."

Maltbie followed up this hypocritical gem with, "I just want you to preserve the existence of your advancement potential."

What? Who talks like that! Did he learn that at an HQ in-service titled "How to Sound Sincere by Spouting Convoluted Bullshit When Screwing with the Field"?

Maltbie's comment *does* provide insight into the HQ mind-set, though.

September 11, 2001

> "The royal penis is clean, your Highness!"
> *—Coming to America*

The World Trade Center is hit for the first time by a 747 jet at 08:46 a.m. Mike Maltbie calls the Minneapolis Field Office and talks to FBI agent Coleen Rowley. When Rowley says it is *essential* that they get a warrant to search Moussaoui's belongings, Maltbie instructs her to take *no* action, because it could have an impact on matters of which she is not aware.

His use of the term "not aware" is both insulting and ironic. Maltbie is *very* aware that Zacarias Moussaoui could be his personal shit bomb. He is currently operating in ass-saving mode and plays the HQ omnipotent bluff—"*We at FBI HQ know things that you in the field could never know*"—to buy some time.

Rowley counters that it would have to be a huge coincidence if Moussaoui were *not* related to the attack. She later recollects that Maltbie disagrees, telling her that the attacks *are* a coincidence. Maltbie later tells investigators that he does not recall using the word "coincidence" in the conversation.

Another Minnesota agent, Chris Briese, contacts RFU chief Dave Frasca. According to Briese, Frasca initially says there is not enough evidence for a criminal warrant, but when they find out the Pentagon has been hit, Frasca consents. He later says that he consented immediately.

Dementia seems to have reached epidemic proportions at FBI HQ as they practice leadership by the three Ds: deny, deflect, and disappear. Minnesota agents finally get the warrant using the same probable cause that Maltbie initially rejected. When they search Moussaoui's belongings, they discover enough information to potentially have prevented 9/11.

CHAPTER 12:

It Wasn't My Fault!

"Always assume incompetence before
looking for conspiracy."

Coleen Rowley later states, "I feel that certain facts…have, up to now, been omitted, glossed over, or mischaracterized in an effort to avoid or minimize personal or institutional embarrassment on the part of the FBI. Perhaps even for improper political reasons."

She wonders:

> Why would an FBI agent deliberately sabotage a case? The superiors acted so strangely that some agents in the Minneapolis office openly joked that these higher-ups had to be spies or moles…working for Osama bin Laden. Our best real guess, however, is that, in most cases avoidance of all 'unnecessary' actions/decisions by FBI HQ managers…has, in recent years, been seen as the safest FBI career course. Numerous high-ranking FBI officials who have made decisions or have taken actions which, in hindsight, turned out to be mistaken or just

turned out badly…have seen their careers plummet and end. This has in turn resulted in a climate of fear which has chilled aggressive FBI law enforcement.

Rowley hit the nail on the head because when Moussaoui's belongings are rushed to an evidence response team, they discover documents linking him to eleven of the hijackers. Rowley later suggests that if they had received the search warrant sooner, "There is at least some chance that…may have limited the September 11th attacks and resulting loss of life."

Harry Samit testifies that the RFU at FBI HQ was guilty of "obstructionism, criminal negligence, and careerism," and that its opposition blocked "a serious opportunity to stop the 9/11 attacks.

Samit says he warned supervisors more than seventy times that Moussaoui was an al-Qaeda operative who might be plotting to hijack an airplane and fly it into a building and that he was regularly thwarted by two superiors, David Frasca and Michael Maltbie.

So, what happened to the individuals whose failed leadership contributed to the deadliest terrorist attack on American soil. Did they get fired, suspended, or receive a reprimand? Nope, they were all promoted.

FBI director Robert Mueller personally awarded Marion (Spike) Bowman with a presidential citation and cash bonus of approximately 25 percent of his salary. Bowman, head of the FBI's national security law unit, was the person who refused to seek a special warrant for a search of Zacarias Moussaoui's belongings before the 9/11 attack. Bowman was among nine recipients of Bureau awards for "exceptional performance." The award came shortly *after* a 9/11 congressional inquiry report saying Bowman's unit gave Minneapolis FBI agents "inexcusably confused and inaccurate information" that was "patently false."

Alec Station, Blee's former director for operations, took the unit's number two position. This was despite the fact that the unit failed to put the two suspected terrorists on the watch list. Some people in the intelligence community and Congress didn't agree with these promotions, offering that the counterterrorism unit they ran bore responsibility for waiting until August 2001 to put the suspect pair on the interagency watch list.

David Frasca, head of the FBI's Radical Fundamentalist Unit, was promoted by FBI Director Bob Mueller. The Phoenix memo, which was addressed to Frasca, warned that al-Qaeda terrorists could be using flight schools inside the United States. Two weeks later Zacarias Moussaoui was arrested while training to fly a 747, but Frasca's unit blocked all attempts to assist.

Dina Corsi, an intelligence operations specialist in the FBI's bin Laden unit in the run-up to 9/11, later became a supervisory intelligence analyst. Corsi repeatedly hampered the investigation of 9/11 hijackers Khalid al-Mihdhar and Nawaf al-Hazmi in the summer of 2001.

Career diplomat Barbara Bodine was named Director of Central Iraq by President George W. Bush shortly after the US conquest of Iraq. Bodine had blocked aspects of the USS *Cole* investigation, which some say could have uncovered the 9/11 plot. She did not apologize or admit she was wrong. However, she was fired after about a month, apparently for doing a poor job.

Michael Maltbie, who removed information from the Minnesota FBI's application to get the search warrant for Moussaoui, was promoted to field supervisor and went on to head the Joint Terrorism Task Force at the FBI's Cleveland Field Office.

These individuals were part of our intelligence leadership and failed by practicing decision avoidance by ignoring the field. The Minnesota agents were fighting in the trenches with real-time intelligence while HQ staff sat inside their HQ cubicles.

This entire incident was indicative of how far the FBI had veered off course, but sadly it did not affect any real change. The FBI's default response to the aftermath of any major screw-up is to investigate what went wrong, apologize, find a soldier to fall on their sword, and mandate remedial training for the troops. How's that working?

CHAPTER 13:

The Legal Repercussion of Words

"Are you going to believe me or your own lying eyes."
—Groucho Marx

Elizabeth Warren got caught with her deerskin loincloth flapping in the wind. Politicians lie, and it's up to their constituents to determine the penalty. But what happens when their fibs break the law? The answer: They lie some more using vague and confusing alibis.

Senator Warren listed her race as "American Indian" on a State Bar of Texas registration card in 1986. One may ask if she benefitted from filing false information on official documents. You bet she did. But when facing political repercussions for her earlier claims, Warren used words to create the image of an honest mistake.

A Warren aide provided this gem: "Senator Warren has said she is not a citizen of any tribe…She is sorry that she was not more mindful of this earlier in her career."

Although not the intent of the alibi, the wording proves that Senator Warren has continued her charade. Being "more mindful" is not an excuse for the lie; it's actually a promise that she'll be more *aware* of her original lie in the future. Warren met with Cherokee Indian chief John Baker and apologized for the "confusion." Neither Chief Baker nor Warren were confused; she simply was caught in an untruth.

But don't try this technique at home when caught in a lie since it insults the listener's intelligence. There are other more serious consequences for claiming a specific ethnicity on forms. For example, filling out a small-business loan and listing yourself as a minority is a crime if you are not in fact a minority.

Warren's use of the terms "more mindful" and "confusion" are thinly disguised justifications for lying.

Perhaps Aristotle worked for the government when he penned this muddled gem: "To say of what is that it is not…or of what is not that it is…is false…while to say of what is that it is…and of what is not that it is not…is true." I actually hurt my brain attempting to follow the Greek philosopher.

But there are some words that cannot be confused, two of which are "yes" and "no." Democratic Virginia lawmaker Kathy Tran sponsored a bill that would allow full-term abortions. Republican lawmaker Todd Gilbert asked if the bill would permit abortions up to the moment of birth. Tran replied, "Yes." After a backlash by anti-abortionists, Tran (the mother of four children) said, "I misspoke."

What Tran is actually saying is, "I didn't expect such a hissy fit from voters, so I'll use some word—'misspoke'—which will sound like an apology, but I really do want to kill babies." Tran did *not* misspeak. She clearly stated her intention with the most direct and unambiguous language even after presented an opportunity to clarify her words. And if further proof is needed, Tran did *not* change the language in her proposed bill.

Tom Krause said that "It is the lie, not the truth, that needs to be proven."

There seems to be a set pattern the media follows after an accusation of wrongdoing by public figures. It either disappears within one news cycle but may regurgitate occasionally like acid reflux, or the story builds momentum with a continuing trickle of damaging information. A third option is that the news item dies a partisan death with the media quoting some politician saying, "This has already been investigated," or "There's no 'there' there," or a relatively new catch-phrase, "This is a nothing burger." This last postscript actually *triggers* acid reflux in many Marines and cops.

None of these paths lead to justice since there is no burden of proof required of the media to report accurately. Anyone with a camera or blog can make heartfelt accusations with no repercussions. The public believes whatever side their ideological bread is buttered on. Many of the truly independent voters are confused and believe the last impassioned plea made by some guy with an expensive haircut and a title scrolling on the television screen. (By the way, where do they find these experts who resemble high school prom kings and queens? They claim to be CEOs, presidents, senior executives, fellows, or emeriti of some vague organization or news outlet. I'd trust very few to walk fire watch, let alone follow their advice during a national crisis.)

I hate to pick on the Clintons as examples of officials whose words are never taken literally but, more importantly, legally. Hillary provided hundreds of hours of slippery sworn testimony before grand juries and Congress in addition to the FBI. During her thirteen-hour testimony before Congress during the Benghazi hearings, she maintained that the attacks were *not* an organized terrorist attack on the consulate.

But emails surfaced from Hillary to her daughter, Chelsea, and an Egyptian official acknowledging that the attack involved a terrorist organization. When Clinton was confronted with her lies, she provided no rational rebuttal. Her words constitute perjury, which is punishable by jail, but she was permitted to deflect and offer a "my dog ate the homework" alibi.

When the guilty can't correct the record by changing their words, an ally in government will correct it for them. This is normally considered criminal, but only conservatives seem to be prosecuted.

When Peter Strzok changed two words on the prosecutorial report following the yearlong email investigation, he downgraded a felony to zip. Strzok tinkered with Comey's original determination that Hillary was "grossly negligent" to "extremely careless." This may seem like an insignificant semantic tweak, but it actually was a "get out of jail free" card. The bottom line is that any individual who is *extremely* careless is also *grossly* negligent, but the federal statute requires exact wording to prosecute. It would be an insult to our intelligence to assume that Strzok wasn't aware that his wordsmithing had no effect on the case given his record of despising Trump and loving Hillary.

Bill Clinton's "I did not have sexual relations with that woman" and Huma Abedin's "I've provided all my emails" are two more examples of perjury minus consequence.

James Clapper is a particularly ballsy liar since he headed the National Security Agency when he told his whopper under oath. The NSA was collecting data on millions of Americans and on March 12, 2013, Senator Ron Wyden of Oregon asked Clapper if it was occurring. The NSA director replied, "No, sir," and "Not wittingly."

Bureaucratic interpretation: "Not wittingly" was Clapper's attempt to qualify the first lie of "No, sir." It was either meant to confuse or intended to be used as a later alibi such as, *I did not deny collecting the data; I qualified the action as being unwitting.*

Wyden later said he provided the question to Clapper *before* the hearing and asked Clapper to correct the record. Clapper told the US representative to bug off.

Public officials lie to Congress to avoid embarrassment or cover wrongdoing. It's a low-risk way to avoid scandal since only six individuals have been convicted for lying to Congress since the 1940s. The number of people who lie to Congress would probably exceed the number of people who *don't* lie. These recent trends establish a not so well-kept secret: Some people *are* above the law.

Perhaps Clapper misunderstood that he fibbed, but Representative Thomas Massie told the *Washington Examiner*, "He [Clapper] admitted to lying to Congress and was unremorseful and flippant about it."

Not so fast, Congressman Massie! Clapper never admitted to *perjury,* but he did admit to making an "untruthful statement." This subtle distinction allows favored individuals to avoid prison since lying is a key element to the crime of perjury.

Clapper's confession of an "untruthful statement" would constitute a trip to the gray-bar hotel for the general public. It seems that lying to Congress or the FBI is only a sin for citizens minus allies in government. Clapper also insinuated that he either forgot one of the largest surveillance programs in the history of this country or he knowingly chose the least untruthful answer.

When Major League Baseball pitcher Roger Clemens was prosecuted for untrue statements before Congress regarding his use of steroids, he was not given the option of providing the "least untruthful" answer. Clemens was eventually acquitted on all charges.

Clapper will establish a standard that will be hard to overcome in the future. Some contend that he had little choice but to lie to Congress given that the question was asked in open session. This doesn't pass the smell test since about 10 percent of all answers provided by witnesses involved in the intelligence community are "I can answer that question in a closed session."

Connecticut Attorney General Richard Blumenthal spoke of an earlier time in his life at a ceremony honoring veterans. He said, "We have learned something important since the days that I served in Vietnam."

"I served in Vietnam" is another straightforward statement and cannot be construed in any other way. But the future US senator *never* served in Vietnam. He obtained at least *five* military deferments from 1965 to 1970 and took steps that enabled him to avoid going to war.

These delays allowed Blumenthal to complete his studies at Harvard, then pursue a graduate fellowship in England and a job in the Nixon White House. Perhaps he didn't violate the law, but he sure as hell violated one of the major ethical lines in the military. It's a form of stolen valor, and having served in Vietnam, I personally find his ruse disgusting. I'm positive that Blumenthal received some votes based on his alleged service in a war zone.

So what verbal damage control did Blumenthal employ when caught? He attempted to clarify his lie by referring to himself as a Vietnam-*era* veteran. Serving your country in war *or* peace is honorable, but Blumenthal desecrated his own military service by lying for political gain. That claim would've got his congressional ass kicked had he been spouting his phony Vietnam exploits at some VFW bar in South Philly.

If the FBI was an independent entity, many of these official perjurers would be arrested. Wouldn't matter if it was a conservative or a liberal, George Clooney or Clint Eastwood. But it's a moot question, 'cause we're not independent anymore.

On Jan. 18, 2011, a small green-energy company named Joule Unlimited announced John Podesta's appointment to its board. Vladimir Putin founded Rusnano, a Kremlin-backed investment fund, which pumped $35 million into Joule.

Podesta appeared on Maria Bartiromo's FOX show. She asked Podesta why he failed to disclose his role in Joule as required by law when he served as counselor to President Barack Obama.

Podesta seemed offended: "Maria, that's not true. I fully disclosed and was completely compliant."

Bartiromo pressed Podesta. "What happened to the 75,000 shares of Joule stock?"

"I didn't have any stock in any Russian company!" Podesta said.

Rhetorical interpretation: Joule is based in Massachusetts, not Russia, making Podesta's statement technically true.

Podesta wasn't finished with his verbal gymnastics and added, "And, by the way, I *divested* [the shares] before I went into the White House."

WikiLeaks documents reveal that when he joined the Obama White House, Podesta transferred his Joule shares to an LLC controlled by his adult children.

Had Podesta murdered someone and transferred the weapon to his kids, would he have legally divested himself from a crime? Podesta resumed communicating with Joule and Joule investors after leaving the White House and joining Clinton's campaign. In 2016, Podesta became Hillary's presidential campaign chairman.

I've always felt that it never hurts if you apologize, *especially* if you don't mean it. Public figures play a delicate balancing act with words. During the Michael Cohen congressional testimony, he accused President Donald Trump of racism, alleging that he had made bigoted statements about black voters. In response, Republican Representative Mark Meadows, who is white, pointed to Lynne Patton, an African American member of the Trump administration who was seated in the audience.

Democratic Representative Rashida Tlaib, the first Palestinian American to serve in Congress, immediately criticized Meadows, calling it "racist in itself" to use a black woman "as a prop" and arguing that it did not disprove the claim. Tlaib also claimed to be a woman "of color."

(At the risk of being tarred and feathered with the "racist" tag, why is a Palestinian American considered to be "of color"? Did I miss something, or as an Italian American am I now eligible for a minority status?)

Tlaib followed up with this gem: "Just because someone has a person of color—a black person—working for them does not mean they aren't racist."

Meadows was outraged by Tlaib's statement and demanded that it be stricken from the record. (Under House rules, lawmakers are not permitted to impugn another lawmaker's motives or insult them personally.) He noted that several of his relatives were "people of color" and that "it's racist to suggest" he would use a black woman as a prop.

After committee chairman Elijah Cummings sided with Meadows, it became apparent to Tlaib that she had crossed the racial divide. Rather than apologize for calling Meadows a racist, Tlaib came up with this whopper of words (note: my use of "whopper" may be offensive and racist to my fellow Italians, so I apologize in advance):

"I did *not* call Representative Meadows a racist but was describing a certain kind of *behavior* as racist." Tlaib added that she was saying that *if* "someone" were to behave in such a way, it would be racist.

Allow me to sort this out, even if I hurt my brain.

Tlaib already knew that the "someone" who invited Patton was Meadows, which Tlaib considered racist. According to Tlaib's logic, his racist "behavior" was the mere invitation, but somehow Meadows himself wasn't a racist. She rationalizes that inserting the word "if" somehow exonerates her from labeling Meadows a racist.

Perhaps an analogy will help. If Tlaib points a gun and intentionally kills someone, her defense may be that the mere act of pointing the gun at the intended target and killing them would constitute a charge of murder, but that the person was not a murderer and should not be considered such.

When Hillary was running for president, she told the following tale about visiting Bosnia in 1996 as the First Lady. I suspect that Hillary was checking the ten-thousand-vote box for combat veterans.

> I remember landing under sniper fire. There was supposed to be some kind of a greeting ceremony at the airport, but instead we just ran with our heads down to get into the vehicles to get to our base.

There's only one problem with this harrowing account: There is actually a video of Hillary being greeted on the tarmac by smiling US and Bosnian officials. An eight-year-old Muslim girl, Emina Bicakcic, read a poem in English. An Associated Press photograph of the greeting ceremony shows a smiling Clinton bending down to receive a kiss.

According to the comedian Sinbad, who accompanied Hillary to Bosnia, "The scariest part of the trip was deciding on where to eat."

CHAPTER 14

I Gotta Take a Leak

"Government is the only known vessel that leaks from the top."
—James Reston

On a Friday afternoon some thirty years ago, I was testifying in federal court on a drug case. I'd used a drug snitch to jam up other drug deal-ers. That's the way the system has worked ever since Epeius, a master carpenter built the Trojan horse. The Greeks rolled the horse in front of the gates of Troy, which bore an inscription claiming it was a gift for Athena. A ruse is part and parcel of winning the war on drugs *or* a beef between Greece and Troy.

During a break in my testimony, I hit the head to take a leak, both literally and figuratively. Some guy in the next urinal looks over and says, "Do you think it's okay to use a dope dealer to catch *other* drug dealers?"

Not in the mood to have any lengthy discussion at this time and place, I resorted to my default as a smart-ass and stated, "Hey, buddy, you can't catch drug dealers with nuns."

I reentered the courtroom with a satisfied smug feeling that lasted until Sunday morning when they delivered the newspaper to my home.

The *Cleveland Plain Dealer*'s Sunday edition had my quote in a bold headline: ***"You Can't Catch Drug Dealers with Nuns."*** The accompanying story was not very complimentary to me or my drug dealing snitch, even though my quote was accurate.

The guy at the urinal was a reporter. I realized that I'd pissed off (no pun intended) several groups with that single sentence: drug dealers and nuns, sure, but most importantly my bosses at the FBI. My phone began ringing within the hour, so I chose to take the family on a nice trip to Mohican State Forest for a day of hiking and hiding.

Monday morning, I was standing tall before several layers of management who took turns reaming my butt about the cardinal sin I committed: Never talk to the press!

They were right, since the FBI should be seen and rarely heard. An FBI agent's TV appearances should be limited to gathering evidence at a crime scene or perp-walking some kidnapper into the courthouse. There's been way too much of Comey, Strzok, and McCabe on camera whining, grimacing, and pointing fingers.

News out of Washington, DC, can be very confusing. News organizations mingle hard news with opinions in similar studio settings. The hosts and guests seem identical in dress, facial expressions, and moral convictions, so the public processes the media info based on their own ideology. We basically accept as gospel any claims made by like-minded mass media outlets. Most of us seem not to hear the preface of "I think," followed by a declarative statement.

There's been a steady drip, drip, drip of accusations concerning the Comey Gang's attempt to overthrow a sitting US president. That's a powerful claim, and to quote an old commercial, I want to know, "Where's the beef?"

Tangible evidence is becoming difficult to ignore. In addition to FISA warrants based on gossip and bogus immunities, evidence has emerged that directly links the Comey Gang to the attempted Trump coup.

A jury's best friend is direct evidence such as a DNA test, finger-prints, electronic surveillance, and the written word of suspects. The inspector general reported that "we identified instances where FBI employees improperly received benefits from reporters, including tick-ets to sporting events, golfing outings, drinks and meals, and admittance to nonpublic social events."

Gifting rules for executive branch officials are strict and exacting. The US Office of Government Ethics provides that "executive branch employees may not solicit or accept gifts that are given because of their official positions or that come from certain interested sources ('prohib-ited sources')." Seems simple enough, but don't bet on any repercus-sions for anyone who violates this rule.

Why would the media provide FBI agents with gifts? Text mes-sages from Strzok-Page and other FBI employees indicate that the FBI was purposely leaking sensitive information detrimental to President Trump to several media outlets. This alone may result in a violation of law, but they added to that tab by accepting swag from reporters. Members of the Comey Gang were receiving gifts—some may say payoffs—from reporters in exchange for the information. Again, these gifts took the form of tickets to sporting events, golf outings, dinners, and possibly some footsies during drinks at swank restaurants.

The biased media was in bed with the biased FBI agents. Their common goal was to get rid of the duly elected president, but even with this shared goal the FBI was double-crossing their media buds. Strzok, Page, and others *knew* that their information was false but needed the press as unwitting dupes. Once the newspapers printed the fake stories, the Comey Gang used the press clippings to bolster their probable cause in FISA warrants. This double-dealing resulted in the rape of the Fourth Amendment (search and seizure) to our Constitution. The FBI was using the judicial branch of our government to approve wiretaps on the executive branch. Think about that for a second.

The process was pretty simple yet so destructive. Strzok or Page calls their *Washington Post* contact and provides information that Carter Page, a Trump campaign advisor, is meeting with Russian intel operatives who offered thousands of Hillary's emails to get Trump elected president. There's your Russian collusion, which they bolster with the Steele dossier, though they were fully aware that both scenarios were unreliable. Agent Strzok then visits a FISA judge (his friend) and uses the dossier *and* the phony newspaper account that he himself planted to obtain permission to violate the Constitution.

The Comey Gang plants the story of Carter Page with the media and says, "Look, Judge! There's even corroboration in the media. The FBI needs to investigate further."

A Strzok text to Page states, "Also, apparently [*New York*] Times is angry with us about the WP [*Washington Post*] scoop and earlier discussion we had about the Schmidt piece that had so many inaccuracies. Too much to detail here, but I told Mike [redacted] and Andy [McCabe] they need to understand we were absolutely dealing in good faith with them."

On April 10, 2017, Peter Strzok contacts Lisa Page to discuss a "media leak strategy." The exact text: "I had literally just gone to find this phone to tell you I want to talk to you about media leak strategy with DOJ before you go."

On April 12, 2017, Peter Strzok congratulates Lisa Page on a job well done while referring to two derogatory articles about Carter Page. In the text, Strzok warns Page that two articles are coming out, one of which is "worse" than the other about Lisa's "namesake" (Carter Page). Strzok added: "Well done, Page."

Strzok texts Page on April 14, 2017: "The FISA one, coupled with the Guardian piece from yesterday."

Aitan Goelman, who is Strzok's attorney, put forth a totally illogical defense inferring "the term 'media leak strategy' in Mr. Strzok's text refers to a Department-wide initiative to detect and *stop* leaks to the media." But subsequent texts dispute Goelman's statement.

While this scenario was proceeding in real time, candidate Trump was complaining about the Trump Tower being bugged. After his election, the press crucified President Trump over his accusations that the intelligence community was leaking and targeting his administration. The Comey Gang were members in good standing of that intel world, and that's *exactly* what they were doing.

Inspector General Michael Horowitz found that at *least* thirteen different FBI agents leaked to the same liberal reporter. The agents leaked fake news to the reporter and then used that column to apply for a FISA warrant.

There are two or three corroborating investigations, one by Catherine Herridge at Fox in addition to Sara Carter and John Solomon. Representative Mark Meadows of North Carolina sent a letter to former Deputy Attorney General Rod Rosenstein saying a "review of the new documents raises grave concerns regarding an apparent systemic culture of media leaking by high-ranking officials at the FBI and DOJ related to ongoing investigations." He was referring to the Strzok-Page texts.

The FBI acknowledged leaking to the press but did the CIA join the party? I previously discussed the unique and different charters of the FBI and CIA. The Central Intelligence Agency mission is to collect, analyze, evaluate, and disseminate *foreign* intelligence. The CIA has no arrest authority within the United States. Simply stated: The FBI is responsible for *countering* foreign nations attempt to spy on US soil and the CIA is responsible for *gathering* intelligence on foreign soil. We arrest spies within the USA and the CIA develops assets abroad. There are obviously some gray areas and overlap between the two intel agencies but did the CIA attempt to overthrow its own government by leaking untrue negative stories about candidate and President Trump?

An April 13, 2017, email from FBI agent Peter Strzok to Lisa Page wondered, "I'm beginning to think the agency [CIA] got information a lot earlier than we thought. They haven't shared it completely with us. They're leaking it. Might explain all these weird seemingly *incorrect* leads all these media people have."

Strzok and Page are enjoying the unexpected support by the CIA to get rid of Trump even though the agency's information about the Trump-Russia is incorrect. Is this important or just some more partisan white noise that the public discounts?

It's evidence that the two most vital US intelligence agencies were working independently to overthrow the government. We now know that there was no evidence of Trump colluding with Russia yet the leaks alleged that Trump *was* guilty. Strzok was aware of the FBI false leaks to the press, and now assumed its sister agency (CIA) joined the revolution.

Rush Limbaugh opines that "This is significant, because we now know that there was no evidence of Trump-Russia collusion. So it looks like—and the source for this is Strzok Smirk and Page, the FBI agents. It looks like the CIA was, in fact, leaking false Trump-Russia stories to the press to undermine Trump. These are leaks that even the FBI agents running their own version of a coup thought were wrong and incorrect, and it was John Brennan running the CIA at the time."

CHAPTER 15

The Curious Case of Thomas McHale

"Do I make a left at the oasis or what?"

"Who the hell is this Tom McHale?"

"Says he's some Port Authority cop from Jersey."

"Not according to *this* file. This guy can't be some local yocal from fuckin' New Jersey."

In the 1990s, I was assigned temporary duty teaching the two-week undercover certification course at the FBI training academy at Quantico. This wasn't your typical in-service where you listen to some subject matter expert for a few hours a day in between meals and frequent coffee breaks. Back in the 1980s, select agents with a minimum of three years' experience could apply to attend the certification school. I use the word "attend" since more than a few were either asked to leave or quit after just a few days of *very* intense training.

In addition to FBI agents, law enforcement officers involved in federal covert cases were also invited. This was (and still is) a "no bullshit" certification school to determine who should be meeting bad guys minus their gun and badge. The ground rules are discussed prior to attending and include strict adherence to issues like punctuality, paperwork, attendance, and weekend duty. The next morning one or two students always test the system and show up late. They are immediately driven to the airport and sent back to their field divisions. This is the equivalent of facing your parents after being expelled from college and is definitely not a career enhancement.

One student who immediately caught my attention was Tommy McHale. He was a NY/NJ Port Authority cop attached to the Newark Joint Terrorism Task Force (JTTF). His mug resembled the map of Ireland and likely met a few fists in its day. Tommy was tough, polite, and willing to learn. He nailed every exercise with street smarts and balls. This guy was good, and at the end of the two weeks, I'd come to like and respect Tommy. The one thing that Tommy and I shared was a willingness to share our thoughts with the higher-ups. I confess that both of us may have occasionally *overly* expressed our opinions.

We kept in sporadic touch over the next fifteen years and I followed his career, which can only be described as remarkable. Detective Thomas McHale became one of the nation's most highly decorated law enforcement officers. I'd get a call late at night and minus any preamble Tommy would say, "Wait'll you hear this bullshit." The Irish kid was working some major covert cases with some serious people. Tommy's concerns sometimes dealt with the bad guys, which was usually an easy fix. But a majority of Tommy's heartburn concerned the bureaucrats running the cases.

I spent eight years in deep cover with mob guys who caused me much less aggravation than the home team. I once had an FBI accountant insist that the strippers at a gentlemen's club provide me receipts after I slipped a fin into their garter belt.

Just seven years after joining the Port Authority Police Department, McHale had his first encounter with terrorism on February 26, 1993, when he was critically injured in the first bombing of the World Trade Center. His heroic efforts during the event and investigations afterward were recognized with the World Trade Center Individual Acts of Valor Medal, and within two years he was assigned to the FBI's elite Joint Terrorism Task Force.

On September 11, 2001, Detective McHale responded to the World Trade Center along with fellow members of the NYPD Major Case Squad. Tommy heard explosions but couldn't determine their source until someone pointed upward. Men and women on the upper floors were jumping to their deaths rather than burn alive. As the bodies struck the concrete they literally exploded. McHale and his team narrowly escaped the second tower when it collapsed and McHale remained at the site for the next ten days. Tommy was eventually ordered back to his JTTF duties but returned to the World Trade Center several times a week as a member of the Ironworkers Union Local 45, spending countless hours cutting through steel and recovering remains. McHale maintained this grueling schedule until the end of January 2002.

Detective McHale was then deployed overseas as part of the JTTF to continue the search for Osama bin Laden and others in the al-Qaeda network. In roughly two months, Detective McHale and his team were instrumental in locating several al-Qaeda safe houses, identifying a possible suicide bomber, and responding to a bombing at a church that took the lives of several people, including two Americans. Before returning to the United States, Tommy and his team worked side by side with US Army Special Forces units in Afghanistan to discover a biological weapons factory.

McHale was also a magician in developing informants, and not many law enforcement officers have that gift. It's a talent, even an art form, to convince someone to betray psychopaths. Sources can smell insincerity, but Tommy was an honest and straight shooter.

You may be wondering about Tom McHale's involvement in a book on the Comey Gang. His story is another troubling example of leaders who'll sacrifice people and cases rather than risk embarrassment. McHale was a hard charger who worked the big cases, but big cases are risky. All bosses fear the shit bomb that's associated with the Tom McHales of law enforcement. When the bomb explodes, even the tiniest piece of crap can stall or end a career.

We had a saying in the *B* that "no good deed will go unpunished." Thomas McHale was a clear victim of that maxim. This hero cop committed the mortal sin of embarrassing the Bureau.

A November 8, 2014, *New York Times* article titled "Getting Close to Terror, but Not to Stop It" was a well-orchestrated hit job on Tommy. The underlying goal was to discredit him for identifying and providing intel on a terrorist group. This may sound illogical and petty, but it's also an accurate description of many bureaucrats. Their reason: McHale did his job, and they were embarrassed.

If you doubt that High Bureau Officials, aka HBOs, will stoop to deception in order to avoid embarrassment, then recall the $70,000 table. Deputy Director McCabe ordered the overpriced conference table and when the expenditure was about to be exposed, he cited national security and redacted the line item.

As reported by the article, a 2007 car bombing in southeastern Iran killed eleven Revolutionary Guard members. A CIA officer noticed something very unusual in the agency's intel files. A report filed months before the bombing warned that something big was about to happen in Iran. The implications suddenly became clear. The United States government knew in advance that a Sunni terrorist group called Jundallah was planning an operation inside Shiite-dominated Iran. The operations officer then noticed the author of the report and it made no sense. It originated in Newark with a detective for the Port Authority of New York and New Jersey, a Thomas McHale.

Tommy McHale pissed people off. He didn't accept fools lightly and was not attuned to the snail pace of federal investigations. Local cops can *run and gun*. Two cops from Brooklyn can leave the office, execute a search warrant, and arrest five people before lunch. Assign them to a federal task force and they'll spend weeks discussing ops plans, SWAT assignments, and Evidence Recovery Teams. McHale traveled to Afghanistan and Pakistan under the umbrella of the FBI and developed informants inside Jundallah's leadership. Every one of his reports was shared with CIA personnel but were inexplicably gathering dust. The operations officer knew that someone within the federal bureaucracy had seriously shit the bed. He dialed Langley and consulted Agency lawyers. Bureaucrats will only seek legal opinions when they're afraid.

Attorneys are in the business of damage control and the CIA began to distance themselves from the one individual who was doing God's work. Their findings are a testament to government absurdity. The CIA attorneys concluded that using Islamic militants to gather intelligence is a bad thing. By providing information on attacks *prior* to them happening, the United States government, through McHale's informants, supported terrorism. According to their convoluted thinking, only the President of the United States could approve McHale's operation or it could represent an unauthorized covert action program. The CIA ended its involvement with Mr. McHale's informants.

Memo to the CIA: *All* law enforcement agencies use bad guys to catch other bad guys. It ain't against the law, and it is encouraged since nuns rarely hang with terrorists and drug dealers. (My old line.) The CIA's hypocrisy is ballsy since it has developed informants inside al-Qaeda and every other country in the world, including Canada.

A *New York Times* article explained that "despite the C.I.A.'s concerns, the FBI and Pentagon continued to obtain intelligence from inside Jundallah…Contacts with informants didn't end when Jundallah's attacks led to the deaths of Iranian civilians, or when the State Department designated it a terrorist organization. Senior Justice Department and F.B.I. lawyers at the time say they never reviewed the matter and were *unaware* of the C.I.A. concerns. And so, the relationship persisted, even as American officials repeatedly denied any connection to the group."

In response to the FBI's continued use of an informant recently jettisoned by the CIA, unnamed (FBI) government officials came up with the following gem of logical confusion: "The goal has always been to use those informants to help dismantle Al Qaeda itself. In the case of Jundallah, the objective was to obtain information, not to combat the group or stop its attacks."

Bureaucratic explanation: The goal of law enforcement when operating informants is to "obtain information" and turn it into action. When done effectively, this action is used to *stop* terrorist attacks.

There is an ongoing turf war among the government agencies involved in the intel business. In fact, United States intelligence agencies had enough information to have prevented 9/11 had they just *shared* what they knew with each other. A sample of US agencies that collect intelligence include the FBI, CIA, Drug Enforcement Administration, Defense Intelligence Agency, National Security Agency, Department of Homeland Security, and even the Commerce Department. The result is a sometimes muddled system in which agencies often operate independently and with little oversight. They protect their territory like jealous children who won't share their milk and cookies.

The *New York Times* reporter met a federal stone wall when requesting on-the-record comments. But a dozen current and former officials spoke on the condition of anonymity, because they were not authorized to discuss the matter.

These anonymous government officials who leaked information to the *Times* had an agenda. My guess is that some of them were embarrassed by or reprimanded for their own incompetence in the case. A few of these anonymous officials did confirm American involvement with Jundallah and McHale's role but downplayed the significance of the operation, "attributing it to lapses in oversight, rather than a *formal* effort to ally with a terrorist group."

MEMO TO CIA

You operate on foreign soil in lands where people would gleefully murder millions of Americans if provided the opportunity. With the advent of available nuclear, biological, and chemical weapons the rules of engagement must change. A majority of Americans would experience no heartburn if you waterboard or whack some scum intent on doing harm to innocent civilians. You can monitor conversations, form naked pyramids, toss them from helicopters or play Soulja Boy rap music on a continuous loop to loosen their lips. Using someone from one terrorist group to snitch on other terrorist groups in a land that has been lopping off heads for seven centuries is good business. Do your job!

MEMO TO FBI

A member of your Joint Terrorism Task Force developed an informant laying the golden egg. There's no telling how many lives this asset could save had you not abandoned ship when attorneys began writing memos. Tom McHale is certainly a brusque individual who cusses and questions authority but, you need him on that wall!

CHAPTER 16:

"Where the Hell Is McHale?"

"If you are a minority of one, the truth is the truth."
—Mohandas Gandhi

The *New York Times* wrote that "those who know Tom McHale paint a contradictory picture—someone whose skill in developing sources was highly regarded by the F.B.I. but who bristled at the restrictions of bureaucracy and whose dealings with Jundallah were conducted largely 'off book.'"

Interpretation: Too many hard-charging law enforcement officers this accusation is actually a compliment meant as a criticism. What it really is saying is McHale is damned good but went "a little" rogue because the bureaucrats are incompetent and cowardly. But McHale *wasn't* operating off the books because he took copious notes and documented everything for the record. He had been around long enough to realize the treachery involved with the home team.

The law enforcement officers who work the streets would seek out the Tom McHales to cover their butts. He became a law enforcement celebrity after 9/11, helping to rescue survivors and recover victims at ground zero and played himself in Oliver Stone's movie "World Trade Center," in which Nicolas Cage starred as a Port Authority police officer. He volunteered for assignments to Afghanistan and Pakistan with the Newark's Joint Terrorism Task Force where he helped capture leaders of Al Qaeda alongside F.B.I. and C.I.A. colleagues. In 2006, McHale received the Port Authority's Medal of Honor for bravery in 2006.

> "If there's a new Greatest Generation, then McHale would certainly define it," *The New York Post* wrote in a 2011 profile. But friends say he could be brash and opinionated.

Interpretation: All cops, especially Irish New York ones, are opinionated. It's especially helpful when dealing with bosses who *lack* an opinion. As retired FBI counterterrorism supervisor Don Borelli put it, "Tommy is not without opinions, and he is generally happy to share them with his colleagues and bosses. As you can imagine, this has ruffled some feathers, especially at the FBI."

It appears that Detective McHale's most grievous sin is being a *fuckin' hard head*. The Bureau careerists manage by decision avoidance. They deflect their inaction by attacking personality rather than moving cases forward. It's a distraction to the real issues.

Immediately after 9/11, information was scarce about terrorist operatives in the Middle East. So, McHale did his homework and developed a source who had been on the FBI payroll since about 1996.

The *NY Times* article carelessly divulged information that put people's lives in danger. They wrote:

> The informant lived in the New York area, according to three former officials, but had friends and family in Baluchistan, a sprawling region covering parts of Iran, Afghanistan and Pakistan. The informant introduced Mr. McHale to these overseas connections, which

included members of the Rigi family, the namesake
of a powerful Baluch tribe based in southeastern Iran.

The arrangement was promising enough that after
9/11 the informant became a joint F.B.I. and C.I.A.
asset, meaning he was supervised by both agencies
simultaneously, with Mr. McHale as the point person.

Interpretation: The *New York Times* reporter put the source in danger by providing information on his general area of residence, but more critical is the specificity of the information on individuals who infiltrated the group and their personal ties back to the New York area. This not only put the FBI informant at great risk but also Detective Thomas McHale.

The *Times* just didn't provide McHale's town of residence but also photos of him and his *wife*. The New York metropolitan area is rife with individuals with ties to terrorist organizations. The question is *why* the need to put Mrs. McHale in danger!

Abdolmalek Rigi, the founder of Jundallah, was executed by the government of Iran in late 2010. Jundallah means "the soldiers of God," and Rigi was their charismatic leader based in southeastern Iran who waged war against the Iranian government in 2003. It was a region where the Baluch people, who are mostly Sunni, have long faced oppression at the hands of the Shiite government. Security forces have demolished homes in the region, and Sunni leaders have been shot dead in the streets.

Washington totally ignored Jundallah though it'd attracted several thousand members. McHale's relationship with the group initially didn't raise any concerns because the United States did *not* consider Jundallah a terrorist organization at the time.

They then threw in the CYA (Cover Your Ass) addendum of, "*it appeared to have no intention to attack the West.*"

"But," says the *Times*, "they [government officials] claim it was also because one of the government's leading experts on Baluchistan, and the one most likely to spot the potential problem, was Mr. McHale himself."

Interpretation: Government bureaucrats were caught with their pants around their ankles and blamed McHale for not crying wolf. Except that McHale was writing reports and cornering FBI supervisors warning that Jundallah *was* a violent terrorist group.

This region of the Middle East was ripe with terrorist groups. One required a scorecard to keep track of the tribes ready to lop off the heads of a rival. In 2005 Jundallah operatives ambushed President Mahmoud Ahmadinejad's motorcade, failing to kill him. The group then initiated a series of attacks, including a massacre at a checkpoint in 2006. In 2007, Jundallah carried out the car bombing of a bus full of Revolutionary Guard members.

Note to the CIA: If you are receiving intel from an asset knowledgeable about terrorist attacks, that individual is *likely* involved in terrorism. The FBI routinely uses Italian Mafia members to provide information on rival families. All criminal gangs are paranoid and tend to be extremely careful on who they share their intent to commit murder and mayhem.

So the CIA determined the group persona non grata due to its violent nature and the bureaucrats began distancing themselves from Detective Tommy McHale. American government officials denied either directing or approving any Jundallah operations. They insisted that they never received information concerning a terrorist attack, which is why they couldn't prevent it. The CIA attorneys went on paper prohibiting US intel agencies from using Jundallah associates as informants. But Tommy McHale didn't get the memo since no one informed the *one* individual who had access to a Jundallah asset.

It is not clear which specific officials authorized the relationship with Jundallah to continue after C.I.A.

> lawyers raised concerns about it. Lawyers at the Justice
> Department and F.B.I. at the time say they were
> unaware of the relationship or the C.I.A. concerns.

When the crap hit the fan, the bureaucrats tossed McHale under the bus and claimed that he worked as a single operator. But documents emerged indicating that senior officials knew of and *approved* of the relationship McHale developed with Jundallah. For example, in 2008, senior FBI officials in Washington approved a trip Mr. McHale made to Afghanistan, where he met with his network of informants. Some CIA official approved that trip and knew that Jundallah was on the itinerary.

Also proof that McHale was no lone wolf is the fact that his reports were "circulated widely" in the intelligence community. In 2009, he was given an award for his work by the CIA's Iranian Operations Division, though the agency could not confirm the reason for or even existence of the award. One gets the picture of "plausible deniability" at work.

In late 2013, McHale's request to meet his contacts in Afghanistan again was denied by the FBI. They provided no explanation nor stated objections to the mission. They simply said no.

The *Times* article explains, maybe "Mr. McHale's brusque personality had caught up with him. He had developed a reputation for being difficult to manage, and F.B.I. managers in Newark complained that he did not keep adequate records of his intelligence operation. Friends said Mr. McHale found himself without support."

Interpretation: McHale guy has penetrated a violent terrorist group killing people in the Middle East, but he's brusque, so we'll show him. We'll let the killings continue, because Tommy McHale may be detonating the shit bomb that will ruin our career advancement.

McHale was unfazed since he was mission oriented and arranged the trip through the Pentagon instead. Tommy McHale informs his FBI supervisors that he's Afghanistan bound and the FBI basically nods and winks. They did *not* object to the trip or order him chained to his desk. It was McHale's fifth trip to that region and McHale met with American Special Forces troops who accompanied him. There's even a photo of Tommy in the sandbox standing beside US forces. Upon his return to the states, McHale dutifully documented his trip and the FBI bounced him off the Newark JTTF. An official admitted that his *unauthorized* trip to Afghanistan was part of the reason.

This is an absurd conclusion. McHale was not a self-employed individual working out of his house. If a law enforcement officer fails to show for work even for a single day, alarm bells ring. At the very least his squad mates will call and ask, "You okay?" There's also a time sheet that in my day required your signature each day unless you were on authorized leave or travel.

Federal officials kicked the blame game into high gear alleging that McHale orchestrated an operation that veered out of control:

> They said that if the United States and Jundallah had too close a relationship, Mr. McHale's go-it-alone attitude was to blame.

Bureaucrats operating in 'ass saving' mode are ruthless. The individuals who worked in federal law enforcement with McHale know that the characterization of McHale as a rogue operator is unfair. They point out that the relationship persisted for more than a decade, and Mr. McHale's actions were approved and *applauded* by several United States agencies over those years.

> Officials say that Mr. McHale's original informant, the one who holds the key to a network of overseas informants, remains on the books as an F.B.I. informant.

Allow me to sum this up. Tom McHale risks life and limb for God and country, yet *unnamed* officials at the FBI shut him down because he was "brusque." They accuse him of a lack of documentation, yet his reports were distributed throughout the FBI and three other intelligence agencies, including the military. And when he doesn't show up for work for a month, they claim no idea about his whereabouts.

FBI leadership needs an overhaul. Between the Ruby Ridge cover-up to the Moussauis tragedy in Minnesota to Jundallah, poor FBI leadership is the one constant. We need bosses who support the hard chargers and don't fear the occasional shit bomb. The good brick agents and cops don't require the "attaboys" from the brass. Let us do our thing and cover our six.

As William Arthur Ward wrote, "Leadership is based on inspiration, *not* domination; on cooperation, *not* intimidation."

What happened to Detective McHale when he returned to Afghanistan at the *request* of the Defense Department to prevent a terrorist attack is an American tragedy.

CHAPTER 17:

FISA

"Here's lookin' at you, kid."
—*Casablanca*

The acronym FISA was basically unknown until the Comey Gang. It stands for the Foreign Intelligence Surveillance Act and permits FBI agents to obtain warrants from a secret court, known as the Foreign Intelligence Surveillance Court (FISC). The basic purpose of a FISA warrant is to conduct electronic surveillance—aka a wiretap—on "an agent of a foreign power." Sounds simple enough. The FBI is legally permitted to secretly listen to spies engaging in clandestine intelligence activities. What can go wrong?

The mechanics to get a FISA warrant are similar to obtaining a criminal warrant. Both are outlined in the Attorney General Guidelines governing FBI investigations. An FBI agent must show probable cause (verified facts) that the target of the FISA is *knowingly* engaging in spying stuff for a foreign government.

Since the FBI lacked legitimate probable cause to obtain a valid warrant to *spy* on candidate Trump, they selected a soft target, Carter Page.

Many of you may be wondering, "Who the hell is Carter Page?" Page served as a naval officer in Europe and the Mideast with a brief stint in Navy intelligence. He earned two master's degrees and a PhD and became a successful investment advisor who worked in Russia from 2004 to 2007. In 2016, Page joined the Trump campaign as an advisor. Candidate Trump didn't even know that Carter Page existed, stating, "I don't think I've ever spoken to him or ever met him."

In September of 2016, shortly before the presidential election, Yahoo News published a story linking Page to Russian operatives. It's good money that someone in the Comey Gang leaked that information to Yahoo because shortly after the story, the FBI received a FISA warrant targeting Page. Information reveals that the FBI used its own leaked media stories to bolster its probable cause in its FISA affidavit. Falsifying a sworn statement is a crime. The Comey Gang may rationalize that the initial FISA warrant was completely factual but leaking info to the media and then using their own leaked material as *additional* probable cause is perjury.

Sorting out this Machiavellian move may seem complicated, but it's actually brilliant in its simplicity. During the Obama presidency, an FBI agent in concert with Justice officials swore under oath that the FBI possessed probable cause to take down candidate Trump with tales of pissing Russian prostitutes and British spies. Carter Page was chosen as the vehicle to bug the Trump campaign in order to corroborate the allegations.

Director James Comey signed *three* FISA applications on behalf of the FBI, and Deputy Director Andrew McCabe signed one. Deputy Attorney General Sally Yates, the acting attorney general, and Deputy Attorney General Rod Rosenstein each signed one or more FISA applications on behalf of the DOJ. Their signatures attested that the FISA applications were verified and reliable. But they weren't, and a few of them *knew* that they weren't. Deputy Assistant Attorney General Bruce Ohr told McCabe, Peter Strzok, Lisa Page, Andrew Weissmann, and others that the Steele dossier was a load of cow manure. *Someone* committed perjury.

If you look at this from afar, it seems like our intelligence apparatus doing their job of protecting America from spies. But the motivation of the Comey Gang was never national security. Carter Page was a pawn in a chess game to subvert our democratic process of electing a president. Page says it was part of a government-led propaganda campaign to leak accusations about him and create an air of suspicion about Trump.

Conducting electronic surveillance on US citizens must pass a high threshold. Did the FBI have evidence that Page was *knowingly* engaging in clandestine intelligence activities? Page *was* meeting with Russian officials, but there has never been any evidence, before or *after* the Mueller report that Page was involved in espionage.

Representative Adam Schiff is guilty of confusing the term "collusion" with "conspiracy." He's adamant that Donald Trump Jr.'s meeting with Russians at Trump Tower during the campaign was treasonous. Counterintelligence investigations *cannot* be opened solely on the basis of First Amendment activities.

In other words, Trump Jr. had a constitutional right to meet and discuss stuff with Russians. The FBI sent me to Russia on diplomatic training missions on several occasions. I met with Russian flag officers and former KGB and GRU operatives and shook hands with Putin. Is the mere act of meeting with Russian intel types sufficient probable cause to gain a wiretap?

Adding insult to injury, Carter Page was an American citizen targeted for the mere act of *meeting* with Russian individuals. In fact, the US government set up some of these meetings with informants and then used that fact as probable cause for the FISA warrant. They orchestrated the probable cause to gain an entrée into Trump's world. The FISA warrant was an acknowledgment that Carter Page was a spy. Since he wasn't, someone committed a crime by swearing that he knowingly was working for the Russians.

The FISA affidavit required some evidence, not suspicion, that Carter Page was knowingly working on behalf of a foreign entity. The key word is "knowingly," and the Bureau failed to ever prove that condition so they massaged rumors and gossip into "knowing."

Had they conducted a legit investigation, their techniques may involve human sources, physical surveillance, bank transactions, or even documents found in the target's trash. These investigative techniques were required *before* going straight to electronic surveillance. Was Carter Page a threat to the United States? Evidently not since Page was never arrested on espionage charges.

The completed FISA application travels through the FBI chain of command. The FISA application must pass muster at the Justice Department by attorneys at the National Security Division, who verify all the assertions made in it. This scrutiny is known as "Woods Procedures" after FBI Agent Michael J. Woods, who developed this layer of approval. The DOJ *must* verify the accuracy of *every* fact stated in the application. Did this happen? The Mueller report indicates that perhaps not.

Somewhere in this process, an agent must raise his right hand and swear, under penalty of perjury, that his affidavit is the verifiable truth, that any sources cited are reliable, and that the facts contained within are not only the truth but the *whole* truth.

None of these requirements were met since the FBI knew that the Steele dossier was bogus, which made former British intelligence agent Christopher Steele unreliable, and they omitted the whole truth that the Clinton campaign had funded their probable cause.

And by the way, that constitutes a criminal act.

CHAPTER 18:

Mueller—The Special Persecutor

"So Mr. Mueller, we already determined that the
Russian collusion thing is bullshit, but can we indict
Sarah Huckabee Sanders for pecan pie perjury?"

The Special Counsel report was bad news. President Donald Trump violated the law multiple times. The breakdown included seven perjury, five obstruction and a witness tampering charge. Oh, wait a minute, that was the result of Ken Starr's findings on President Bill Clinton.

Mueller found no collusion and no obstruction. Nada. Non. Khong. Zip. And Vladimir Putin would chime in with an emphatic "Neit!" Not that it matters since special counsels are basically ineffective and inefficient. A black hole of money, time, and aggravation. Mueller's interview of five-hundred-plus witnesses may seem thorough but there was *never* any evidence of Russian collusion by Trumps team.

Mueller did create the *illusion* of obstruction but that even lacked the genuineness of a magician sawing a lady in half.

Here's a look at the sprawling two-year-long Mueller investigation and report by the numbers: 675 days, 448 pages, 40 FBI agents, 500 search warrants, 2,800 subpoenas, and 500-plus interviews. Mueller ultimately indicted, convicted, or got guilty pleas from 34 people and three companies.

Ding dong, the witch hunt is dead. The Mueller special counsel probe shot craps on Russian collusion, which paralyzed the Trump administration agenda for two years. The not-so-secret probe dominated the president's attention his entire time in office and continues with no end in sight. Mueller's original mandate was Russian collusion but he quickly realized that was a dry hole. Comey was fired in May of 2107 and a few months later Mueller interviewed him shortly after being appointed special counsel. Comey provided no evidence of collusion since he, along with McCabe and Peter Strzok, made public comments confirming no evidence existed that the President or his staff engaged in espionage. Collusion was always the sexy accusation with images of Russian pissing hookers and Trump in the role of the Manchurian candidate.

***

The Department of Justice's official announcement appointing a special counsel states: "Deputy Attorney General Rod J. Rosenstein today announced the appointment of former Department of Justice official and FBI Director Robert S. Mueller III to serve as Special Counsel to oversee the previously-confirmed FBI investigation of Russian government efforts to influence the 2016 presidential election and *related* matters."

The initial scope was limited to the Ruskies attempt to sow discord via our presidential election. The caveat "and *related* matters" allowed Mueller to veer off course and deal with obstruction. It was Rod Rosenstein who decided how far Mueller could stray from the election and he provided the special counsel a wide channel.

Mueller had the responsibility after two years of grand jury testimony, wiretaps, etc. to either recommend an indictment *or* exonerate the president. His job was *not* to equivocate but "poop or get off the pot." Attorney General Barr summed up the Mueller report with a basic "no collusion, no obstruction." End of story.

But it wasn't an end but rather the beginning of a plot to impeach President Trump. Mueller's report dangled *obstruction* of justice like a Damocles sword by not drawing "*a conclusion—one way or the other—as to whether the examined conduct constituted obstruction.*" He carefully set out evidence for *both* sides of the legal argument leaving the question unanswered. Mueller set a trap that will paralyze the government for the next few years using the Democratic Congress as his weapon of choice.

Obstruction of justice was always the vehicle, ever since the fired FBI director informed Special Counsel Robert Mueller that there was no Russian collusion but Trump was vulnerable to obstruction of justice. Mueller believed Comey but required corroboration since James Comey had a problem. He previously lied under oath and would be brutalized on the witness stand. Mueller solved this problem by offering the Democratic Congress a road map to impeachment. The Mueller report identified additional obstruction witnesses like Don McGhan, the president's counsel, who Trump allegedly ordered to fire Mueller.

The below 2017 court finding indicates Mueller adding *obstruction* to his collusion investigation. (lines 8-9-10). The *bombshell* are lines 23, 24, and 25, which confirms that President Donald Trump is the *only* target listed within the scope of obstruction of justice.

> Before the appointment of the Special Counsel on
> May 17th, the FBI has opened an investigation into
> obstruction of justice. That investigation entailed
> matters that were covered in the Comey memoranda,
> which explored and recorded Mr. Comey's recollections
> of meetings, including one-on-one meetings with
> the President of the United States. In those meetings,
> events occurred that led the FBI to conclude that an

investigation was appropriate under its authority to consider matters such as obstruction of justice.

The subject of that investigation would be defined by reference to the United States Attorney's manual's consideration of what is a subject of an investigation. That is a person whose conduct is within the scope of the investigation.

In this instance, a person whose conduct is within the scope of the investigation is the President of the United States.

Reporters from the *New York Times* and *Washington Post* won Pulitzer Prizes for their investigative work on the Russian collusion case. They printed the gossip and rumors as facts since former CIA directors, FBI agents, congressmen, and national security advisors told them that Trump was a traitor.

The Russian collusion issue boils down to a simple semantic misunderstanding. Liberals mistake the mere act of *speaking* with Russians as *collusion*. Legally there is no collusion statute. Technically the crime would be a *conspiracy* to violate the Espionage Act, but a conversation alone is not a crime. It requires an overt *action* following the conversation. When Donald Trump Jr. met with the Russians at Trump Tower during the campaign, they engaged in a conversation on opposition research. Trump Jr. did nothing further upon the conclusion of that conversation. There were no campaign violations, espionage acts, or urinating Russian prostitutes.

The Mueller probe was no more than a morality play that ran two years in the Washington theater. The lead characters were the antagonist Robert Mueller and the antihero Donald Trump. The cast of characters included villains like Comey, Strzok, and McCabe, victims like

General Flynn and Carter Page, and the media critics who kept rewriting the script.

Now that the special counsel has issued his report and touched off several more years of chaos, let's discuss the fruit of the poisonous tree. This legal term may result in every special counsel conviction being tossed in the trash. Mr. Mueller put the squeeze on President Trump's orbit of friends, making them collateral damage. They were never the target since the charter of Mueller's special counsel statute was Russian collusion. The fruit on the tree is the evidence gathered based on a bad affidavit for a warrant. It makes the tree and all branches poisonous and thus any evidence gathered inadmissible in court. Since the predication for the original FISA warrant was bogus, the evidence gathered is poison and should be inadmissible. It was based on the lies of Christopher Steele.

Special counsel statutes are barbaric in nature and rarely accomplish the predication on which they were initiated. The Starr chamber went after the Clintons for improper real estate dealings and ended up convicting some Arkansas Bubba doing what Bubbas do. Whitewater was identical to what New York City hucksters do, which is basically increase their profits by shorting the IRS and filing creative financial forms. It never rises to the level of special *persecutors*.

But what special counsels *do* accomplish is destroying the lives of the remora fish that attach themselves to sharks. They eat the leftovers of the shark's prey. It's a good gig, but not without risks.

Here's a brief summary of the accomplishments of the Starr special counsel investigation. The taxpayers got hosed on this one. These dangerous criminals could've been dispatched by two IRS agents in Tupelo, Mississippi, rather than spend almost $50 million to come up empty on the alleged target, the Clintons.

Webster Hubbell was a Clinton friend from Arkansas and former law partner of Mrs. Clinton. He pleaded guilty on December 6, 1994, to mail fraud and tax evasion and admitted stealing almost $400,000 from his clients and partners in Little Rock's Rose Law Firm. He was sentenced to twenty-one months in jail.

James McDougal was a Clinton friend and Whitewater business partner who operated Madison Guaranty Savings and Loan. He was convicted in May 1996 of eighteen felony counts related to bad loans. McDougal agreed to cooperate with prosecutors against Mr. Clinton, but not until after his conviction. He died in prison, and Mr. Clinton retired as one of America's most popular presidents.

Susan McDougal and her husband, James, were partners in the Whitewater land deal with the Clintons. She was convicted in 1996 of four felony fraud counts. She served a two-year sentence.

Larry Kuca, a business associate of the McDougals, pleaded guilty to misdemeanor charges in connection with a federally backed loan. He was sentenced to probation and community service.

Robert Palmer, a land appraiser in Little Rock, was sentenced to probation in 1994 for filing false papers in connection with Madison Guaranty.

John Haley, a lawyer for Arkansas governor Jim Guy Tucker, was accused of bankruptcy fraud but pled guilty to a misdemeanor charge of failing to provide correct information to the government.

This Haley guy is a great example of the point I'm attempting to make. He failed to provide correct information to the government. Has anyone ever filled out an SF 86 for a security clearance without unintentionally omitting information or getting a date wrong? How about an application for a small business loan or even employment at McDonalds? And who has the courage to do their own taxes?

Haley is analogous to Richard Pinedo, a minor character in the Mueller probe who pled guilty to one count of identity fraud. This is a clue that Mr. Pinedo was indeed a means to an end. Mueller's team could hang outside any bar in Cleveland on a weekend and round up a few hundred eighteen-year-olds and charge them with identity fraud.

Starr didn't land a *glove* on the Clintons, although there was a soiled blue dress involved. This stain caused a lot of unnecessary heartache but no indictment. Mueller basically came up just as dry on his anticipated Russian collusion. Starr spent about the same amount on the Clintons, $48 million, as special counsel Lawrence Walsh did on the eight-year investigation of Reagan administration officials involved in the Iran-Contra affair.

Walsh, Starr, and Mueller went big-game hunting for Reagan, Clinton, and Trump, but all they got was a few squirrels who hid some seeds from the government.

Think about this. If we only had an independent and incorruptible federal law enforcement agency, there'd be no need for any special counsel. Oh wait, we do. It's called the Federal Bureau of Investigation, and when we find our balls and assert our independence from politics, America will never require another special counsel.

But I have a grudging admiration for Mr. Mueller's chutzpah. This Jewish word is defined as audacity, insolence, impudence, gall, brazen nerve, effrontery, incredible guts, and arrogance. All of these words pretty much describe the special counsel's techniques. They psychologically beat confessions out of General Flynn, George Papadopoulos, Michael Cohen, Paul Manafort, Republican lobbyist Sam Patten, and Rick Gates. I'll concede that Manafort and Cohen are sleazy *and* guilty, but we didn't need to spend $25 million to get those two. A couple of H&R Block tax preparers could have found the financial evidence of Manafort and Cohen.

The scope of the special counsel was Russian collusion/interference in the election. None of the above fit that bill, but Mueller did lay hands on a few people who did. Unfortunately, their indictments were strictly symbolic. The special counsel indicted, in absentia, thirteen Russian nationals and three Russian entities accused of interfering in the 2016 US election by mounting an elaborate and multifaceted social media influence operation meant to sow political discord during and after the race. Just for the record, millions of Americans attempted to sow political discord during the 2016 presidential race every single day on social media. It's called Facebook.

There's been an amazing amount of indignation on both sides of the aisle over Russian interfering in our election. People equate it to an act of war. Having survived twenty-two days at Hue City during the 1968 Tet Offensive, I can say with certainty that sowing political discord through social media is not even close to war. Half of Alpha Company were killed or wounded during the first six hours of that battle. Any one of those Marines would have traded their fate for time in front of a computer portraying Trump or Clinton as undesirable. This may be a simplistic view of the entire Russian collusion issue, but if some guy named Boris in a chat room can influence the outcome of our election, then we're doomed anyway.

If you are facing bankruptcy, imprisonment, and loss of reputation, there is little consolation knowing that you were simply in the wrong place with the wrong person. In the movie *The Godfather*, Michael Corleone says, "Luca Brasi held a gun to his head, and my father assured him that either his brains or his signature would be on the contract." Though Mueller's Ivy League attorneys in their $1,000 suits didn't have actual guns, their tactics were identical to Brasi's.

Charles Colson, President Richard Nixon's aid, had a wooden plaque on his wall that read, "When you got them by the balls, their hearts and minds will follow." This basically sums up the credo of a special counsel with the proviso "One size fits all."

Once an investigative agency places you in its crosshairs, you will be questioned (remember perjury trap), served subpoenas, followed, and embarrassed, and eventually someone will offer, "If you cooperate, we can get you a few years at some country club prison." At this point you're broke, petrified, and exhausted and very likely to take the deal.

It's like shooting ducks in a barrel. Comey knew that General Flynn had spoken with the Russian ambassador and was aware that Flynn was unsure if that conversation was illegal, inappropriate, or merely embarrassing to the president.

Strzok knew the meeting with the ambassador was *not* against the law but was pretty sure Flynn would lie. Strzok, Page, and Comey could not care less about Russian collusion. Their words and actions indicated that it was *always* about nailing the president. If it wasn't, then Strzok would've handled General Flynn differently.

This questionable strategy was identical when President Clinton was asked if he had had sex with Monica Lewinsky. The special counsel had the blue dress after beating up on Monica with similar threats of indicting her on some crime. The Clintons had enough criminal exposure (no pun intended) that they needn't embarrass a young intern into a lifetime of ridicule. Mr. Starr spent years pressuring President Clinton into perjuring himself over oral sex. This is not a good use of our money and manpower while terrorists plot jihad.

The Rosenstein appointment of Mueller as special counsel is questionable for two specific reasons: It was prematurely enacted, and there is a blatant conflict of interest.

Rod Rosenstein initiated the special counsel, though there was no evidence of a crime. The statute *requires* evidence of underlying criminal activity, but there existed zero evidence of any Russian collusion involving the Trump campaign. The special counsel statue would have been better suited investigating Hillary Clinton's ties to Russia. In addition, the statute calls for the recusal of the special counsel or his staff if there's a conflict of interest. The statute defines a conflict of interest as "a personal or professional relationship with a target or witness."

James Comey was both a witness and suspect in the investigation, so Mueller's impartiality must be questioned. I would be more predisposed to believe my friend and former coworker than the friends of a president I despise. Considering Mueller's role in much of this, it makes him a bizarre choice to lead the heated Russia investigation.

James Kallstrom is a former assistant FBI director and Marine Corps hero. He wondered who investigates the investigators. Kallstrom felt that "Bob Mueller should have never been offered nor accepted the job as special counsel, as he has a huge conflict of interest," Kallstrom told Breitbart News. "He should have recused himself." Not only are Mueller and Comey friends but the special counsel pursued an investigation heavily involving the bureau he once led. The article went on to say:

> How one maintains detachment in leading a team that includes numerous anti-Trump partisans in a probe involving one's close friend and the former bureau for which Mueller served as director goes unexplained.

Both Comey and McCabe led the FBI when a FISA order was granted to spy on Trump officials. They also helped procure the dossier. Kallstrom stated:

> This whole matter with the dossier and the investigations that ensued, including FISA surveillance and the unmasking of hundreds of names, in my view, will prove to be violations of the rules set down by the Congress for unmasking, or worse, will be found to be violations of federal law. The Justice Department should find out if the FBI paid for this phony dossier and should inspect the affidavit that was given to the FISA court to determine the accuracy of their probable cause.

Comey, Mueller, Rosenstein, Wray, and a chunk of the special counsel staff share a long professional and personal history. In a series of questionable coincidences, Comey leaks his investigative memo to pressure the appointment of a special counsel. Bam! Rosenstein appoints his bud Mueller, who hires *his* buds, all of whom share a hatred for all things Trump. Had this team been voir dire'd for jury duty, all would have been excused for cause.

We *know* that the McCabe Strzok FBI team essentially manufactured evidence and that the Justice Department team of Bruce Ohr and Loretta Lynch were the Bureau's coconspirators. According to Rod Rosenstein, the appearances of impropriety caused him to appoint a special counsel. The word "special" indicates someone incorruptible, impartial, and with no agenda. But the *political* Justice Department *appointed* the counsel, so we basically had the fox picking the guards protecting the henhouse.

Though I agree with Mueller's finding of no collusion, the road traveled was filled with cow manure. Mueller hired a team of Trump haters and then ignored all things Russian *not* tied to the Trump group. The special counsel never asked too many questions about Hillary's uranium deal, Podesta's ties to Russia, and the Clinton campaign financing the Steele dossier that, though fiction, accused Trump of Russian collusion.

Another issue involves fairness. Many people in the Justice Department's orbit claimed that Mueller and his team would *never* allow their personal views to influence their objectivity. That claim has some large *buts* attached.

Facts surfaced in late 2018 that several key members of the Mueller team had knowledge that the FISA warrant was based on gossip and lies. Follow the bouncing ball.

On January 30, 2016, Assistant Attorney General Bruce Ohr met with Christopher Steele, who told him that Trump was a Russian agent who shared a bed in Moscow with pissing hookers. Ohr did not believe Steele and when he pressed for facts, Steele had nothing to offer other than "I hate Trump."

In August 2016, Ohr briefed Peter Strzok, the Bureau's lead investigator, and then met with senior personnel in the Justice Department's criminal division. These included Deputy Assistant Attorney General Bruce Swartz, prosecutor Zainab Ahmad, and fraud unit head Andrew Weissmann.

Ohr was adamant with both the FBI and Justice Department officials that the information came from the Clinton camp and warned that it was likely biased and certainly unproven. Yet the FBI swore on an affidavit that this biased and unproven information was fact provided by a reliable informant (Steele).

After Mueller was appointed as special counsel, he hired both Weissmann and Ahmad to investigate Russian collusion, aka President Trump. Both attorneys knew from the beginning that the predicate act of the entire investigation—the Steele dossier—was tainted. Yet they basically went on a search-and-destroy mission and harassed anyone inside Trump's tent. They destroyed families and used Gestapo techniques that were designed only to intimidate. The early-morning raids of Manafort and Stone with automatic weapons and armored vehicles were more suitable for Venezuela.

Those individuals, which include Strzok, Page, Weissmann, and Ahmad, may be guilty of federal crime(s). Other top officials who also shared this knowledge were Andrew McCabe, Bruce Ohr, Bill Priestap, James Comey, and additional FBI and Justice officials who are yet unknown.

All of the individuals who shared this "fruit of the poisonous tree" information were attorneys and/or FBI agents, so Ohr's buzzwords of "biased" and "unproven" were legal caution flags. Yet they either declared under oath that Steele was a reliable source or approved the application knowing Steele was untrustworthy.

Comey stated under oath that he approved the FISA application based on written assurances contained in the document that Christopher Steele was a reliable source. Comey, ever the coward, couched his signature as being *procedural*. Try that excuse on the IRS should your cousin prepare your taxes with a Bernie Madoff calculator.

Ohr testified that, "When I provided [the Steele information] to the FBI, I tried to be clear that this is *source* information."

Bureau interpretation: Don't believe a f★★★★★g word of it.

Let's make the conspiracy even more sexy. Mueller promotes Weissmann as his second in command. What's Weissmann's reputation as an objective and fair arbiter? According to Sidney Powell, a federal prosecutor who wrote *Licensed to Lie: Exposing Corruption in the Department of Justice*:

> Weissmann creatively criminalized a business transaction between Merrill Lynch and Enron. Four Merrill executives went to prison for as long as a year. Weissmann made sure they did not even get bail pending their appeals, even though the charges Weissmann concocted, like those against Andersen, were literally unprecedented. Weissmann's prosecution devastated the lives and families of the Merrill executives, causing enormous defense costs, unimaginable stress and torturous prison time. The 5th Circuit Court of Appeals reversed the mass of the case.

If Robert Mueller is ever questioned under oath there is only one question of consequence to ask him: "Did Andrew Weissmann tell you when you hired him that the entire Russian collusion case was based on unverified information?"

If Mueller knew that the kindling wood that ignited the special counsel statute was phony, then he was part of the problem. What we *do* know is that Mueller later became aware, independent of Weissmann, that the original FISA warrant was based on lies and *never* blinked.

Kevin Bacon, playing Marine Captain Jack Ross in the movie *A Few Good Men,* concluded his opening statement of the court martial with "These are the facts in the case, and they are undisputed."

CHAPTER 19:

The Perjury Trap

"You have the right to remain silent, but if you do so,
I'll just make up a bunch of incriminating stuff..."

As an FBI agent, I've conducted a thousand-plus interviews. That may seem a high number, but interviews are the bread and butter of law enforcement. If you're doing it right, one interview often leads to five more. The interviewees vary from hysterical victims to Mafia hit men, so your technique must be flexible.

The term "perjury trap" has been in the news lately, with experts offering contradicting explanations of what it means. And to be honest, perjury can be a confusing legal concept when liberally interpreted. Perjury essentially is lying, and though lying may seem a straightforward concept, it has many gray areas.

General Flynn pled guilty to lying to the FBI. This is a violation of Title 18, Section 1001 of the federal code. Sounds like an open-and-shut case, since he admitted to the crime and lying is an absolute. Or is it?

Some of the misconceptions floating around the Flynn case center on entrapment and Miranda warnings. The FBI agents who interviewed

General Flynn (one of whom was Peter Strzok) had no legal obligation to advise him of his right to remain silent. Miranda warnings are *only* required in situations involving custodial interrogation, meaning when you restrict the freedom of an individual, usually through an arrest.

Since Strzok didn't place General Flynn under arrest, there was no legal requirement to say, "You do realize that if you lie to the FBI, you'll go to jail." Should he have done so? Yes, because at the exact second Flynn uttered a fib, Strzok had a moral and ethical responsibility to stop the interview and ask for clarification. The crux of Flynn's legal problem is not if he spoke with the Russian ambassador but rather did they discuss *sanctions*. The word "*sanction*" could be interpreted in different ways. I'm not defending General Flynn but would want to assure myself that the national security adviser completely understood the issue. My follow-up questions would include:

1. "Were these the sanctions currently enforced on Russia by the United States?"
2. "Who brought up the sanction issue?"
3. "Did you make any promises?"

I've been in similar situations and would caution, "You may want to think about what you just said." This alerted the individual that the truth would best serve him. That is, if it's the truth that you seek. But Strzok and Comey were never after the truth but rather viewed Flynn as a stepping-stone to Trump.

Individuals *can* refuse to answer questions and walk away, leaving law enforcement limited options. The majority of interviews are for information-gathering purposes and are generally nonconfrontational. At the FBI Academy, we role-played scenarios that had us presenting our credentials and declaring the familiar acronym "FBI" to instructors posing as interviewees. I'll admit to feeling a mild flush of self-importance whenever I'd introduce myself with a "Special Agent Ligato,

FBI." One could imagine trumpets blaring accompanied by string instruments following that pronouncement.

But the real world didn't get the memo. When I was a baby agent, I had a lead to interview an individual in connection with a case. The interviewee wasn't a suspect in the case but was the type of lead that rookies are assigned.

I knocked at the door and waited, then knocked a little harder and waited some more. I could hear a conversation inside the home and banged on the door. Tired of the open defiance, I uttered the three initials that I figured would end this standoff: "FBI!"

There was a slight delay, and then a female replied in a clear and confident voice, "Go fuck yourself!"

I stood still and considered my options. This *never* happened at the Academy. My initial impulse was to kick the door down, which I rejected because I lacked a warrant to require this drastic action. Other options included waiting until someone left the house, calling my supervisor for advice, or going back to the office and claiming, "Nobody was home." I picked the fourth option but felt emasculated feeling my superpowers gone. It took a while to recharge them.

Was General Flynn entrapped by the FBI? Entrapment is basically making somebody do something that they normally wouldn't do. This was not the case with Flynn, so he wasn't entrapped.

As an FBI agent, I found Section 1001 an interim investigative tool but not the end goal. In the wrong hands, it can also be a questionable breach of due process. It's about as sporting as shooting ducks in a barrel, especially when you have transcripts of the duck's conversations. A majority of people cannot recall the *exact* wording of conversations held ten minutes prior to being asked again about what was said. This is the reason why the word "trap" follows "perjury."

Law enforcement officers rarely deal with Mother Teresa types, so it's safe to say that many of our interviews are with individuals who wander the fringes of society. Although I have no supporting data, it would be safe to say that a significant number of the interviews I conducted during my career had Section 1001 implications. Most individuals will shade, slant, skew, invent, and outright lie to mitigate their role in any investigation. Many of them may have a minor or no role in criminal activity, but there's a survival instinct to distance yourself from the fire.

How easy is it to trap someone into committing perjury? It's not too difficult if that's your end goal. Say you suspect an accountant of cooking the books for some mob associate. The FBI has a wire on the mobster and overhears the accountant say, "So Vinnie, how do you want me to claim the $100,000 from your loan company?"

Two FBI agents appear at the accountant's door at 9:00 p.m. and ask two questions:

"Is Vinnie Bagadonuts your client?" and "Does Vinnie have a loan company?"

Game, set, and match since any reply will constitute a felony. Mr. CPA has no idea that he is essentially under oath since lying to the FBI is a federal crime.

There was a seventh-floor conversation with the Comey Gang. Words to the effect of, "Hey, Andy (McCabe), let's take a shot. Call Flynn and tell him we're sending a couple of agents over to talk to him."

"What if he wants an attorney present?"

"Assure him he can have an attorney present but it's just an informational chat and a lawyer will slow things down."

Comey later admitted that protocol demanded the FBI contact the White House counsel *prior* to interviewing a national security advisor. He never believed the agents would get anywhere near Flynn.

Comey was quoted, "This would have never happened in the Bush or Obama White House."

McCabe contacted Flynn directly and in between some friendly BS throws in, "We [FBI] need your help on a sensitive matter. Can I send some agents over? And by the way, you won't need an attorney present because then we'd have to get the Justice Department involved."

McCabe hooked General Flynn, who had no idea that he was about to be the catch of the day. As an investigator, this admission tells me that the Comey Gang had *already* determined President Trump's guilt in *some* crime. They kept fishing with a massive net since they lacked any specific evidence.

At the time of the interview, Strzok had information on Flynn considered embarrassing but *not* illegal. Flynn had spoken with the Russian ambassador during the transition, which is business as usual but became a crime when Flynn lied about the *context* of the meeting. Flynn believed the subject matter would be an embarrassment to Trump due to the fever of Russian collusion. It's a similar situation when President Clinton lied under oath about Monica Lewinsky. Oral sex is not a crime but highly embarrassing given the circumstances, so he fibbed.

As an FBI agent, I'd feel a hollow victory and a waste of the government's resources to coerce a blow job confession from *any* married guy. Bill and Hillary Clinton had plenty of substantive violations of law to pursue instead of Monica Lewinsky. And the sole purpose of the Flynn interview was to legally extort him into flipping on Trump.

The time line in any investigation is important since any action will produce a *reaction*. Consider this sequence of events. On July 5, 2016, the same day of FBI Director James Comey's press conference exonerating Hillary, Christopher Steele flew to Rome to meet an old government contact. A week or so later Deputy Assistant General Bruce Ohr informs Peter Strzok, Lisa Page, and Andy McCabe, in addition to high-ranking Justice officials, that Christopher Steele has salacious information on candidate Trump. Ohr categorizes the information as gossip, rumors, and *unverified* adding that it was financed by the Clinton campaign. In the fall of 2016, the FBI fires Christopher Steele as an FBI informant for lying. The FBI forbids any further contact since Steele is unable to testify in court, but the FBI and Justice Department officials later swore in the FISA application that Steele was a *reliable* source. In October of 2016 the first FISA warrant was approved as part of an overall Russian hacking investigation. The entire hierarchy of the FBI and Justice *knew* at that time that the probable cause used was false (perjury).

In January of 2017 Comey and McCabe sent Strzok to jam up Flynn, realizing that White House protocols were not in place yet. Comey later explained that a Bush or Obama White House would never have permitted a cavalier interview with their national security advisor. They would be required to go through the White House legal counsel.

The fact that Comey chose to bypass Trump indicates his conviction that the president of the United States was *not* to be trusted, though they had no evidence to warrant the distrust. It was a *feeling* based on a deep hatred and fear of Donald Trump.

I'm doubtful that Comey notified his boss, Rod Rosenstein, that he was sending agents to the White House to question the national security advisor about Russian collusion. Rosenstein seems like the joker in this deck of cards and his role as villain or hero is yet to be determined.

The Flynn interview occurred *prior* to the special counsel while Rosenstein had the helm at Justice. On May 17, 2017, Deputy Attorney General Rod Rosenstein appointed former FBI Director Robert Mueller to investigate Russian efforts to influence the 2016 presidential election and *related* matters. The term *"related matters"* was interpreted by Mueller to mean, "*Any* individual, financial record, or third cousin to Donald Trump is *related* to Russian collusion."

Collusion in the 2016 election was the special counsel's scope but Mueller ventured far off course. Did Rosenstein approve Mueller's *witch hunt*?

A recently released special counsel report shows there were *two* additional scope authorization memos. Rosenstein allowed Mueller to veer off course and select targets of opportunities *not* directly tied to Russian collusion, but with connections to President Trump. This is further proof that Russian collusion was merely the excuse to end or cripple the Trump presidency. The first scope memo was August 2, 2017. The second scope memo was issued by Rod Rosenstein to Robert Mueller on October 20, 2017. This memo provided Weissmann and Mueller authority to investigate specific targets, for specific purposes. One of those targets was General Michael Flynn's son, Michael Flynn Jr.

Once Mueller was allowed to free style he targeted Paul Manafort, Roger Stone, and Michael Cohen for financial crimes. Their convictions were *not* related to Russian efforts to fix our election. Rosenstein did not act as a neutral arbitrator when he authorized Mueller to act outside the original special counsel's scope.

The two agents sent to interview Flynn were Peter Strzok and Joe Pientka. Only one agent is tasked with writing the FD 302 for both agents and my guess is Pientka was the guy. Strzok's stated excuse for not advising Flynn of his constitutional rights was a desire to maintain the rapport. Hostage negotiators depend on rapport to achieve safe outcomes to crappy situations. But there's a very subtle difference to the Flynn interview that makes the Comey Gang particularly rotten.

The guilty sometime incriminate themselves during the course of a routine interview with a skilled interrogator. At that moment, agents generally stop the conversation and advise them of their rights. There is no legal duty to do so at this point, though some judge may cite the interviewee's Fifth Amendment rights against self-incrimination.

When FBI agents interviewed Martha Stewart and General David Petraeus, they specified that it was in relation to questionable stock market trades and mishandling of confidential documents, respectively. They were aware of their criminal exposure and chose to talk anyway, believing they could wordsmith their way through the conversation. (Exhibit A is Hillary Clinton, who has successfully double-talked her way through four scandals.)

The Flynn interview particularly smells because it skirted the line of entrapment by a microscopic atom. At the time, Flynn was the newly appointed national security advisor arranging the family photos on his White House desk. The deputy director of the FBI called and asked for his help. McCabe and Flynn had previously met, so it wasn't a faceless official with a stern voice demanding an interview.

Peter Strzok and FBI Agent Joe Pientka described Flynn as "being very open" and noted that he "clearly saw the FBI agents as allies." Their report included Flynn shooting the bull about Trump's "knack for interior design" at the hotels he stayed at during his campaign.

According to Strzok, "Flynn was so talkative, and had so much time for them, that he wondered if the national security advisor did not have more important things to do than have a such a relaxed, non-pertinent discussion with them."

Sandwiched between the guy talk, Peter Strzok began a series of questions concerning national security (Flynn, after all, *was* the national security advisor). Flynn attempted to recall an exact conversation with the Russian ambassador. Strzok had verbatim transcripts of that conversation between Flynn and Sergey Kislyak. Flynn never denied the Kislyak conversation, but he denied discussing *sanctions* with the Russians. Mueller charged him with lying or misleading federal investigators under 18 U.S.C. 1001.

The bottom line is that Comey, McCabe, and Strzok set up Flynn with a perjury trap to get to Trump because Flynn speaking with Kislyak was *not* a crime.

If the above doesn't raise your suspicion hackles, then consider that the judge who took Flynn's guilty plea was Rudy Contreras, who is a *personal* friend of Peter Strzok. The FBI deliberately chose to entrap General Michael Flynn, knowing he'd lie over something that *wasn't* criminal. Remember Comey's words when charging Martha Stewart for "a *minor* securities charge." These crimes only become *major* when the subjects are nationally known or pathways to bigger fish.

There was another significant misstep that could have criminal exposure for some FBI agent. According to sworn testimony, the Flynn interview concluded with Agents Strzok and Pientka's belief that Flynn "didn't display any of the normal physical manifestations of lying." Someone with access and motive *modified* their original report to *change* that opinion. That edit made Flynn guilty of a Title 18, Section 1001 violation, which led to his plea.

FBI agents *never* place opinions in reports, as in NEVER! Strzok was either incompetent or *very* incompetent. If I had written that 302, no supervisor would dare place it in an FBI file. They'd probably ask, "If you knew Flynn was lying, why would you contradict your own conclusion with an opposite *opinion*?"

The only individuals permitted to provide *opinions* are expert witnesses. If Flynn was being interviewed by a psychiatrist, even that specialist would have to present a long vita citing their specific qualifications on recognizing deception, to include personal research, professional articles, and cases where they successfully identified the "manifestations of lying."

The motto for the Comey Gang could be "Anyone can convict the guilty, but it takes hard work to convict the innocent." The recurring pattern of agents altering official documents to fit their desired narrative would be frowned upon by the management during my days in the Bureau. The Flynn amendments seem a reverse déjà vu happening of the Hillary Clinton email case, when Strzok changed the wording to make Hillary *innocent*.

Had Flynn not pled guilty he may have beaten the case. Recent court filings by DOJ clarified that in order to prove a defendant acted *willfully*, federal prosecutors must show beyond a reasonable doubt that the defendant *knew* his or her statement was unlawful, not just that the statement was false.

Bottom line: You can lie all you want to federal agents if you didn't know you were breaking the law by lying. This is a material change in the government's position that could have had a significant impact on the Flynn case and many others. Flynn chose *not* to vacate his guilty plea and was sentenced to probation. It seemed less expensive, faster, and saved his son from prosecution.

If I take someone into custody ("You're under arrest"), then I *must* advise them of their constitutional right to remain silent *before* I ask a question lest they incriminate themselves. But if I knock on someone's door and interview them, they are essentially "under oath" anyway given Title 18, Section 1001.

Some judges and commentators have criticized Section 1001 as a "catchall" and an unfair trap for the unwary. It is not unheard of for prosecutors to charge people with making false statements even where the government lacks sufficient evidence to indict on the underlying offense under investigation. The breadth and flexibility of Section 1001 makes it attractive to prosecutors, particularly in investigations where the suspected crimes are complicated and difficult to prove. In 1998, US Supreme Court Justice Ruth Bader Ginsburg went so far as to state that Section 1001 gives prosecutors "extraordinary authority" to "manufacture crimes." Prosecutors have brought Section 1001 cases on the basis of statements people made in their living rooms without any opportunity to talk to a lawyer, compose themselves, or prepare their comments.

As an undercover agent I lied *all* day and *every* day. When a case went to trial, I'd be decked out in my conservative FBI suit, and the first question the defense attorney would ask after I took the oath to tell the truth was, "Are you a liar, Agent Ligato?"

This is a trick question since if I reply *no*, the next series of questions deal with the lies I told his client, but if I answer with a yes, then the attorney smiles and says, "No further questions." I'd just admitted that I am a liar in front of a jury. I never allowed the attorney to box me into that perjury corner. I'd look at the jury and explained that undercover work is similar to actors assuming character and saying lines but I have never lied in a courtroom.

Ethically, Strzok was aware of statements previously made by Flynn as a result of a questionable wiretap, so this is a classic perjury trap, *but* it is not entrapment. Strzok definitely abused the spirit of the law, but Flynn lied and is technically guilty of violating Title 18, Section 1001.

Full disclosure: I have lied to my supervisor during my career. The fibs were never case related, but they were lies nonetheless. I think one had to do with my whereabouts on the golf course. Agents routinely lie to their supervisors. Though technically not a crime, it does demonstrate how slippery Title 18, Section 1001 can be.

CHAPTER 20

"Is that Bigfoot, Mommy?"

"What's important at this time is to re-clarify the
difference between hero and villain."
—J. Edgar Hoover

How did James Comey assemble a group of like-minded folks and trash the reputation of an American institution whose motto is Fidelity, Bravery, and Integrity? Perhaps the more relevant question should be *why* Comey did it.

At first blush Comey resembles the poster child for the Boy Scouts. But it's a Boy Scout who earned badges in treachery and backstabbing. When Comey was nominated by President Barack Obama for FBI director, the *Wall Street Journal* headlined an article with "The Political Mr. Comey." They went on to make the case that Comey had a record of *excess* and *bad* judgment.

It appears that Comey has made a habit of prosecutorial overreach that culminated in the Russian collusion case, his finest career moment.

Comey's MO could be described as the "carpet bombing" approach to criminal justice. Upon selecting the enemy compound, it's bombs away. Screw the collateral damage on who gets an ass full of legal shrapnel. Michael Flynn, George Papadopoulos, Martha Stewart, Frank Quattrone, Steve Hatfill, and Scooter Libby be damned. Jam them up on something even if it's felony stupid, then offer a deal. I will probably repeat this mantra several times, but if the government wishes to indict you, you *will* be indicted.

The Federal Bureau of Investigation *had* been one of the few enduring American institutions. The words "solid" and "steady" come to mind. I've always been proud of the three institutions that defined my life. After attending Catholic school for twelve years, I joined the United States Marine Corps and retired as a special agent of the FBI. These institutions are certainly not perfect. All three had their share of scandal involving flawed individuals who chipped away at the bricks, but their foundation was always stronger than any one person.

In 1836, the fifth commandant of the Marine Corps, Col. Archibald Henderson, left a note pinned to his door. It read, "Gone to Florida to fight the Indians. Will be back when the war is over."

Colonel Henderson's message says plenty about Marines and their sense of mission. Versions of this note have been uttered by Marines in every skirmish since 1775. Marines are *very* direct and result oriented, and that's why we respond to simple commands like "Charge" or "Take that hill."

The Marine Corps and FBI traditionally share many outstanding virtues. Excellent leadership and a clarity of mission were two constants until lately. The Corps and the Bureau understood that the troops in the field were the key to mission success. The role of any headquarters is to select an objective and then support the field. It's a formula for many successful campaigns, whether the villain is Adolf Hitler or Pretty Boy Floyd. The Mueller-Comey eras changed that dynamic and tarnished the shine of an FBI that glowed brightly for over a hundred years. The reasons are many but not too complex. I'll discuss them in detail, but allow me to provide a quick snapshot into the mind-set of FBI HQ under the Mueller-Comey reign.

Special Agent Joseph Pistone (retired) is one of the most recognizable names in FBI history. You may know him from his undercover identity as "Donnie Brasco." A movie starring Johnny Depp and Al Pacino chronicled Joe's undercover experience in the Mafia. His sacrifice and valor led to over one hundred arrests, including numerous Mafiosi capos, and disrupted their criminal enterprise for a decade.

In September 1976, Pistone walked out of the FBI office and did not return for the next six years. He infiltrated the Bonnano crime family as a deep undercover operative. After his retirement, Joe occasionally returned to the FBI Academy to teach undercover techniques to agents involved in active cases. This proved an invaluable experience having the FBI's most successful UCA (undercover agent) providing real-life experiences dealing with the most dangerous investigative technique.

In 2015, Pistone was informed by FBI HQ that his expertise was no longer needed. The *exact* two words used were that he was no longer "current" and "relevant." How could Donnie Brasco become irrelevant with an expiration date? The FBI managers who reached this conclusion probably weren't aware that Joe *wrote* the undercover program that is used today. There is also a subtle irony in their decision to discard Joe on the undercover scrap heap. He is the most sought-after subject matter expert on covert operations internationally. Joe continues to provide his hard-earned wisdom to many foreign governments at their training academies. But he is no longer welcome at his alma mater, the Federal Bureau of Investigation.

I was fortunate enough to work in an undercover capacity with Joe, and there is no such thing as *currency* when dealing with bent-nose psychopaths. Without discussing techniques, successful undercover operations are dependent on crucial skills that are timeless. Joe's supposed lack of "currency" is like benching General George S. Patton from teaching tactics and leadership skills to today's West Point cadets.

Leadership expert Warren Bennis said, "Failing organizations are usually overmanaged and under-led." Leadership involves courage and the responsibility to admit mistakes.

One of the first lessons Marine recruits learn at boot camp is to accept your screwups. The words *"No excuse, sir!"* are seared into every Marine's gourd. Even when Comey is presented with proof of his fibs, his two default replies are "I don't recall" or "That's not correct." He has never accepted *any* responsibility for the shit storm in which the Bureau finds itself. Could Comey believe his own untruths?

Law enforcement officers conduct many interviews and within the first minute can generally tell if the subject's lying. Fox News reporter Catherine Herridge once asked James Comey, "The FBI's reputation has taken a big hit over the last year. Do you share any of the responsibility for that?"

A smug Comey defensively shot back, "No, the FBI's reputation has taken a big hit because the president of the United States has lied about it constantly. And a whole lot of good people who watch your network believe that nonsense. That's a tragedy. That will be undone eventually, but the damage [to the FBI] has nothing to do with me."

When President Trump fired Comey as FBI director in May 2017, some retired agents defended Comey's record, and active-duty agents felt that their boss was a victim of politics. Some even denounced Trump's self-serving decision and circled the Bureau wagon around Comey.

But slowly those opinions did a 180 as the man who self-professes his own humility and sacrifice began to talk, and talk, and then talk some more. Comey transformed from Clark Kent to Alex Forrest. Glenn Close played Alex in the movie *Fatal Attraction*, and for the first half of the film she was a bright, well-spoken, and rational professional. But as the movie progresses Alex boils a kid's pet rabbit on the stove, pours acid on a car, and chases Michael Douglas with a kitchen knife.

Many of the agents who'd previously supported Comey scratched their heads and now view him as an arrogant, self-centered politician who damaged the Bureau. One retired agent stated, "His testimony in June of 2017 *sickened* me." Others felt him a coward when Attorney General Loretta Lynch ordered him to call the Clinton email investigation a "matter." But what sealed Comey's fate in the eyes of the retired agents was leaking an investigative memo to the *New York Times*. This was the final act in Comey's transformation from Batman to the Joker since it included using a shill to do his dirty work. Comey's lame excuse was a desire to avoid the media camping out on his driveway. This transparent bullshit was my personal last straw.

Many years ago I was part of a conversation while working undercover in the Italian mob. Four of us sat at a small cocktail table inside the VIP room at a high-end gentlemen's club. Two young wise guys were arguing about who was more handsome. Both wore the standard Guido uniforms of open silk shirts, 10 pounds of gold dangling from their neck, and greased-back hair.

"I'm the handsomest guy in this joint."

"Whatta you outta you mind?" his friend countered. "You look like a fuckin' rotten zucchini."

The girls were circling the table like vultures about to pounce on some Italian cuisine.

The third wise guy was old, obese, bald, and wearing a Nike sweat suit. He took out a hundred dollar bill, spit on it, and stuck it to his forehead. Then he announced, "Now *I'm* the fuckin' handsomest guy in the joint."

The moral of this story may seem muddled, but work with me. It seems that the old Guido was correct since two girls immediately sat on his lap. There's a weird similarity between Comey and the obese wise guy. Both bent the rules based on a pompous arrogance, but only the wise guy was aware that he wasn't playing fair.

James Comey's an enigma. He appears a polite, soft-spoken, capable guy who cut down the cherry tree and could not tell a lie. But

Comey's very convincing when staring at the camera while dispensing half-truths, verbal gymnastics, and outright lies.

We've all watched Hillary and Bill lie, and it's a cringeworthy experience no matter your politics. The Clintons lie when it helps them out of a jam and *after* careful calculations. They aren't very convincing, but they do try hard. When Bill Clinton stated that he "did not have sexual relations with that woman," I understood that his lie was to prevent major embarrassment and political damage. Got it.

Their lies are Machiavellian in nature, whereas President Trump's fibs are more impulsive and less calculated. His whoppers deal with porn stars and his golf handicap. Got that too.

But Comey is different. The thought occurred to me that Comey *believes* his lies because I believe *him*, even though I *know* he's lying. Disclaimer: I am not a psychologist, though I have an M.ED. in educational psychology. I dusted off some old textbooks, and my unofficial diagnosis is that Comey is an arrogant bullshitter.

A real psychologist might use the words "narcissistic pathological lying" to describe the condition. It's characterized by an inflated ego and disdain for what one considers inferior. That'd be the rest of society, including you and me.

There are many other factors that contributed to the Bureau's fall from grace. One lies squarely on the back of every president from Coolidge to Trump. Chief executives *falsely* believe that FBI directors should be recruited from the Justice Department or federal bench. *Every* FBI director has been an attorney, and only Clarence Kelley and Louis Freeh had actual law enforcement experience. Most of the public incorrectly assume that FBI directors are former agents.

There's a subtle but critical difference between prosecutor and cop. Our common goals are to rid society of bad people, but that's where the similarities end. FBI agents attend the FBI Academy, where we learn how to shoot, fight, and attain the mind-set of a predator. Perhaps a politically incorrect term by today's standards, but it's also an accurate description of good cops and agents. We are the hunters, and this tag involves long hours in bad neighborhoods, eating cold chicken nuggets while peeing in McDonald's coffee cups. Our language is coarse, our patience strained, and we'll occasionally fart in the presence of coworkers. Justice attorneys belch. When presented with a decision, a lawyer will default to why something *can't* be done.

"The first thing we do, let's kill all the lawyers" is a line from William Shakespeare's *Henry VI*. Though that may be extreme, it would clear the way for a non-attorney FBI director.

Prosecutors sit around their office and discuss how the agents *may* have violated some poor mope's rights who resisted arrest and got their nose bloodied. Justice Department attorneys do *not* understand the culture of law enforcement officers. We are a team who plays the same sport, but in different leagues.

The system had always worked when the FBI had been an independent entity. The Mueller merge ended our sovereignty, and it's resulted in the Justice Department both conducting *and* prosecuting cases. That's *exactly* what Comey did in the email case. The FBI investigated the case and the FBI director granted clemency. He must've gotten confused because a few weeks later the Justice Department very quietly agreed with Comey's verdict. *Surprise!*

The Justice Department is a political entity, and its decisions sometimes reflect that condition. Eric Holder and Loretta Lynch are two prime examples of politicians masquerading as unbiased prosecutors. The FBI initiates cases through informants, crime scenes, complaints, and referrals from local police departments. We conduct the investigation and the Justice Department prosecutes. It was a division of labor that worked, but only if the FBI retained its autonomy. Once the Bureau effectively merged with Justice, attorneys jumped into the pilot seat and steered the course of FBI investigations.

The practice of *exclusively* appointing Justice Department attorneys as FBI directors caught up with the Bureau with Mueller. You'd think we'd learned our lesson, but after Comey's firing, President Trump appointed yet another Ivy League attorney, Christopher Wray. He's a good guy, but he seems perfectly content to sit in the copilot's seat. The FBI needs a reboot, and it starts with flying our own plane.

When I retired in 2003, I would have argued that there was no earthly way that a group of eight to ten FBI agents and Justice Department attorneys could conspire to nullify the people's will.

There's a line in the movie *Goodfellas*: "After a while, it got to be all normal. None of it seemed like crime."

My guess is that Comey and his gang didn't just meet and instantly plot betrayal. It was likely a group seduction, beginning with warm and fuzzy conversations about the environment and the proper wine choice to accompany Maine lobster. But at some point, their conversations approached treason, and not one individual rose and declared, "Not on my watch!" That's what *leaders* do. Newspaper articles referred to them as a "secret society," but that would be an insult to any reputable secret society. If you think about it, the Comey Gang was actually an episode of *The Gong Show.*

Strzok and Page, both high-ranking members of an intelligence agency, traded personal texts on their government phones. Lisa seemed concerned about their using official phones to insult presidential candidates and asked, "So look, you say we can text on that phone when we talk about [redacted] because it can't be traced." In addition, the two felt safer detailing their sexual liaisons on their government phones in obvious codes that wouldn't require a super computer to decipher. It was a combination of pig Latin and high school shorthand.

One should not confuse the rank-and-file FBI agent with the Beltway gang that couldn't tweet straight. James Comey, Peter Strzok, Andy McCabe, Lisa Page, James Baker, and other inhabitants of headquarters shared a tangible arrogance. Comey's belief that the field agent had his back is an example of his vanity. He surrounded himself with like-minded folks who either shared his ideology or *pretended* to be in lock step rather than risk a transfer to Guam.

Headquarters duty has always been considered an unwanted, but obligatory, stop along the management journey. Two-hour carpools in DC traffic is the Catholic's version of purgatory. Supervisory agents spend a few years initialing stuff and attending meetings until they can escape back to the field. It's like being in the penalty box. The end goal for supervisory types is to lead the troops on the battlefield.

This system of a continuous flowing stream can prove a valuable experience by exposing supervisors to diverse locales and circumstances. But when the stream stops moving on the seventh floor of headquarters, the water becomes stagnant and can morph into a rancid cesspool of conspirators who plot bloodless coups.

We keep tinkering with our system of justice, but the problem is not the machinery but the humans pulling the levers. The FBI and Justice Department have successfully prosecuted bad guys for a hundred years. What's changed in the past thirty years is the politicization of the FBI. Individuals who place handcuffs on someone and put them in cages for twenty years should *never* be red, blue, *or* green.

The FBI's basic mission is to put bad people in jail, so consider these two simple questions:

If FBI HQ disappeared tomorrow, would the field still be able to fulfill its mission?

But what if the *field* disappeared tomorrow?

CHAPTER 21:

The Politicization of the FBI

"Mr. Rogers did not adequately prepare me
for the people in my neighborhood."

The FBI has been infected by politics, similar to First Officer Chekov in the *Star Trek* movie *The Wrath of Khan,* when a slime-covered slug-like creature enters his skull through his ear and wraps itself around the cerebral cortex. We recruit from the human race, so we're not a perfect institution, but for a long time, we were *damn* close. That was before Robert Mueller and his illegitimate son, James Comey, injected their politics into the Bureau's DNA.

FBI agents had always been the knights in shining armor riding white stallions and saving damsels in distress. We'd flash our credentials, say, "*FBI*," and the bad guys would assume the position. The Bureau's reputation transformed average individuals into superheroes, but that was prior to James Comey leaking government documents to the press. Other senior managers are suspected of leaking, including Deputy Director Andrew McCabe, chief legal counsel James Baker, and one or two of the lovebirds. It's no surprise that the seventh floor of headquarters sank.

The institution of the FBI will survive this scandal, but only if we return to our roots. That requires a divorce from the Justice Department. What earned the FBI's reputation for excellence was a fierce independence from outside political influences. The FBI had always been a sovereign entity *until* Robert Mueller became director.

Although the FBI is technically an agency that reports to the Justice Department, we'd always maintained an arm's-length distance. This separation assured the public that FBI agents were not influenced by the current occupant of the White House and his attorney general. Many AGs mask their partisanship, but recent appointees such as Eric Holder and Loretta "Tarmac" Lynch have openly ripped Lady Justice's blindfold off and placed Lois Lerner on her scales.

How did the FBI become politicized? It didn't happen overnight. During his twelve-year term as FBI director, Robert Mueller marinated the FBI into Justice. He accomplished this union slowly but surely. Since *all* FBI directors came from the Justice Department or federal bench (except for Clarence Kelley), their priorities are not viewed through a law enforcement prism no matter what they claim at their confirmation hearing.

Prior to Mueller's tenure, FBI agents could open and investigate most cases minus interference from Justice. If an agent received credible information that the Clinton Foundation was a criminal enterprise, they'd initiate an investigation. At its conclusion, the agent would submit the results to the Justice Department, which had three options: indict, decline prosecution, or request additional evidence.

After Mueller's tenure at the FBI, the Justice Department's approval was required to open specific cases, recruit informants, and conduct sensitive investigative techniques. This additional bureaucratic layer would be a mere pain in the butt if Justice based its decisions on evidence. But it appears that recent leadership has practiced selective prosecution based on their political beliefs.

I believe that every government agency requires oversight. The Comey Gang is proof that checks and balances are needed. So some may believe that the Justice Department *should* have veto power over what cases the FBI investigates. But they'd be wrong. The Bureau had always been a self-contained entity. Our informants received code names, and their files are secured in safes. If an agent entered the informant room, they were required to sign in and could only retrieve their own source file. If a Justice Department attorney visited our building, they required an escort and couldn't roam freely. The Justice Department is more cavalier about their security.

By compartmentalizing and separating our functions, it takes politics out of the equation but still permits the Justice Department its oversight function. It begins *after* the FBI completes its investigation. By *not* allowing Justice to exercise veto power, it prevents them from engaging in selective prosecution.

Released emails reveal President Obama's Justice Department initially rejected the FBI's request to investigate the Clinton Foundation's relationship with the State Department. There are numerous other examples of the Justice Department putting the kibosh on FBI investigations.

Eric Holder and President Obama had an agenda. For example, both men often claimed that white cops were targeting and killing young black males. Besides conducting investigations, the Bureau is also responsible for compiling national crime statistics. Even though the data failed to support their personal beliefs, Holder ordered the FBI to investigate local police agencies for civil rights violations.

Director Mueller caved to Holder's pressure, resulting in more than twenty civil rights investigations into local police departments between 2009 and 2014, more than doubling the number of reviews from the previous five years.

Many in law enforcement, including FBI agents, were demoralized by the probes, believing they were risking their lives without any support from Main Justice or FBI HQ. Law enforcement morale hit rock bottom as officers on the street played a prevent defense. They refused to be proactive crime fighters lest they find themselves fired or indicted for doing their job. Many cops wouldn't even write traffic citations fearing they'd be accused of racism. There was no line of demarcation between the attorney general and FBI director since both Mueller and Comey were born and raised in the Justice Department.

The FBI director *and* attorney general are appointed by the president, and there has *never* been a non-attorney to serve at either position. Furthermore, every director and AG served at the Justice Department or on the federal bench. This is a small fraternity borne of similar backgrounds, careers, and life goals. It's only natural that Justice Department attorneys who become FBI directors would bring not only their prosecutorial experience but also the culture of the Justice Department to their new post. And that's one of the contributing factors that led to the Comey Gang. Comey immediately hired James Baker, also a Justice attorney, which continued the tunnel vision.

The Comey firing, leading to the Mueller special counsel appointment, has some loose ends. Comey, Mueller, Rosenstein, Ohr, Baker, and even current FBI Director Christopher Wray all worked together at Justice. Comey referred to Mueller as a mentor and a trusted public servant.

FBI agents generally conduct investigations and take them wherever the evidence leads. This Russian collusion investigation resembled a jockey leading a horse with blinders to the starting gate. It required criminal activity to enact the special counsel statute, but there was nothing but hearsay, rumors, innuendos, and gossip. The FBI should have been awarded a first-place prize for fiction based on the FISA warrant affidavit. But the fix was in, and there was not one impartial player in the chain of checks and balances.

One of the many unknowns in the Comey Gang saga is the role of former Deputy Attorney General Rod Rosenstein. He's the hub with many bent spokes encircling him. There's an old saying that applies to Rosenstein: "He knows where all the bodies are buried."

Andrew Weissmann worked for Rosenstein at the Justice Department, and so did Bruce Ohr, who confided to Weissmann that the Steele dossier was a load of bullshit paid for by the Clinton campaign.

If an impartial FBI brick agent got the ticket on this collusion case, their first step would be to meet with Rod Rosenstein and ask, "Whatta you got?" Though this may seem like a simplistic approach, the entire case would rest on his reply.

Since Rosenstein likely knew that the Steele dossier was bogus, an honest reply may have been, "We got squat, but what I'd do is jam up everyone around Trump and get something impeachable. Fuck the Russians."

And that's exactly what *almost* happened.

If you doubt that the FBI has been politicized, then follow this bouncing ball. Peter "I hate Trump" Strzok interviews General Flynn and jams him up on lying. The special counsel arrests George Papadopoulos for lying, Michael Cohen for lying and financial crimes, Paul Manafort for lying and financial crimes, and Roger Stone for more of the same.

These supporting actors were pressured to dime out Trump not with evidence of Russian collusion but with allegations involving pay-offs to Playboy models and porn queens and some financial shenanigans. They never could place a Russian military hat on the president's head. The special counsel failed to even put him in bed with the pissing Russian hookers, which is exactly what the Steele dossier claimed. That document was a tawdry dime-store novel that the FBI elevated to a best seller.

The man who began the FISA ball bouncing was Carter Page, who was an investment banker and oil industry consultant with ties to

Russia. In 2013, Russian intelligence officers targeted Page as a source for *economic* information since he had no political currency at that time.

The Ruskies eventually determined that Page was unreliable and low level, referring to him as an "idiot." The FBI was aware of Russia's belief that Page knew nothing of value and was an unreliable, insignificant player. They had recordings of the Russians voicing those *exact* doubts on a wiretap, from an earlier espionage case involving three Russian spies working undercover for the Kremlin in New York. Page only became a super-reliable Russian spy *after* he visited the Trump Tower.

Remember that the FBI had closed Christopher Steele as an informant, also deeming him unreliable. Once an FBI informant is considered unreliable, it is documented in their file, and they are considered persona non grata. It would be difficult for such an untrustworthy person to take the witness stand or even use their information for warrants.

So, Peter Strzok had a problem, which he solved with Deputy Assistant Attorney General Bruce Ohr. Bruce's wife, Ellie, worked for commercial research firm Fusion GPS, which was contracted by a law firm to get information that would embarrass candidate Trump. Fusion retained Christopher Steele, which led to his eventual production of the "dossier." The law firm was paid by the Clinton campaign. This convoluted sequence actually places Hillary Clinton in closer proximity to the Russians than Trump. Deputy Attorney General Ohr slips the Steele dossier to the FBI, and all of this culminates in special counsel Robert Mueller. Very convenient.

There exists a major problem for everyone who signed their name and verified that the FISA application was proper. That list includes Comey, Rosenstein, Sally Yates, Bill Priestap, and several more as yet unknown FBI agents. The affidavit stipulated that Steele was a reliable informant, but the FBI's own files say otherwise.

There is a great irony that the two men (Page and Steele) most responsible for the entire Russian collusion hoax had both been designated as unreliable by both US and Russian intelligence officers.

The FBI cited Page's involvement with Russian intel types from that 2013 New York case in their applications for the FISA warrant. They conveniently omitted the Russian opinions that Page was undependable. Withholding material and exculpatory evidence from the FISA applications may have violated Page's Fourth Amendment protections against omissions of material facts that would undermine the FISA warrant.

"It is illegal," said veteran FBI agent Michael Biasello. The affiant "*cannot* cherry-pick only information favorable to the case."

Based on the dossier, the FBI swore to the FISA court that it believed Carter Page, working for the Trump campaign as an advisor, was conspiring with the Russian government to influence the 2016 election. This melodramatic allegation came from Christopher Steele, the former British spy. What the FBI and Justice Department neglected to inform the court was that Steele's allegations had never been verified.

The public may not be aware that the October 1, 2016, original FISA application, *and* the three renewals were labeled "**VERIFIED APPLICATION**" [bold caps present in original]. In addition, each application states:

> *The FBI has reviewed this verified application for accuracy in accordance with its April 5, 2001 procedures, which include sending a copy of the draft to the appropriate field office(s).*

This was obviously a fib, otherwise known in legal jargon as perjury, because the applications were *never* verified for accuracy. FBI procedures to verify a FISA application require that all paperwork be sent to the appropriate field office for review. This requirement is spelled out in the Bureau's *Domestic Investigations and Operations Guide* (DIOG), which mandates that information contained on a FISA application has been thoroughly vetted and *confirmed*. I suppose you can verify anything, but *confirming* a document full of half-truths and omissions may trip one up.

Carter Page was the primary predication of the collusion case, but the poor guy had absolutely no involvement in espionage. This supposition is sound since the FBI has yet to arrest Page years after the allegation on the warrant. There's no way that our government would allow a Russian spy to be roaming the streets of America had they evidence of his treason.

Comey admits that he reviewed and signed the October 21, 2016 FBI wiretap application against Carter Page. After the Steele dossier became Comey's kryptonite he claimed he didn't know any details of the affidavit. "I simply signed off *procedurally*," he said.

Bureaucratic translation: I'm in a world of shit since I either didn't read the application or I wanted Trump's ass on a platter. I'll just use the word "procedurally," which sounds like I'm just an incompetent idiot instead of a coconspirator. I'd sign any piece of paper placed in front of me, and that's my defense. "My bad."

The former director can't remember if the paperwork was entitled "VERIFIED APPLICATION" but remembers the FBI alleged Page was working for, or with, the Russian government. And most importantly, Comey doesn't recall if the application mentioned "probable cause." (He later did recall that it was labeled "verified.")

Would a former deputy attorney general and current director of the FBI lack the interest in assuring the probable cause of an affidavit that would change history?

Let's put this in some perspective. The director of the FBI is asked to sign an application to spy on the incoming president's political aide who is suspected of being a Russian spy. Comey's thought process evidently wasn't, "Russia has more nukes than the United States, and the incoming president may have a Russian mole in the White House, so

I'll just ignore the whole mess." That would make the director of the FBI a disinterested rubber stamp to a potential constitutional crisis on his watch. His claim that he signed this document minus knowing the details should peg the bullshit meter of any past or present FBI agent.

Comey's amnesia is interesting given that in his book, *A Higher Loyalty*, big Jim displayed a photographic memory for detail. In his congressional testimony, Comey was not sure how Steele's dossier got to the FBI and doesn't know what steps the FBI took to verify Steele's information before or after the FBI presented it to the FISA court. He just kept signing his name to stuff, and when asked if the information was reliable, his response was "the FBI was still evaluating" the information.

Now this is either another case of incompetence or a gigantic lie. I was the affiant in many warrants, and it's required you document the informant's reliability so the judge can evaluate whether to approve it. For example, if a snitch has never been used before, then you must state that the informant has "unknown" reliability. If your source has been successful in providing info leading to arrests, seizures, etc., then you provide the number of times. For example, "Source 1234 has provided information resulting in the seizure of ten kilograms of cocaine and ten arrests."

Presentation of any unverified material to the FISA court to justify a wiretap would appear to violate the Woods procedures designed to protect US citizens. Comey acknowledged that he signed off on the wiretap as "verified" even though the information was unverified. He said he did so because the information came from "a reliable source" (Steele) with "a good track record."

Allow me to sum up the bottom legal line. Someone violated the Woods procedure since the Steele information used to gain the wiretap was unverified. Someone perjured themselves since they stamped "verified" on the original warrant and subsequent renewals. If they had attempted to actually verify the information contained in the FISA application, the word "verified" would never have been attached to it. Someone may have committed *double* perjury by claiming somewhere in the affidavit that Steele was reliable and then didn't tell the whole truth on who financed the dossier.

Comey's lack of oversight when it came to the controversial wiretapping of a political campaign associate in an election year is a strong indication that he had a political agenda.

In September of 2016, Director Comey said, "Public corruption is the FBI's top criminal priority. The threat—which involves the corruption of local, state, and federally elected, appointed, or contracted officials—strikes at the heart of government, eroding public confidence and undermining the strength of our democracy."

It's ironic that Comey selected public corruption as the Bureau's *top* priority since his statement seems to describe the Comey Gang. They were top public officials who attempted to undermine our democracy. As James Wedick, a thirty-four-year Bureau veteran, said, "If people start looking at the FBI as a political organization, the taint will be incredible."

Agents should always seek the truth and not fabricate, omit, or massage facts on warrants. Our political ideology should never bleed into our integrity. This applies equally to field agents as well as headquarter types.

The Comey era was all about politics. Deputy Assistant Attorney General Rod Rosenstein recommends that President Trump fire Comey, laying it all out in a memo. Rosenstein knew that the president was looking for cause to dump Comey ever since he exonerated Hillary. Remember that Comey and Mueller are professional buddies.

Trump fires Comey, and the former director leaks the alleged obstruction of justice memos to the press. Under oath, Comey confesses to leaking the memo with the expressed intent of initiating a special counsel. Mueller wants his old FBI job back now that Comey is gone and schedules a job interview with Trump for the vacant FBI directorship. Mueller calls his old friend Rod Rosenstein, who personally escorts Mueller to the job interview with the president.

Trump decides not to appoint Mueller, and the very *next* day Rosenstein appoints Mueller as special counsel. If this Machiavellian drama gets too confusing, remember that Rosenstein gets Comey fired and then appoints Comey's dear friend as special counsel to investigate the president. Since Comey was both a witness and subject in the special counsel's investigation, Rosenstein may have considered selecting a more impartial individual to lead it. Perhaps Judge Judy.

I am a very loyal person to my friends and would be predisposed to believe a buddy over a guy who just rejected me for a job. Where was the adult who said, "This is unfair to place Mr. Mueller in this difficult position." I guess that Rod Rosenstein was either sucking his thumb or planned it that way.

And if further proof of a stacked deck is necessary, Mueller then assembles an anti-Trump team that includes Peter Strzok and Lisa Page. The scope of the special counsel was technically Russian collusion in our 2016 election, but its true purpose was *always* to end the Trump presidency.

The investigation with that limited scope of collusion should have been wrapped up in ten months max. The computer forensic part had already been completed, which indicated that the Russians *did* attempt to influence the election. The intelligence agencies determined that these attempts did *not* affect the outcome and did not change votes.

I am reluctant to burst the public's bubble on the entire issue of spying. Every nation has an intel or spying program. It's been going on since Joshua sent two spies to Jericho in biblical times and will continue forever. At this very moment, CIA agents are spying on the Russians, Chinese, and maybe the Lithuanians. Jonathan Pollard was a former intelligence analyst for the US government. In 1987, Pollard pleaded guilty to spying when he provided top-secret classified information to Israel. He was sentenced to life in prison for violations of the

Espionage Act. Israel has been, and continues to be, one of our greatest allies and views these espionage attempts against the United States as business as usual.

The point is, this latest Russian incursion into Facebook and Twitter is nothing new. Russia's electronic attempt to influence our elections is merely an electronic form of spying. Indignant legislators declaring this an act of war are beyond hypocritical.

THE OPTICS OF POLITICS

On July 26, 2017, in the predawn hours, Mueller ordered FBI agents to conduct a "no knock" raid on the home of former Trump campaign chairman Paul Manafort. Agents appeared in Manafort's bedroom as he slept next to his wife. The FBI does not normally arrest white-collar criminals with no history of violence in this manner.

On January 25, 2019, at 6:00 a.m., Roger Stone was arrested at his house in Fort Lauderdale, Florida, after being indicted by special counsel Robert Mueller. Twenty-seven armed agents in ballistic vests and automatic weapons surrounded Stone's home and hauled him off to jail. Stone's been charged with five counts of false statements, one count of witness tampering, and one count of obstruction of an official proceeding. Stone has no history of violence and is not a flight risk. This is highly unusual treatment for white-collar criminals.

On March 4, 2015, Hillary Clinton received a subpoena from the House Select Committee on Benghazi. The committee wanted emails related to its investigation into the September 11, 2012, deadly attack on US facilities in Libya. Three weeks *after* the subpoena, Hillary deleted over thirty thousand emails. Hillary has lied before Congress, to the media, and to the mother of a slain American killed in Benghazi. There was no predawn raid on her home, no indictment, but she did get a book deal.

CHAPTER 22:

The Obstacle Course

"I'm from the government and I'm here to help you."

The new deputy assistant director of the criminal division of the FBI climbed the steps to the auditorium stage. Tony Daniels convened this get-together a few days after his arrival at headquarters. Tony is an Italian guy from Western Pennsylvania who graduated from Slippery Rock State College and quarterbacked their football team.

Mr. Daniels began his introductory remarks with, "The sole function of FBI Headquarters should be to support the field."

He followed up by describing their role as headquarters supervisors when interacting with the field. "If you receive an undercover proposal or Title III, and it needs some work, just don't reject it out of hand. You work with the agent to get it right."

Tony knew that brick agents viewed FBI HQ as an obstruction to overcome. Field divisions are staffed with senior executive service–level agents who are capable of making many decisions, but instead agents are now required to contact HQ for a variety of approvals, and do not expect any words of wisdom or encouragement. What they get is convoluted explanations, unnecessary hurdles, and delays. It's like contacting a call center in India for a simple computer problem and two hours later you hang up and head to Best Buy.

FBI headquarters has become top heavy and obsolete. Law enforcement is a fluid beast that requires an ability to respond quickly. The current model requires multiple approvals by many individuals of the same rank and experience level. We've created a parallel dimension of checks and balances that results in delays and failure. Many first-level supervisors at headquarters have minimal field experience and still have their training wheels attached to the bicycle. All FBI HQ types spent time as field agents but seem to have short-term memory loss soon after reaching the Puzzle Palace.

FBI headquarters obstructs field investigations under the ruse of oversight. Dealings with the seventh floor of the Hoover Building can trigger frustration, aggravation, anger, and an occasional tragic outcome. Headquarters was warned on seventy occasions that terrorists may be planning attacks involving airlines and US skyscrapers just *prior* to 9/11. They rejected evidence from the Minneapolis FBI office and threatened an agent's career who persisted. As the first World Trade Center tower was collapsing, FBI HQ called the attack a coincidence. It was only after the second plane struck that HQ approved a warrant that led to uncovering information that may have prevented the deaths of over three thousand Americans.

These factors may be considered blips on the radar of any large institution, but there's been a recent history of circling the wagons around the executive suite when things go bad, and *all* their fingers point downward.

There is a major disconnect between the field and HQ that affects morale and operations. For example, immediately after Comey was fired, acting FBI director Andrew McCabe flatly denied the White House's assertion that Comey had lost the confidence of FBI agents.

Had he asked agents outside the Beltway, "Whatta you guys think?" he would've been shocked by their reply.

I've used the term "Beltway delusion" when referring to this mirage. Within the DC Beltway, headquarters staff, in *all* government agencies, eventually become deluded into believing that the field is in total agreement with them. They rarely hear the seeds of discontent from the prairie outposts for a variety of reasons. Many FBI directors conduct "wellness checks" during Monday morning conference calls with some or all of the Special Agents in Charge of the fifty-six field divisions. These are generally cordial events when the director or his deputy pontificates from Mount Olympus. Comments from the SACs generally run from "Yes, sir" to "I agree totally." The rest of them are doing crossword puzzles.

The transition from the field to headquarters reminds me of a werewolf metamorphous when the new arrival slowly transitions to a creature with a hairy face, claws, and fangs. They suddenly feel the urge to stamp *No!* on incoming documents and tinker with *any* request from the field. During their spare time, they create unnecessary policies, unwanted procedures, and confusing guidelines.

FBI headquarters is seriously afflicted by the Wyndham Effect— the sudden need to obstruct, delay, and frustrate the field. Most of us have never heard of this virtually unknown phenomenon, but it contaminates FBI HQ supervisors.

In July of 1940, Adolph Hitler planned the Nazi invasion of Great Britain. It included an amphibious landing of 67,000 troops supported by an airborne division that was to be parachuted into Sussex. British officials recognized that they couldn't stop the German invasion once Panzer tanks arrived. Churchill basically conceded a Nazi occupation of southern England.

A handful of former British military officers and inventors trained a guerrilla battalion capable of infiltrating occupied France and preventing the Germans from pushing north to the invasion launch point. The unit developed several weapons such as the sticky bomb, a nitroglycerine bomb that attached itself to a tank. It created a deadly inward blast that sent high-velocity shrapnel into the tank's interior. This resulted in crispy Nazis.

But the consensus of some British officers was revulsion that the mother country would use such a dirty weapon. One of these officers, Brigadier General Everard Humphrey Wyndham, did everything in his power to obstruct the program, which included denying funds, losing requisitions, and bad-mouthing the program to senior officials.

FBI headquarters has become a collection of General Wyndhams who were dragged reluctantly into the dirty world of terrorism and then demand a fair fight. The Bureau was totally unprepared for the aftermath of the attacks of 9/11. There were sufficient warnings that radical Islamists were our new frontier, yet we had no urgency to deal with the issue.

The information available to the FBI and other US intelligence agencies prior to the 9/11 attacks was sufficient enough to prevent the attacks. Part of the problem was ego and the inability to transfer raw data into actionable intelligence. There are literally hundreds of tiny government offices within major departments that have *some* intelligence-gathering responsibility. Departments like Commerce, Treasury, Transportation, and Energy have someone in some cubicle gathering intelligence, while other departments like Defense (DIA, NSA), State (INR), Homeland Security (Secret Service), and Justice (FBI, DEA) have major intel duties.

The problem pre- and post-9/11 is that these agencies do not fully share their intelligence with each other. When they occasionally do share, some supervisor will ignore legitimate threats based on their personal ideology.

During the Obama administration, more than fifty intelligence analysts working out of the US military's Central Command formally complained that their reports on ISIS and al-Qaeda were being inappropriately altered by senior officials. Two senior analysts signed a written complaint that their reports had been changed by CENTCOM higher officials to conform with the Obama administration's line that the United States was winning the battle against the Islamic State in Syria. The reports were altered to make two terrorist groups appear weaker than they were according to their intelligence. (This type of manipulation of intelligence is not new. In 2002 and 2003, senior US officials deliberately cherry-picked intelligence on Iraqi dictator Saddam Hussein's alleged weapons program.)

Congress issued a 371-page report documenting serious shortcomings in the performance of various US government agencies in the months leading up to the 9/11 hijackings. The report stated, "We believe that widespread and longstanding deficiencies in the FBI's operations and Counterterrorism Program caused the problems we described in this report including a shoddy analytical program, problems sharing intelligence information and the lack of priority given to counterterrorism investigations by the FBI before September 11."

The report focused on three major episodes before the September 11 attacks, one of which was the handling of a July 2001 memo theorizing that al-Qaeda leader Osama bin Laden might be sending operatives to US flight schools. Although the memo from Phoenix FBI agent Kenneth Williams was proposed as "a theory rather than a warning or a threat," the report concludes that the Bureau "failed to fully evaluate, investigate, exploit and disseminate information related to the memo because of shortcomings in the way its analysis and intelligence programs were set up and run."

Regarding conclusions about Zacarias Moussaoui, the report says that Minnesota agents "did not receive adequate support from the field office or from FBI headquarters." Previous investigations have found that Moussaoui's laptop computer and other belongings were not searched in the weeks after his arrest in Minneapolis because FBI headquarters mistakenly believed it did not have enough evidence to obtain a warrant."

The FBI issued a statement agreeing with many of the report conclusions but claimed it "has taken substantial steps to address the issues presented in the report."

But they *hadn't* taken any steps to address these issues. A year after the 9/11 attacks, I had a domestic terrorism case. I cannot discuss the specific facts of the case due to security issues, but it concerned a domestic group with national implications. I was working a source who had infiltrated the group hierarchy. There were recordings of high-level meetings between the source and major players. It was time to move the undercover operations to a "Group I" undercover case, since this designation would allocate additional money and equipment and permit investigative techniques required to take down the entire organization. I had worked several Group I undercover cases and attended meetings in DC where agents provided input on the program. I knew the policies pertaining to the probable cause needed for a Group I.

My supervisor, who shall remain nameless, provided no support and in fact dissuaded my efforts to move the case forward. The guy had been in the news for screwing up a major case at headquarters, so they shipped him back to the field. He was running scared and unwilling to make a decision. Traditionally, covert op cases are feast or famine and can make or break the career of the supervising agent. Undercover cases are shit bombs waiting to explode, and as I said, even a small piece of poop can end careers.

With that said, my supervisor was a necessary ingredient in making my case happen since his signature was required on many thick documents.

He demanded additional probable cause to support the proposal, which wasn't a problem. I had the source meet with the president of the domestic terrorist group at their national compound. Not enough. The source then recorded a conversation with a card-carrying member discussing blowing up a government building under construction. I believed this development significant enough to contact FBI HQ directly. The supervisor there asked this question: "Is the building occupied?"

"Nope," I replied.

"Well, let's wait awhile, get some more PC [probable cause], and resubmit the proposal."

Had there been real leaders in my chain of command, they would've supported my efforts and fought with the obstructionist at headquarters.

Angelo Codevilla, a professor of international relations and national security expert, blames careerism and an out-of-control bureaucracy on the FBI's problems. Codevilla said, "I'm afraid that the explanation is all too simple: bureaucrats—employees of large organizations—figure out on which side their bread is going to be buttered. They learn to think, feel, and do what advances their careers."

Even if the guilty remain threats to our nation.

The Marine Corps leadership model places the responsibility on its field commanders to adapt, improvise, and overcome. Rear echelon military commanders determine the mission to be accomplished, and the field commanders take it from there. Once the troops leave the perimeter the brass' role is supporting the mission with resources.

On the other hand, here is how FBI whistleblower Coleen Rowley describes the situation at FBI HQ in a CNN report.

> The FBI is a bureaucracy rife with "risk aversion," "roadblocks" to investigations and "endless, needless paperwork," FBI agent Coleen Rowley told a Senate panel Thursday.
>
> Rowley testified before the Senate Judiciary Committee on Thursday, her appearance greeted with an explosion

of camera flashes. Her blistering letter to FBI director Robert Mueller about the bureau's headquarters has become a focal point of congressional probes into apparent intelligence failures preceding the September 11 terrorist attacks…

Rowley, the chief legal advisor in the FBI's Minneapolis field office, said she wrote her letter because she was concerned that after September 11 the FBI was moving in the direction of more bureaucracy and micromanagement from headquarters…

Mueller conceded FBI headquarters did not adequately respond to some internal memos and clues about terrorism prior to September 11. Mueller said that his agency "must change" and needs more resources, points he said are underscored by the devastating attacks of September 11.

Milton Friedman said, "The government solution to a problem is usually as bad as the problem."

CHAPTER 23

The Pursuit of Political Correctness

"How do you make things fair?"
—Al Sharpton

The FBI's New York Field Office went to war over the death of Eric Garner in New York City. Mr. Garner died in July 2014 after a New York City police officer confronted him for selling untaxed cigarettes. The officer was seen on video using a chokehold, prohibited by the New York Police Department, to subdue him.

FBI agents investigated the case and opposed charging the officer, a recommendation supported by New York federal prosecutors. Attorneys at the Justice Department's Civil Rights Division also agreed that there was no clear evidence to charge the officer.

But Attorney General Loretta Lynch disagreed with her own Justice Department and removed the FBI agents who investigated the case. She replaced them with agents from outside New York.

Think about this for a second. This case was a proper example of how the FBI and Justice Department *should* interact: Agents conduct the investigation and bring the facts to federal prosecutors, who review them and decide whether to prosecute. But AG Lynch desired a different set of facts and essentially accused the New York agents of incompetence when she ordered other FBI agents to do it again.

This is disgraceful and yet is another example of a political ideology pushing Lady Justice left. The move was described as "highly unusual." Ultimately, a federal grand jury decided *not* to indict the officer, Daniel Pantaleo.

In December of 2018, the New York Patrolmen's Benevolent Association (PBA) issued a press release stating that the autopsy report on the death of Eric Garner "demonstrates *conclusively* that Mr. Garner did not die of strangulation of the neck from a chokehold which would have caused a crushed larynx (windpipe) and a fractured hyoid bone."

The PBA report noted that Garner's windpipe and hyoid bone were both intact. PBA president Pat Lynch said in a statement, "This case demonstrates the danger that is inherent in prejudging incidents absent all of the information that must be considered in order to come to a truthful and accurate conclusion. The death of Eric Garner was tragic and we feel for the family's loss, but there has been a *false* narrative built against PO Pantaleo by the emotion on the street instead of the facts. Sadly, Mr. Garner's health was so poor that it is highly likely that if he had decided to flee police instead of fighting them, the end result would have been the same. The exertion and stress would have overcome his already seriously ill body and would have resulted in his death."

The autopsy report was made available to attorneys involved in the disciplinary case against Officer Pantaleo. I would bet that Pantaleo did not receive an apology call from Lynch.

Stress from the Garner skirmish was still fresh at the Justice Department when the Clinton Foundation investigation began. FBI officials worried about how much Washington would interfere with their work.

"Holder and Lynch totally politicized the Justice Department," said Hans von Spakovsky, a former Justice Department attorney who now works with the Heritage Foundation. "There was no compunction about interfering with a criminal investigation."

Having spent my entire career in the field, I occasionally ran the FBI HQ's bureaucratic gauntlet but was happily spared from interacting with the DC Justice Department. That changed shortly after the 9/11 attacks, when I uncovered evidence of an "honor" killing in a Muslim family. My jurisdiction in the case was under federal civil rights laws, and the penalties could exceed a state murder conviction. This required the approval of the Justice Department, with a final determination by its Washington civil rights division.

I can't discuss the specifics of my investigation, but my eighteen years as an FBI agent (at the time) coupled with unofficial conversations with assistant US attorneys (AUSAs) indicated that a grand jury should be convened. I traveled to Los Angeles after identifying a key witness and secured statements from witnesses who observed the suspects with a handgun that matched the caliber and make of the murder weapon.

I recall meeting the victim's parents on a cold winter evening at their home. Their little girl had been murdered and tossed in a dirty snowbank. Sarah (not her real name) loved America and wanted to assimilate by attending college and dating non-Muslims. Her parents cried as they pointed to statues of angels that Sarah collected and shared stories of their daughter's love of America.

The call came one morning from the civil rights AUSA, who quickly got to the point. The following conversation is not verbatim but it's damn close.

"We're declining prosecution."

"Why?"

"Insufficient evidence."

I immediately ticked off the evidence and cited the elements of the violation. She listened minus comment, and when I finished the AUSA simply stated, "Not enough for a conviction."

I had had several conversations with one or two local attorneys who felt that there was sufficient evidence to convene a grand jury. My gut was screaming that something else was going on besides justice, so I pushed. "Bullshit," I countered, then appealed to her humanity by putting a face and personality on Sarah. The response was silence, which pissed me off as a father of two girls.

I finished with, "Look, this case deserves to be heard by a jury, and I'm not letting it drop. I'll lobby every bureaucrat that'll talk to me. You and I both know that this family deserves some justice, and the evidence is there."

The AUSA's voice lost its officiousness, and she said, "Look, John, there's a lot of anti-Muslim sentiment going on, and this may not be a good time to go forward."

This is a classic example of political correctness and the loss of the Bureau's independence to Justice Department agendas. My appeals all fell on deaf ears.

Just for the record, there is no statute of limitation on murder cases, so it would be sporting if someone in authority will review this case. The vicious murder of as beautiful twenty-one-year-old child should be given its day in court. Her only sin was a desire to assimilate into the American fabric. By refusing to prosecute Sarah's murder, the Justice Department was an unwitting accomplice in further segregating the Muslim community. It reinforced to the killers and everyone else that sharia law has a place in America minus repercussions.

Danny Defenbaugh, a thirty-three-year FBI veteran, agreed with this sentiment when he said, "I know from talking to some agents in the FBI that there were conflicts between the Holder DOJ and its priorities on how the FBI wanted to work cases. The FBI had always taken pride in following the evidence to where it would lead and never allowing politics into their investigation decisions. But then the DOJ at times would say, 'We don't want you to do this.'"

Much of the public believes that attorneys are investigators. Mueller's special counsel staff was composed of FBI agents who did the actual investigations. The attorneys direct the agents and whine a lot about "predicate acts." During the Hillary email investigation, so-called experts on television kept implying that Comey himself was conducting interviews and "investigating." Law school doesn't include classes in the bread-and-butter tools of criminal investigations. The FBI Academy does.

An unintentional consequence of a US attorney or judge becoming the head honcho of the Federal Bureau of Investigation is political pollution. Since the Justice Department is an ideologically contaminated agency, they introduce that infection into the FBI's bloodstream. Directors from William Webster to Bob Mueller, James Comey, and Christopher Wray falsely believe they understood our culture, but their entire frame of reference was viewed through a lens of a bystander. The FBI recruits a significant number of attorneys as agents, but they are required to attend the FBI Academy and spend time working criminal investigations in the field as brick agents. *Their* frame of reference is viewed through a law enforcement lens.

If you've never sat on a twenty-hour surveillance surrounded ankle deep in fast-food wrappers or busted through a door executing a drug warrant, then you shouldn't get to second-guess split-second decisions from inside the Beltway. You have no frame of reference to understand the options available. FBI directors and attorneys general routinely perform these autopsies on law enforcement operations. It's similar to NFL analysts who second-guess every play with the benefit of slow-motion replay.

During my undercover days with the Mafia, I set up a gun deal with a mob associate who was connected to Sal V. (now deceased), a made guy and high-ranking member of the Detroit family. The plan was to meet at a mob warehouse where the deal would take place. I told Joey that I'd like an assortment of weapons and he said, "No problem, and you can test fire the guns. It's a blast."

I mentioned all this to my contact agent, since I'd be spending thousands of government dollars to purchase the weapons. The day of the meeting, my pager vibrated an emergency code alerting me to call my contact agent. The conversation was bizarre. It seemed that my FBI bosses contacted an assistant US attorney, who asked, "Is the warehouse an *approved* gun range?"

"You're shittin' me, right?"

My contact agent was a good guy who could only offer, "I wish I was."

"Tell them that it's a deserted mob warehouse."

"I did, but they said that you can't fire weapons inside a building within the city limits unless it's an approved firing range."

Unfortunately for the mob, I have a serial case of insubordination and ignored this ridiculous condition. I fired and purchased several guns, which led to the arrest of the made guy. Sal eventually flipped and testified against the entire hierarchy of the Detroit mob.

This incident was just another example of losing our independence resulting in an unwanted merger with the Justice Department. SES staff at the FBI field office level should be able to make operational decisions on active cases.

It's time to piss a few people off and end the political correctness inside the FBI. Cut the umbilical cord with the Justice Department and be the FBI that America wants and needs.

The Swamp Fox

"Hey, at least I won't have to lie to you anymore."
—*All That Jazz*

My comfort zone is in the company of Marines, cops, and *most* Italians. Whether we admit it or not, most people will gravitate to like-minded folks. Normally, homogeneous groups involve themselves in activities that entertain or provide some benefit to society. Examples from my world are the Purple Heart Society and USO.

But there's also a potential danger when that sort of single-mindedness gets together and possesses the authority to hurt people or subvert due process. That's apparently what happened when the Comey Gang met the Department of Justice Gang.

What's evident is that the FBI director, deputy director, assistant director, deputy assistant director, and legal counsel either conspired with or ignored attempts by others to shred our Constitution. If that sounds like an extreme statement, take off your partisan cap and draw your own conclusions.

Not all the individuals on the seventh floor were actively involved in this rebellion, but their silence made them passive participants and just as guilty. There wasn't one leader in that entire gaggle of careerists who stood up and screamed, "Bullshit," or even a milder version of "Maybe we shouldn't do this."

Sir Edmund Burke stated, "The only thing necessary for the triumph of evil is for good men to do nothing."

How did Comey assemble a core of like-minded staff within the seat of power? To answer that question, we must first answer this one: Who is the *real* James Brien Comey Jr.?

Comey's arrival at FBI headquarters was originally thought to be a breath of fresh air—a man of integrity and sincerity. But now, his legacy will forever be that of one who played fast and loose with the values that ensured an institution's character. Comey claims to have been a good Republican until recently, but his words betray his actions. Here are some indisputable facts.

His hero is James Clapper, a man who perjured himself by lying to Congress. Comey's family were passionate Hillary and Obama fans, and his wife worked for the HRC campaign. Comey ignored Clinton's violations of the law with an indefensible conclusion while ignoring the clear words of relevant law. Since Comey is *not* a fool, then there must be a logical explanation for his decisions.

Comey had numerous ties to the Clinton political machine. His brother Peter is an executive at DLA Piper, the law firm responsible for filing the Clinton Foundation's taxes. Comey holds the mortgage for his brother's mansion, tying a direct financial connection between Comey and the Clinton Foundation while he was investigating Hillary.

The former FBI director has had connections to the Clintons since 1996. He acted as the deputy special counsel for the Senate committee investigating the Whitewater scandal involving shady real estate loans authorized while Bill Clinton was governor of Arkansas. People connected to the Whitewater company were charged with over forty crimes, yet the Clintons remained unscathed. James Comey acknowledged that Hillary Clinton obstructed the investigation and destroyed evidence, yet he decided not to prosecute due to lack of "intent." Does that sound familiar?

The second in command at the FBI was Andy McCabe, the accused perjurer. McCabe coincidently also had a Clinton connection. A political action committee run by former Virginia governor Terry McAuliffe, a close political ally of the Clintons, gave half a million dollars to McCabe's wife's campaign for Virginia state senate in 2015. McCabe was the assistant director of the FBI's Washington Field Office while his wife was running for office. After she lost the election, he was promoted to HQ as deputy director, giving him direct oversight authority of the Clinton email case. McCabe has somehow rationalized that since his wife was no longer a candidate, he could now impartially oversee the case.

This is flawed logic. McCabe's wife received a significant amount of cash tied to the Clinton machine. That fact alone makes the deputy director indebted to Hillary Clinton. What did Andy do? He refused to recuse himself, citing an HQ ethics official's opinion. Whoever provided this opinion should be convicted of malfeasance. The *appearance* of impropriety is off the charts. The FBI deputy director is supervising a criminal case on a subject *after* his wife received money from the subject's friend. Just for the record, the *only* opinion that McCabe required was his own, though his boss, Comey, could've said, "Hey, Andy, you may wanna sit this one out, bud."

What has not appeared in the media is that on April 29, 2015, officials at the Washington Field Office warned McCabe that his wife's candidacy could pose a conflict of interest. McCabe conveniently dismissed the field division's opinion and was appointed the number two man in the FBI. While in this position McCabe presided over the Clinton email case *until* just a few days before Comey waved his absolution wand when he unexpectedly recused himself. The timing of McCabe's recusal insults the intelligence of anyone with common sense and a notion of fair play.

Both Comey and McCabe had direct ties to the Clintons that tainted the email and Russian collusion investigations, but there were *other* high-level managers roaming the seventh floor of the Hoover Building. They couldn't *all* be card-carrying liberals. Could they?

On December 21, 2015, Director Comey appointed William E. "Bill" Priestap as assistant director of the Counterintelligence Division. Bill happened to be Peter Strzok's boss and was in daily contact with McCabe and Comey. He supervised the entire counterintelligence program that was the basis for the original FISA warrant on the Trump campaign. Consequently, every single piece of paper on the matter passed through his fingers.

Knowing the chain of command in the FBI, I find it implausible to believe that Priestap was unaware of the activities of Peter Strzok. It is also highly unlikely that Priestap didn't brief his immediate supervisors, Andy McCabe and James Comey.

During the 2016 campaign, Priestap was one of several officials at the center of two politically volatile probes: the investigation into Hillary Clinton's handling of classified information and a counterintelligence inquiry into whether associates of then candidate Donald Trump colluded with the Russian government.

Bill Priestap had to approve any payment or reimbursements to Christopher Steele for his information used in their counterintelligence operation and subsequent FISA application. Without Bill Priestap's involvement and approvals, the entire Russian/Trump counterintelligence operation doesn't happen.

If you doubt Priestap's role in the entire scandal, then look at James Comey's congressional testimony. When the ship began to sink, Comey went Benedict Arnold on his buddy. He blamed Priestap as the individual responsible for making the decision not to inform congressional leadership—the so-called Gang of Eight specifically—about the July 2016 FBI investigation.

The Gang of Eight are responsible for congressional oversight of *all* intelligence agencies and are briefed on classified intelligence matters by the executive branch. Anything intelligence-related *must* be shown to this committee. If there is a US covert operation, these eight members of Congress must approve it. So how did Priestap get to sidestep these statutory obligations and constitutional checks and balances and exclude the Gang of Eight? The answer is that Comey desired they be excluded and then pushed Priestap on the sword. My bet is that Bill is singing to the inspector general as I write this.

Priestap was also at the epicenter of the Clinton email and Trump campaign investigations. Hundreds of the texts and emails between Strzok and Page referred to or were copied to Bill Priestap. He reviewed and approved the Clinton exoneration talking points delivered by James Comey. So why isn't his name and mug plastered all over Fox News and the *Washington Times*?

We know that Comey, McCabe, and others have ties with the Clintons, but perhaps Priestap is a Reagan Republican and closet Tea Party supporter. He certainly couldn't have any Clinton connection. Yep, he did.

Priestap's spouse, Sabina Menschel, graduated Harvard in 2005 with an MBA and immediately became a special advisor at the FBI. She left that position shortly after 9/11 and became president for the investigative firm of Nardello & Company. Menschel was a heavy contributor to the Hillary for America campaign and the Hillary Victory Fund.

There's another lead character in this Shakespearean drama, and it's the deputy attorney general, Rod Rosenstein. His fingerprints are all over the murder weapon, starting with his signature on the bogus FISA warrant. Approving an affidavit based on omissions and half-truths would have most of us in the exercise yard at Lewisburg, but not the deputy AG.

Rosenstein then appoints his buddy Bob Mueller as special counsel, who in turn appoints an array of Clinton allies to his team. It would be highly suspicious if Rosenstein had any Clinton connections given this central role, since this would constitute a clear conflict of interest. But let's take a look anyway.

Lisa Barsoomian represented Bill Clinton in a 1990s case. She works for R. Craig Lawrence, who himself has represented Mueller, Obama, Bill Clinton, Hillary Clinton, and former Health and Human Services secretary Kathleen Sebelius. Lisa Barsoomian is also Rod Rosenstein's wife.

The man who sat a few doors down from Rosenstein was Deputy Assistant Attorney General Bruce Ohr. Marc E. Elias, a lawyer representing the Clinton campaign and the Democratic National Committee, retained Fusion GPS, a Washington investigative firm, to conduct opposition research on Trump. Fusion hired dossier-writing Christopher Steele, a former British intelligence officer with ties to the FBI and the US intelligence community, and then they hired Ohr's wife, Nellie.

James Comey admitted in testimony that he knew the FISA applications were based on information provided by British spy Christopher Steele, who was financed by Democrats who opposed President Trump. Yet that information was not included in the FISA affidavit. A House Intelligence Committee memo released in February 2016 documented that as FBI director, Comey signed *three* FISA applications to spy on Carter Page, with the Steele dossier serving as part of the basis for the warrant.

As an affiant on numerous warrants, I've stood before judges and magistrates and swore to tell the truth, the *whole* truth, and *nothing* but the truth. We do not know who the affiant was on the FISA warrant, but that person is a perjurer. But we *do* know that Comey approved the application and could be charged with conspiracy to commit perjury.

Comey stated repeatedly that as director of the FBI, he never knew that Fusion GPS had been hired to do its anti-Trump research by the Perkins Coie law firm, which represented Clinton and the DNC.

Yet the FISA application verified by Comey, stated the FBI had information that Steele had been hired by a "U.S.-based law firm" to conduct research regarding Candidate #1's (Trump) ties to Russia." Maybe Mr. Comey was confused and never was briefed or read the FISA application. Maybe Comey is being unfairly tarred with the "liar" tag. Most FBI directors would be given every benefit of the doubt, but *this* particular FBI director is a liar and leaker.

CHAPTER 25

The Fissure King

"Don't worry, we got some guy on the jury."
—John Gotti to Sammy "the Bull" Gravano

The depths of the antagonism within the FBI were exposed in an inspector general's report that disclosed former FBI deputy director Andrew McCabe's perjury and his misleading multiple investigations. McCabe was fired from the FBI and is awaiting indictment. The report cited examples of McCabe lying during questioning, some of it under oath, and went much deeper, describing the rift between the Bureau and the Justice Department.

The relationship cracked under Attorney General Eric Holder as agents in all fifty-six field offices lost trust in Justice Department attorneys. They viewed many of them as DC bureaucrats orchestrating FBI cases for political advantage. Consequently, the Justice Department became frustrated with the field FBI agents for not always following its directives on cases. The Bureau's loss of its independence and weak leadership created this fissure.

FBI agents in the New York Field Office requested authority from the Justice Department to investigate corruption in the Clinton Foundation. There are very strict laws governing not-for-profit corporations like the Clinton Foundation, and there was an abundance of direct and circumstantial evidence to justify a criminal investigation.

Doug Band was a trusted Clinton associate and the former head of the Clinton Foundation. Band made a direct request that the DOJ open an investigation into a potential pay-to-play relationship between the State Department and the Clinton Foundation. He alleged that the foundation only spent a very small fraction of its funds on actual charity work.

In addition to these allegations, Judicial Watch, a nonprofit integrity group, obtained State Department emails that indicated Clinton aides granted favors for Clinton Foundation bigwigs during Hillary Clinton's tenure as secretary of state. For example, Clinton aides Huma Abedin and Cheryl Mills arranged a meeting with a US ambassador to Libya and a Clinton Foundation benefactor who was convicted of international money laundering in 2000.

Doug Band also alleged some interesting business practices by Chelsea Clinton, a primary officer in the Clinton Foundation. He accused her of "using foundation resources for her wedding and personal life for a decade, in addition to Chelsea's getting paid with foundation money while campaigning for her mother." Band alleged that Chelsea's husband, Marc Mezvinsky, abused the Clinton Foundation's influence and his wife's family name to help him find sources of cash for his hedge fund, Eaglevale Partners. These included seed sponsors such as Goldman Sachs CEO Lloyd Blankfein.

Marc also had a bright idea to put together a poker night for the foundation to raise money. His own fund hadn't been going well, so he had Chelsea make some calls for him to arrange meetings with some Clinton people. Marc invited several potential investors to the poker night who Band assumed were contributors to the foundation.

This activity blurs the line between the nonprofit Clinton Foundation and the for-profit hedge fund, which may or may not be criminal but certainly is unethical.

Don't try any of this at home unless your last name is Clinton.

The Justice Department refused the FBI's request to probe the Clinton Foundation's use of the State Department, citing a lack of evidence at hand. But Band's statements and Judicial Watch emails constitute direct pertinent evidence. There's also an abundance of circumstantial evidence like the timing and size of donations to the Clinton Foundation after meeting with Secretary of State Clinton. The DOJ justified its refusal, stating the Bureau had already tried and failed to probe the organization in 2015.

And there's a good reason why the FBI failed: The same Justice Department had pressured the FBI to *halt* the investigation. If this situation happened outside the Beltway, it may be considered obstructing justice, but not in Clinton's world.

In 2016, the FBI New York Field Office opened up a case on the Clinton Foundation. It's not clear if they requested permission from the Justice Department since the New York FBI office is a collection of free spirits. I know this from working organized crime in New York City, which is a target-rich environment of bent noses on guys named Bruno.

Soon after, Deputy Director McCabe received a call from an angry senior Justice Department official. Basically, the conversation was a one-way ass chewing complaining that the FBI's overt actions could hurt Hillary Clinton's chance to become president. The official didn't seem all that concerned that Hillary may be operating a continuing criminal enterprise but rather that the news may damage her reputation. Did McCabe object and inform the Obama Justice Department that the FBI would continue this legitimate inquiry? Nope.

Inspector General Michael Horowitz released a report revealing McCabe lied four times to investigators, twice while under oath, about authorizing an FBI spokesman to tell Devlin Barrett of the *Wall Street*

Journal (just days before the 2016 election) that he had not issued a similar "stand-down" order on the reported FBI investigation into the Clinton Foundation.

The allegations surrounding the Clinton Foundation are well known. As I've mentioned, they include a quid pro quo trading of donations to the foundation for favors of the secretary of state. The timing of the following events coupled with an expected outcome can be powerful circumstantial evidence proving politics at play within the Justice Department.

Loretta Lynch was appointed as a US attorney for the Eastern District of New York by President Bill Clinton. President Obama then selected Lynch to succeed Eric Holder as attorney general. Multiple reports indicated that Hillary would likely retain Lynch as attorney general if elected president, and she was heavily favored to win. You can be sure, then, that Lynch was aware that her continued employment was dependent on Hillary's victory. There were also unconfirmed reports that Lynch would eventually sit on the Supreme Court should the Justice Department disappear the email case and block a Clinton Foundation investigation. Perhaps this is the reason why Comey felt that Lynch was compromised.

A week or so before Hillary was exonerated in the email case, Bill Clinton met with Lynch on a private plane in Phoenix. When asked about the meeting, the director of the FBI, James Comey, stated that he had no interest. The suspicious timing of these events coupled with prior relationships would lead a reasonable individual to believe that politics were in play. A political FBI is an impotent FBI.

The fissure formed between the Justice Department and the FBI outside the Beltway has some interesting sidebars. The legal wrangling leading to the impeachment of Bill Clinton offered some great examples of why special counsels never hit their intended target. It proves why they are a barbaric and unnecessary waste of time. Once enacted, special counsels will stray light-years from their original charter, determined to put some trophies on their mantel. The cross-examination reprinted below is a humorous example of the legal repercussions of words.

On August 17, 1998, Deputy Independent Counsel Solomon "Sol" Wisenberg questioned President Bill Clinton about Monica Lewinsky. The following is an abbreviated excerpt of the transcript.

> **Q:** Mr. President…Counsel is fully aware that Ms. Lewinsky has filed an affidavit…saying that there is absolutely *no* sex of any kind in any manner, shape or form, with President Clinton. That statement is made by your attorney in front of Judge Susan Webber Wright, correct?
>
> **A:** That's correct.
>
> **Q:** That statement is a completely false statement…the statement that there was "no sex of any kind in any manner, shape or form, with President Clinton" was an utterly false statement. Is that correct?
>
> **A:** It depends on what the meaning of the word "is" is. If the… if the…if "is" means *is* and never *has* been that is not—that is one thing. If it means there is none, that was a completely true statement. But, as I have testified, and I'd like to testify again, this is…"

And that exchange is why we *really* need to consider a do-over in DC.

CHAPTER 26

Only Two Undersized NVA Companies

"What the fuck are *those* guys smoking?"

There's always a price to pay when headquarters ignores intel from on-site field commanders. Moral superiority within command centers is not exclusive to the FBI.

The Radical Fundamentalist Unit (RFU) at FBI headquarters may have contributed to the 9/11 attacks by ignoring the Minneapolis Field Office, but there's historical evidence of Beltway delusion.

Hue City, Vietnam, 30 January 1968

Army warrant officer Al DeMilo is behind the stick of his Huey (UH1) gunship on 30 January 1968 patrolling at an altitude of 1,500 feet near Hue City, Vietnam. He spots a large contingent of friendly ARVN troops double-timing down Highway 1. DeMilo pushes the stick forward to get a closer look and can't believe his eyes.

It isn't ARVNs (South Vietnamese soldiers) but a battalion-size force of NVA troops boldly operating in broad daylight. This is highly unusual since the NVA usually operate in snoop-and-poop mode this far from home. The US rules the skies, so these guys are either lost or smoking something. He alerts his M60 door gunners, "Stand by, gentlemen, we may be busting caps soon."

Confused, DeMilo radios back to his command and asks, "Any intel on significant NVA troop movement around Hue City?"

"Negative."

"Well, I'm looking at hundreds of NVA regulars diddy bopping down Highway 1. Permission to engage."

"Negative. Do *not* engage. Repeat, do *not* engage! These are likely friendlies."

"Stand by."

Maybe DeMilo *hasn't* spotted a shitload of NVA troops. His command seems positive that no hostile troops are in the area, so Al decides to get a better look. He drops the Huey to an altitude of about three hundred feet and maneuvers the ship astride the tail end of the formation. At this height there is no mistaking the enemy, but if he requires further confirmation, it's the AK-47 rounds that whiz past.

DeMilo does a 180 and gains altitude. He cues his radio and says, "Have confirmed the large formation is North Vietnamese troops, repeat the *bad* guys...permission to engage."

The reply is the same: "Do *not* engage. There is *no* intelligence placing an enemy force of that size in your area of operation."

The Air Cav officer from western Pennsylvania has had enough of the bullshit and screams, "I'm giving you the fucking intel right now, you dumb fucks!"

The Next Day, 31 January 1968

Military Assistance Command, Vietnam (MACV) is totally unprepared for the Tet Offensive. Task Force X-Ray estimates the enemy strength at Hue City at two "undersized" NVA companies. The ARVNs at the

Citadel are surrounded by the NVA and requesting assistance from the American Marines.

X-Ray dispatches Alpha and Golf Companies under the command of Marine Lieutenant Colonel Marcus Gravel to dispatch these pests. The Marines engage two NVA battalions just getting into Hue, with Alpha Company losing half of their numbers in the ensuing firefight. Awaiting Gravel and his remaining Marines inside Hue proper are eight thousand crack NVA troops. When Lieutenant Colonel Gravel disputes the "two undersized" NVA company number, X-Ray insists, "Our intel boys say you're wrong. I am ordering you to attack the Citadel now!"

The Perfume River separates north and south Hue City. The Citadel is a large fortress located on the north side and visible by the Marines staging on the south side. Alpha Company acting CO Gunny John Canley radios Gravel with enemy troop strength estimates of "a battalion of NVA, maybe more."

Gravel relays the eyewitness accounts to X-Ray, who now order Gravel to order the attack or be relieved of command. Alpha Company provides suppressing fire while Golf Company crosses the Nguyen Hoang Bridge and is decimated.

Benghazi, Libya, 11 September 2012

Fox News reported that former acting director of the CIA Mike Morell confirmed that he ignored guidance from the top CIA officer on the ground in favor of believing analysts in Virginia. Morell then crafted the flawed "talking points" that asserted the attack on the consulate in Benghazi, Libya, sprung from a spontaneous protest. Morell confirmed that he overruled the eyewitness account from the CIA chief of station *in* Libya that the attacks were "not an escalation of protests."

In ignoring the on-site intelligence, Morell may have also been complicit in stopping any rescue attempts. State Department whistleblowers presented three main arguments for why the military could have responded to the assault on the US mission in Benghazi. There were special operations teams outside of Libya that could have made it to Benghazi in time to save Americans from the second attack on the annex facility. There were four active-duty special operations personnel based in Tripoli who could have also made it to Benghazi but allegedly got the order to "stand down." And there were F-16 fighter jets in Italy that could have flown over the fight in Benghazi and scared the militants away.

Morell explained his odd decision to ignore a high-ranking on-site CIA officer and challenged the email evidence his chief of station sent him a few days *before* the attack. Morell said the claim of terrorists was based only on "press reports" and reports from officers who arrived in Benghazi *after* the attack had already started.

Morell's testimony was met with disbelief in some corners. One source who was on the ground in Benghazi wondered, "Why would he ever believe that people who weren't there hold credence over those of us that were…and even his own respected chief of station?" the source said. "It makes no sense."

Legislators challenged his statements that it was a "protest and not a terrorist attack," which was in keeping with the Obama White House mantra that al-Qaida was no longer a viable fighting force.

Morell explained away the discrepancy on who to believe in this bizarre way: "The suggestion that I made edits for the political benefit of the administration is false." He finished with this gem of irrefutable logic: "I consider the attack to have been *both* a protest and a terrorist attack."

Interpretation: I got caught with my pants down and just threw out some total bullshit that demonstrates both my convictions and my ability to change them or be committed equally to opposing absolutes. So there!

Why would any individual trade lives to fit their political agenda? It's inexcusable and immoral, and yet it'll happen again and again.

CHAPTER 27:

A Flawed Organizational Model

"Mama says, 'Stupid is as stupid does.'"
—Forrest Gump

"Hey FBI HQ, I gotta suggestion that will save the Bureau millions of dollars."

"Let's hear it."

"Well, you can transfer half the supervisory special agents back to the field while increasing your effectiveness at Headquarters."

"That won't work!"

A contributing factor to the current state of the FBI is a system flaw. This defect disrupts the effectiveness and chain-of-command decisions that trickle down to the field. Many new FBI directors promise to reduce the number of staff at headquarters. None do. Their original intent is an indication that they recognize the benefits of reassigning manpower out of downtown DC and back to the field.

I had a supervisor who'd loudly announce to the agents still sitting at their desk after 10:00 a.m., "I don't see any criminals in the office." Louie Allen was encouraging us to hit the bricks.

FBI headquarters is overstaffed and top heavy. There are too many supervisors trolling the hallways of HQ searching for SES types who may be on their next career board. I'd estimate that 50 percent of HQ managers spend a chunk of their day plotting an exit *out* of HQ and back to the field. Reassigning this glut of managers increases the number of agents in the field, where crimes occur, while reducing the number of carpal tunnel cases from all the signing, typing, and glad-handing.

The current management model is based on a false premise. It requires multiple tours of duty at FBI HQ for agents choosing the management track. These agents are required to yo-yo back and forth from the field to HQ if they wish to climb the ladder. The overwhelming majority of FBI agents view time at HQ as a hardship. They lose the use of a Bureau car, pay higher living costs, and spend ten-hour days attending meetings and signing shit. At the conclusion of the day, they get sandwiched in between two other high rollers in the back seat of a carpool on I-95.

The headquarters complex itself reminds me of a straw Halloween maze where children get lost and begin to sob. After the first few months in headquarters, new supervisors begin to believe that their work is not only terribly important but also challenging. I've had several HBOs (high Bureau officials) confide that the system sucks but since *they* had to walk the punishment tour, others should also suffer multiple moves.

Another contributing factor leading to the current crisis was the promotion of agents to HQ with minimal field experience. This experience drought affected leadership and effectiveness up and down the chain of command. Inexperienced agents are reluctant to make decisions, and if they do, it's likely to be wrong.

One doesn't join the FBI to sit in an office all day writing interrogatories, conducting file reviews, and attending meetings on diversity in the workplace. The personality drawn to a career in law enforcement is an individual who craves the action of car chases and slapping cuffs on bad guys. The FBI is unique since the first step into management chains an individual to a desk for as long as they remain a supervisor.

The military or police departments require an occasional stint behind a desk before being promoted back to the field, but *not* the FBI. The usual career track for supervisory agents is to gain experience in the field until that time you apply for management. The rest of their career consists of bouncing back and forth between desks at HQ to desks in field divisions, but *rarely* back on the street. You never leave the office, except for meetings with other agency managers. FBI field supervisors have the authority to *occasionally* leave their desk, but most stay behind and monitor the action. This is due to a great FBI tradition involving the case agent.

A field supervisor will O&A (open and assign) every case to an agent on their squad. The more complicated cases will be assigned to more experienced agents. That agent theoretically calls the shots, and the role of managers is to support the agent. Managers offer advice, encouragement, and occasional suggestions, but the case agent has the wheel.

I had a SAC attend a pre-raid brief on a case that I'd worked for over a year. We were about to make multiple arrests and execute search warrants citywide. As the case agent, I had developed an operations plan that included arrest team assignments, SWAT involvement, surveillance units, and a multitude of details based on my knowledge of the case. This SAC began to "suggest" changes to my plan two hours before the raids. I nodded and made concessions, but the plan eventually morphed into a cluster fuck. I called a time out and with my supervisor by my side we spoke privately to the SAC.

We discussed his suggestions and why they wouldn't work. I ended the conversation with, "Boss, we got this covered. You're the SAC and I'm the case agent."

He understood, smiled and said, "OK, but don't fuck up."

Agents sometimes choose the admin track, but after a few years they miss the field. They are required to resign from management to get back into the action. A majority of agents choose to remain in the field for a variety of reasons. The pay difference is not significant enough to uproot your family four to five times for the few dollars added to your pension. Supervisors come and go but seasoned brick agents know the major players and become the subject matter experts in their geographical area. These agents are generally left alone to do their thing, and they'll have little patience when some careerist begins their babble about missing commas.

This system worked for many years due to mentoring of new agents and the promotion of experienced agents to headquarters. It produced an uninterrupted flow of subject matter experts who passed down their expertise to field agents. If you contacted the organized crime section and asked about some Guido in NYC, they knew him, his mother, and his aunt Carmela. These agents understood that the seat of power existed to assist the field. Forty years ago, headquarters was staffed by grisly veteran agents who had made a ton of arrests and knew how to bob and weave administratively.

Sometime around the late 1980s, the FBI began promoting supervisors with minimal field experience, some of whom had *never* made an arrest, testified in court, or were affiants in a warrant. These are the bread-and-butter experiences of any law enforcement officer.

FBI headquarters attempted to *"paper over"* the problem by requiring probationary agents to complete a "to do" checklist. This probationary book included tasks such as arrests and testimony, but it was merely putting people through the motions. Senior agents would tell the rookie, "Okay, you can put the cuffs on and check off 'arrest.'" The problem was never check marks on some probationary book but rather that inexperienced agents were being sent off to the Puzzle Palace who were unprepared to lead. They required a few more years of mentoring and seasoning, because once they reached headquarters, they were expected to offer real-time advice to field agents in fluid situations. Many of the conversations were stilted with these boy wonders, who were reluctant to make decisions when the field *needed* a decision.

This group of headquarters supervisors weren't equipped to pass on any worthwhile advice to the field. This resulted in management by decision avoidance, which caused delays, tension, and perhaps the 9/11 attacks.

I'd worked in the undercover world both as an operative and case agent. headquarters assigned me TDY (temporary duty) to the FBI Academy to teach the quarterly undercover certification course at Quantico. New Scotland Yard in London requested that I be temporarily assigned to assist them in the development of their covert program. The Bureau sent me to Moscow, Siberia, Estonia, Budapest, and other locations to conduct undercover seminars. When agents gathered at FBI headquarters to write guidelines, policies, or procedures for undercover work, I was there.

During my last assignment on the Joint Terrorism Task Force, I contacted FBI HQ requesting approval for an undercover operation. The new supervisor with minimal undercover experience began quoting policies that I'd helped write while denying the request. We had numerous conversations and exchanged communications, most of which had nothing to do with the merits of the domestic terrorism case in question.

I crossed every T and dotted every I, yet not once did FBI headquarters offer any constructive guidance or clarify their reluctance. The recommended changes weren't substantive to the case, and HQ sometimes would wait weeks before they'd recontact me. All the while, the domestic terrorists *weren't* sitting behind desks and having abstract discussions.

After weeks of telephonic bureaucratic babble, I screamed, "It's because of people like you that terrorists succeed!"

This comment was not received well at headquarters. The word "insubordination" was tossed around, but hey, I'm a hot-headed Italian Marine.

FBI headquarters is composed of units that mimic the squads in the FBI field offices. For example, the organized crime squad in Pittsburgh will communicate with the organized crime unit at HQ on many issues requiring approvals and guidance.

As I've mentioned, the Marine Corps leadership model places the responsibility on its field commanders to adapt, improvise, and overcome. Once Marine units leave the perimeter, leaders in the field will make the operational decisions since the situation is fluid and plans frequently change once you go live. But FBI HQ can't help themselves and will either make no decisions or the wrong decisions from their desks. They can't help themselves.

The problems arising out of headquarters that delay and restrict field agents from accomplishing the mission are organic. We've all had to deal with plugged toilets. A combination of too much toilet paper and poop will prevent flushing. The current duplicitous paper flow required for a brick agent to gain approvals plugs the bureaucratic outhouse.

Field agents are required to gain approvals from multiple levels of HQ supervisors for many investigative techniques. If a Los Angeles agent sends HQ a request on a time-sensitive investigative matter, there is no urgency on the other end. Many HQ types have lost any empathy to place themselves back into a field operation mode and sense the importance of an active investigation. The communication will usually sit in the electronic queue awaiting the supervisor's return from lunch, the gym, or a two-week vacation.

FBI officials justify such delay and obstruction under the guise of needed oversight, but much of their arrogance is served with a side of careerism. A *bad* decision may stall their career, but a *stalled* decision can be blamed away.

To further complicate matters, the Bureau has unintentionally created a parallel system of approvals requiring both the field *and* HQ. This duality causes delays and hurts morale. I can cite many examples of decisions delayed by HQ that prematurely ended cases. Each field division is staffed with Senior Executive Service–level agents who are of comparable rank with 95 percent of headquarters staff. These local SES staff are capable of making *many* of the decisions now required by HQ.

The following fictitious example is *not* an exaggeration in detailing the delays caused by this dual system. I'll caveat it with a disclaimer that I retired seventeen years ago and that the process may be less cumbersome now, but it's probably still a cluster fuck.

Agent Booker in Cleveland has probable cause to apply for a Title III, which is a request to wiretap a phone or location. After he completes the mini novel, he meets with his immediate supervisor, who must review and approve the document. (Hint: The supervisor is in no rush to read a Title III application.) Then the agent must duplicate the meeting with the Assistant Agent in Charge (ASAC), the Special Agent in Charge (SAC), and the principal legal advisor for the division. Schedules generally preclude a "one meeting fits all" outcome.

When they finally get back to Booker, one or all supervisors involved will have questions or request revisions. This brings about the second round of meetings (schedules permitting). A conservative estimate is that we're at the three- to five-month mark at this point in the process. We're not even close to the finish line because Agent Booker requires the approval of the US attorney for the Northern District of Ohio. He meets with the assistant US attorney (AUSA) who will handle the affidavit. That AUSA will meet and seek approval from their supervisor and eventually the United States attorney, all of whom are in no rush since their court calendars are full. Throw in some vacations, road trips, the flu, some type of emergency, and the seasons change.

If by some miracle Agent Booker gets a local "Go," he must seek FBI headquarters approval, starting with the unit that has authority over the subject matter. The approval process continues at headquarters, who toss more poop down the toilet.

You get the idea—the system is no longer efficient for the fluidity of law enforcement. I'm not suggesting that we eliminate all oversight, but the redundancy equals paralysis. There *are* some provisions for emergency approvals, but delays on nonemergency situations often turn them into emergencies.

This is a very simple fix. You reduce the number of eyes that must approve the finished product and put everyone on the clock. HQ must learn to trust the field to make many of the decisions that now require HQ approval. Another systems failure is the trend to designate brick agents as "office coordinators." The FBI's fifty-six field offices staff agents who work full- or part-time in media, applicants, informants, firearms, and other areas who are all gun-toting FBI agents who *never* leave the office except for lunch.

They have no rank or authority and, when confronted with a problem, respond with, "I'll get back to you." They rarely do.

Many of these coordinator positions can be eliminated, combined, or performed by support staff. The agents can then be reassigned to the field along with all the other dead weight from FBI headquarters. The Bureau can probably add five hundred agents to the field if it streamlined operations.

For example, the media coordinator can be an ASAC or SAC. Every FBI field division has one or more SACs as well as several ASACs. They all receive training in dealing with the media and should be the face of that office. A media coordinator is *not* a full-time job. If you think about the usual reply provided by the FBI to the press, it's the two words "no comment."

That leads to another recent problem. The FBI should step back from the cameras. You should only see FBI agents when they perp-walk some criminal from a car to the jail. We lose our image as super crime fighters when an agent like Peter Strzok opens up his arrogant mouth and wails like a spoiled child on national TV.

If an agent somehow finds themselves sitting in front of a congressional committee, then tell the truth and the *whole* truth. When the Bureau receives a legitimate subpoena, quit blacking out every word except for adjectives. Take your lumps, and the public will forgive you. Rather than come clean, the Mueller and Comey eras delayed, ignored, and redacted documents while FBI SES-level staff repeated a mantra of "I don't recall."

The FBI justifies redactions under the guise of national security, but that's a Trojan horse. If a judge orders unredacted documents, FBI HQ often gets caught with its redacted pants down. Remember the $70,000 conference table purchased by Deputy Director Andy McCabe redacted for "national security reasons." No apology or explanation followed the inflated table issue. Whatever happened to "low bid" in government purchases? It's not that McCabe didn't have less-expensive options. He could have called the Amish to make one for him, visited IKEA, or ordered the exact $70,000 table from China for three hundred bucks.

When astronaut Alan Shepard was asked how it felt to be shot into space, he replied, "It's a very sobering feeling to be up in space and realize that one's safety factor was determined by the lowest bidder on a government contract." Perhaps Shepard had a point for rockets, but it doesn't apply to a conference table. Except for my last three years, my desks were dented metal hand-me-downs from some government warehouse in Peoria. The drawers stuck and the whole thing wobbled, but it never occurred to me that I needed a better desk. I always considered my desk in the same way I consider hotel rooms on vacation—I plan to spend as little time as possible at either, which illustrates another FBI problem: agents who spend all day and *every* day at their desks.

The FBI's operational flaws requires an engine overhaul in lieu of an oil change. The proof is evident, and I'll submit Comey, Strzok, McCabe, and Page as the exhibits to be admitted as evidence.

The following is another excerpt from Special Agent Coleen Rowley's letter to then FBI director Robert Mueller. It highlights flaws in our business model and how the Comey Gang evolved. It refers to this systems failure that worsened under Comey and follows the tried-and-true headquarters response to any incident that embarrasses the Bureau.

Dear Director Mueller: May 21, 2002

An honest acknowledgment of the FBI's mistakes in this and other cases should not lead to increasing the Headquarters bureaucracy and approval levels of investigative actions as the answer.

Most often, field office agents and field office management on the scene will be better suited to the timely and effective solution of crimes and, in some lucky instances, to the effective prevention of crimes, including terrorism incidents. The relatively quick solving of the recent mailbox pipe-bombing incidents which resulted in no serious injuries to anyone are a good example of effective field office work (actually several field offices working together) and there are hundreds of other examples. Although FBIHQ personnel have, no doubt, been of immeasurable assistance to the field over the years, I'm hard pressed to think of any case which has been solved by FBIHQ personnel and I can name several that have been screwed up! Decision-making is inherently more effective and timely when decentralized instead of concentrated.

Sincerely
Coleen Rowley, Minneapolis Division

The FBI should consider looking at retired agents as assets. Immediately after the 9/11 attacks, retired agents from across the nation volunteered their services. Whereas other federal agencies welcomed their ranks back with open arms, the Bureau basically said, "Thanks, but no thanks." The FBI agents weren't expecting to conduct inter-views or knock down doors but would man phones and do other duties to free up active-duty agents for the field.

The Bureau could still be using this valuable resource since most retired agents have the time, desire, and experience to contribute. A side benefit would be mentoring and passing down the FBI's values and culture to the active-duty agents.

As previously discussed, the president should avoid naming future FBI directors from the Justice Department or federal bench. The FBI has thousands of attorneys within its ranks. Many field agents have law degrees, and each field office has a principal legal advisor who does nothing else but provide legal guidance. Headquarters boasts a general counsel office filled with the best legal minds in the country. Prior to Comey appointing James Baker as the chief counsel, this unit was our break wall preventing the Justice Department from drowning FBI operations.

CHAPTER 28:

Hoover, JFK, and Alvin "Creepy" Karpis

"He's not the Messiah. He's a very naughty boy."
—*Monty Python's Life of Brian*

The Office of the Attorney General was created by the Judiciary Act of 1789. Its mission statement is simple: "To enforce the law of the United States; and to ensure fair and impartial administration of justice for all Americans."

This lofty goal has been ignored by several attorneys general with political agendas. The result is an edited mission statement that appears to affirm a *biased* Justice Department that is *unfair* and partial to only *some* Americans.

Eric Holder, Loretta Lynch, and Rod Rosenstein all placed personal ideology over their mission statement, just as Attorney General John Mitchell did during the Nixon administration. But during those periods when the Justice Department became a political arm of the executive branch, there was always the Federal Bureau of Investigation serving as the break wall of integrity.

Politics has frequently been viewed as the enemy of law enforcement and the military. The Vietnam War was a prime example of politicians involving themselves in operations. President Lyndon Johnson began selecting enemy targets in Vietnam from his White House desk based on the politics affecting his reelection.

In the spring of 1936, Democratic senator Kenneth McKellar was the chair of the Appropriations Committee, which funded the FBI. The senator publicly humiliated J. Edgar Hoover during a hearing and then attempted to gut the FBI of needed funding. The senator's ire had little to do with his publicly stated budget objections.

McKellar began by asking the FBI director, "Have you ever *personally* made an arrest?" The senator already knew the answer to that question and had Hoover stammering about the number of cases he supervised.

Feeling somewhat emboldened, McKellar declared that FBI agents should *not* be armed when apprehending criminals. He elicited testimony that in the Bureau's short history, eight criminals had been shot resisting arrest and four agents died in the line of duty. The senator concluded with this gem of logic: "Even if a law enforcement officer knew a man was a murderer, he shouldn't have authority to kill him."

Hoover challenged, "Even if he pulls a gun on you?"

Unphased, McKellar responded, "We have courts to take care of that situation."

Several senators of McKellar's own Democratic Party challenged this insane statement, but the Tennessee senator repeated the mantra that only the courts had the right to take a man's life and not an FBI agent. It was obvious that McKellar had another agenda.

The backstory to this exchange was Hoover's refusal to hire several of McKellar's constituents as agents, considering them to be hacks. The senator chose revenge served cold and was willing to accept any consequences *not* in the best interest of the country. This is nothing new in

DC, as today's politicians routinely make decisions detrimental to the safety of the nation rather than agree with a political opponent.

On April 30, 1936, Hoover flew to New Orleans to prove Senator McKellar wrong and arrest public enemy number one. Alvin "Creepy" Karpis bragged that "my profession was robbing banks, knocking off payrolls, and kidnapping rich men."

The field agents surrounded the Canal Street apartment where Karpis was hiding and made plans to knock the door down. But law enforcement is fluid, and as the agents were getting into position, Karpis strolled out the front door and into his car.

The following scenario has been disputed by some, but it is the *official* report. J. Edgar Hoover ran to the open car window and grabbed Karpis by the throat. Public enemy number one immediately surrendered, and Hoover described Karpis as "folding up like the yellow rat he is."

There are two humorous side stories about the arrest. Not one agent remembered to bring their handcuffs, so Karpis was bound by an agent's necktie. (I was guilty once of that exact sin and requested that my arrestee sit on his hands.) Also, while transporting Karpis back to the FBI office, the out-of-town agents got lost and asked *Karpis* for directions.

I cite these two incidents not as a criticism of brick agents but rather as a testament to their ingenuity. We may shoot it out with the bad guys, but we can experience occasional brain farts while planning.

At the press conference, a reporter asked Hoover, "Now that you captured Karpis, who takes his place as public enemy number one?"

J. Edgar stared earnestly at the assembled group and said, "*Politics* itself is public enemy number one. Politicians continue to hamper and *interfere* with federal and other police and are the real menace at present."

What was *not* said: "Fuck you, Senator McKellar!"

Washington, DC, Six Years Later, 1942

"You're up, Fred."

Special Agent Fred Ayer had hit the jackpot. New agents usually get the crap details, but Director Hoover was personally monitoring this technical surveillance. If it was successful, then Agent Ayers' name would be all over the logs.

The senior agent hands the earphones to the rookie and begins typing up the summary of his hour-long shift. He offers, "You may have a tough time understanding them."

"Is it an equipment failure?"

The agent chuckles and says, "I haven't detected any equipment failure, but you may wanna ask Inga."

Fred positions the earphones on his head and immediately overhears…moans, groans, and a few squeals. The agent may have been new to the FBI but not to the sounds of passion. The subject of the case is a twenty-eight-year-old former Miss Denmark who parlayed that title into Miss Europe. Inga Arvad's personal friends include Hermann Göring and his boss, Adolf Hitler, who proclaims Inga "a perfect Nordic beauty."

The former Miss Europe is a suspected Nazi spy with a mission of compromising a young naval intelligence officer. The lovebirds seem to pick up the pace judging by the volume, culminating in a noisy conclusion and then quiet. A full minute later the two begin an innocuous conversation that comes through loud and clear. Ayer jots down the time and notes, "non pertinent conversation."

After a moment of postcoital banter, Fred cocks his head the way puppies do when they hear a new sound, then presses the earphones tightly over his ears. It couldn't be, but it was! He recognizes the male's voice as his former Harvard classmate Jack Kennedy, currently an ensign in the United States Navy.

JFK has friends in high places, and rather than derail his career, the Department of the Navy transfers Kennedy out of DC to a small naval outpost at Charleston, South Carolina, and restricts his access to low-level confidential information. But Inga travels on weekends down to Charleston to see her "Johnny."

The FBI bugs their hotel room, and one summary log states, "Surveillance maintained upon subject [Arvad], from 2-6-1942 through 2-9-1942. John Kennedy, Ensign, United States Navy spent each night with the subject at the Ft. Sumter Hotel engaging in sexual intercourse on numerous occasions."

J. Edgar Hoover makes copies of the tapes and stashes them inside his safe. The director then calls his old friend Joseph P. Kennedy and explains the situation. Both men agree that this would be a career-ending incident to a young man with political ambitions. Hoover suggests that the young Kennedy be shipped overseas and ends the conversation with, "Don't worry about those incriminating tapes, Joe. They'll never see the light of day."

Joe Kennedy realizes that this is code for blackmail, but his immediate concern is salvaging his son's career. The senior Kennedy contacts his old Wall Street buddy Assistant Secretary of the Navy James Forrestal. Ensign Kennedy is summarily shipped to the South Pacific and becomes a war hero, which propels him into the presidency.

(As a side note, it's ironic that J. Edgar Hoover somehow contributed to the appointment of Attorney General Robert F. Kennedy. Two decades later the two men shared a deep hatred for each other but were forced to play nice. Over the decades people have speculated that Hoover had something on JFK, and they were right. It was the Inga tapes.)

Jack Kennedy somehow became aware of the sex tapes (perhaps through Fred Ayer) and wanted the originals. He made attempts as a freshman congressman in 1947 and then again as a senator but had no idea how to accomplish the mission. J. Edgar Hoover was the most powerful man in government. The *Inga* matter stayed on JFK's mind even after his election as president. A few months before his assassination, Kennedy was the grand marshal at the Harvard commencement and in attendance was his former classmate and FBI agent Fred Ayer. As Kennedy walked down the aisle in tails and silk top hat, Ayer called out, "How's Inga?"

The president smiled and mouthed, "You son of a bitch."

I have a deep respect and admiration for the Kennedys, but I recognize that naming your brother attorney general stretches the credibility of a supposedly fair and impartial Justice Department. This appointment seems to be the start of the overtly partisan attorneys general, which includes both Republican and Democratic administrations.

Hoover had many enemies within President Kennedy's orbit. The day after his 1960 election, the president-elect was celebrating at his family's Hyannis Port retreat with *Washington Post* reporter Ben Bradlee. After a few drinks Kennedy says, "OK, Ben, I'll give you one choice to name for an appointment, *one* job to fill.

Bradlee was adamant: "Get rid of J. Edgar Hoover!"

Kennedy shook his head and said, "You can't fire God."

CHAPTER 29 :

The Reign of Bob Mueller

"You fellas wanna a badge and gun too?"

Robert Mueller is described as utterly incorruptible, unbiased, and principled by major Washington, DC, political and media players, but there's a murkier side to his shiny coin.

"We'd like to meet with Director Mueller."
"What is the nature of the meeting?"
On February 8, 2011, the FBI chief met with two Islamist organizations to listen to their demands. The Council on American-Islamic Relations (CAIR) and Islamic Society of North America (ISNA) accused the FBI of compiling racist training manuals and demanded that all *offensive* references be purged. The groups cited books at the FBI Academy library claiming that counterterrorism experts were promoting "Islamophobia." In addition to censoring training materials, the Muslim groups *demanded* that specific FBI subject matter experts be prohibited from conducting any further lectures.

Mr. Mueller agreed to this rank censorship and then banned the FBI staff who authored the offensive materials from publicly defending their work. This capitulation not only resulted in document censorship but also allowed the two Muslim organizations to effectively reassign FBI staff. Imagine coming home from work and mentioning that you are no longer a counterterrorism subject matter expert in the FBI.

"Yeah, honey, a few terrorist groups didn't agree with my curriculum."

Director Mueller ordered the removal of offensive or racist oral presentations and written curricula on Islam from FBI offices worldwide. The purge was part of a broader Islamist operation designed to influence the opinions and actions of persons, institutions, governments, and the public at large. The irony is that the FBI's role as the primary US agency charged with counterterrorism makes these redactions tantamount to surrender.

During the 2007 Holy Land Foundation (HLF) terrorist financing trial, FBI agent Lara Burns testified in court that CAIR was a front for Hamas. One trial exhibit submitted by federal prosecutors—and stipulated to by the defense in the case—explained that these organizations were dedicated to a "civilizational-jihadist process" to destroy America from within and replace the Constitution with sharia (Islamic) law.

Federal prosecutors specifically cited an internal Muslim Brotherhood planning document as incorporating the strategic goal of these US-based Islamic groups—the very same groups advising the Obama administration. The federal judge in the Holy Land Foundation case agreed that "the government has produced ample evidence to establish the associations with CAIR, ISNA, and NAIT [North American Islamic Trust] with HLF...and with Hamas."

Based on evidence from his own agency, Director Mueller should have been prosecuting CAIR and ISNA and not partnering with them. The FBI was sitting on a mountain of evidence against these groups as a result of the largest terrorist funding trial in our nation's history.

Hamas is a front for terrorist activities, and you can squirt all the perfume on top, but it still smells like monkey feces.

ISNA and CAIR were named by the US government as unindicted coconspirators in the Holy Land Foundation case. The fact that Mr. Mueller gave carte blanche to two identified radical groups to edit FBI training manuals is confusing at best. It's like asking the Mafia to rewrite the racketeering statutes.

FBI counterterrorism experts created that training material based on their expertise and research. The only logical reasons for any redactions would be that the existing material was racist, unfair, *or* inaccurate. But it wasn't. The information contained in the training books represented an accurate and fair depiction of terrorism post 9/11.

Mueller justified his decision to purge training material by providing examples of the offensive material. One sample was an FBI article Mueller deemed highly inflammatory that argued the Muslim Brotherhood is a terrorist organization. It's interesting to note that Mueller himself had previously described the Muslim Brotherhood as a group that *supports* terrorism in the United States and overseas.

The Muslim groups selected words or terms *they* deemed offensive. Examples include the word "jihad," which is defined as a holy war waged on behalf of Islam as a religious duty. "Islamist" is defined as an advocate or supporter of Islamic militancy or fundamentalism. These are dictionary definitions and seem straightforward, but the Muslim groups objected anyway. They also nixed as offensive such adjectives as "radical" and "extreme."

The groups falsely argued that "the FBI is teaching its counterterrorism agents that 'main stream' [sic] American Muslims are likely to be terrorist sympathizers; that the Prophet Mohammed was a 'cult leader'; and that the Islamic practice of giving charity is no more than a 'funding mechanism for combat.'"

CAIR and ISNA charged that at the FBI Academy, agents were shown a chart contending that the more devout a Muslim, the more likely he is to be violent. They contended that those destructive impressions could not be reversed. Sounds a little bit like the image of the devout Muslim terrorist who handed a nine-year-old a gun to shoot nonbelievers.

The Muslim groups cited a specific FBI instructional presentation that stated, "Any war against non-believers is justified" under Muslim law, and "a moderating process *cannot* happen if the Quran continues to be regarded as the unalterable word of Allah."

The irony of these charges is that the Quran preaches these *exact* beliefs. It may be unfair to believe that "the more devout a Muslim, the more likely he is to be violent." Not all Muslims are terrorists or *support* terrorism, but devout Muslims would be in spiritual crisis if they accepted the American way of life. This goes far beyond religion since Jews, Catholics, and Protestants maintain their unique faith but assimilate into the American fabric. Here's why devout Muslims have difficulty doing the same.

Theologically, a good Muslim's allegiance is to Allah, and no other religion is accepted except Islam. Scripturally, a good Muslim's allegiance is to the Quran. Good Muslims must submit to the mullahs (spiritual leaders), *some* of whom teach annihilation of Israel and America, the great Satan. A good Muslim believes the Bible to be corrupt and therefore cannot accept the American Constitution since it is based on biblical principles. Democracy and Islam appear to have trouble coexisting since every Muslim government is either dictatorial or autocratic. So many *devout* Muslims would have difficulty in being both good Muslims and good Americans.

Additional training material that offended the terrorist groups, according to the FBI files, was an article claiming al-Qaeda was "clearly linked" to the 1993 World Trade Center bombing. This was an interesting claim since al-Qaeda *was* involved in the 1993 terrorist attack. A bomb built in Jersey City was driven into an underground garage of the World Trade Center and detonated, killing six people and injured

1,500 others. The architect of the attack was Ramzi Yousef, who trained in al-Qaeda camps. The splitting of hairs between being "officially" linked is like claiming Hitler wasn't a Nazi since he was born in Austria.

Other complaints included the Quran not being the revealed word of God but rather the teachings of Mohammed. They disputed a sweeping generality that "those who fit the terrorist profile best are young male immigrants of Middle Eastern appearance," and conflating Islamic militancy with terrorism.

The list goes on and on and is both contradicting and illogical.

The outcome of this training overhaul was a subtle reprogramming of the mind-set of future FBI agents. It wouldn't occur overnight but over several generations of new agents receiving training at the FBI Academy. These same agents attend in-service counterterrorism training throughout their entire careers. The result is that the FBI terrorism training manuals may be politically correct but are worthless in combating terrorism.

The Obama administration ordered the review of FBI training materials in 2011–2012. It's fair to say that President Obama had a more sympathetic view of the Muslim faith than President Trump. But many experts felt this action was driven by an alliance between the administration, Islamic organizations, and sympathetic media outlets. This resulted in subject matter experts, books, and training materials being blacklisted from offering an opposing view to radical Islamists.

In essence, the purge of the FBI training materials resulted in a single view of a complicated two-sided issue. The FBI organized crime training materials refers to the Italian Mafia. There's very few Italians who are offended by that ethnic prefix since it's factual in describing the La Cosa Nostra. But, *Islamic* militancy was deemed offensive since it doesn't concede that some followers of Islam are *not* militant. That's also true, but you'd have to consider the context and concede that some followers of Islam are *very* militant.

One of the individuals offering input on what constitutes offensive training materials was Mohamed Elibiary. Elibiary served on the Department of Homeland Security Countering Violent Extremism Working Group. In 2010 he was appointed to the Homeland Security Advisory Council and became a senior fellow for the agency, where he was encouraged to purge *old* offensive guidelines. Then DHS took this questionable step further by allowing Elibiary to develop their *new* guidelines.

During his time developing America's guidelines on counterterrorism, Elibiary actively supported brokering a US partnership with the Muslim Brotherhood. The FBI considers the Brotherhood a terrorist group, but that didn't stop them from awarding Elibiary one of the top civilian prizes for "*combating* extremism."

CHAPTER 30:

The Fallout of Capitulation

"Your title gives you claim to the throne, but men
don't follow titles, they follow courage."
—*Braveheart*

What's the harm in editing training material? It's done all the time as information becomes obsolete or things change. My seventh-grade history book referred to the forty-eight states, but by the time I entered ninth grade there were fifty states. Is keeping up with history the precedent FBI director Robert Mueller used in justifying the changes in FBI training materials? Probably, but it's a rabbit hole filled with faulty logic. The admission of Alaska and Hawaii to the United States was factual and not a matter of opinion.

Mueller boasted that more than seven hundred documents and three hundred presentations of material from the Bureau's counterterrorism training curriculum were deemed unusable. The criteria for tossing the material was if it (1) included factual errors, (2) was in poor taste, (3) was stereotypical, or (4) lacked precision. End of story.

There is an inherent danger in having others judge what's in poor taste for you. This is especially true when their findings cannot be discussed, rebutted, or factually corrected. The Muslim redactors would be highly motivated to neuter the one law enforcement agency with jurisdiction over counterterrorism. This is especially true if the groups offended by the curriculum are targets of FBI investigations into terrorism.

The FBI counterterrorism experts who generated the training material could not appeal or even dispute any change. How's that for fair play? The subject matter experts became victim of political correctness gone amok. Essentially, CAIR and ISNA revised our history much in the same way that many Muslims deny that the Holocaust took place during World War II. According to the George Washington University, History News Network, the Middle East has the largest percentage of doubters, with only 8 percent of the population believing the descriptions of the genocide of Jews during World War II.

What were a few of the inaccurate and offensive words or phrases in the FBI training manuals? The nameless editors purged an article because it "inaccurately argues that the Muslim Brotherhood is a terrorist organization." Duh? Another document was deleted to "remove references to mosques as radicalization incubators." Double duh?

Mueller's actions had a widespread effect because several other law enforcement agencies followed the FBI's lead in allowing Islamic groups like CAIR to dictate what anti-terrorism material could be used to train officers. Among them were police departments in three Illinois cities—Lombard, Elmhurst, and Highland Park—as well as the New York Police Department (NYPD). The NYPD purged a highly acclaimed report that proved to be a critical tool in terrorism investigations after three New York Muslims, two mosques, and an Islamic nonprofit filed a lawsuit.

In the case of the Lombard Police Department, CAIR asserted that the instructor of a training course called "Islamic Awareness as a Counter-Terrorist Strategy" was anti-Muslim, though there was no evidence to support it. Like the FBI, Lombard officials got rid of the "offensive" course.

After the FBI purge, complaints from inside the intelligence and law enforcement community were loud and clear: "What the hell is wrong with Mueller?"

Rank-and-file cops as well as FBI agents wanted to know the identities of the individuals making the changes. It was a reasonable request, and perhaps an open discussion could result in a compromise. But the FBI *classified* the names. This was an unprecedented move that suggested two inferences: either the FBI feared that law enforcement officers would harm the redactors or the Bureau would be embarrassed. Maybe both.

In May of 2012, Congressman Louie Gohmert used a graph demonstrating to Congress the hypocrisy of Mueller's purge. The graph compared words and terms used in *The 9/11 Commission Report* with the words and terms redacted from the FBI counterterrorism training documents. Terms such as "jihad," "Islam," and even "al-Qaeda" that were used hundreds of times by the 9/11 Commission had been virtually removed from the training documents.

Former FBI agent John Guandolo wrote that Mueller and other FBI leaders joined a number of Muslim Brotherhood groups to discuss "inflammatory training" that offended Muslims. This illustrates Mueller's odd taste in partners for the FBI, which is *not* a new phenomenon.

In 2000, Abdurahman Alamoudi, head of the American Muslim Council (AMC), shouted at a rally in front of the White House, "We are all supporters of Hamas…I am also a supporter." The AMC was identified by several law enforcement experts as having ties with terrorist organizations. But that didn't stop Director Mueller from speaking to the AMC in 2002. Mueller asked the group for their help in fighting terrorism. They would definitely know how.

In September 2010, Kifah Mustapha, a known Hamas cleric, attended a six-week FBI Citizens Academy. Mustapha got the royal treatment with a visit to the FBI Academy, FBI headquarters, and the top-secret National Counterterrorism Center (NCTC). A year before, Mustapha was named as an unindicted coconspirator in the Holy Land Foundation trial. Mueller would not discuss Mustapha's participation in the FBI Academy when asked.

All of the above is further indication of a lack of leadership in the executive suite of the FBI. Where was the lone voice who suggested, "Hey, Boss, we may not want to invite a terrorist to attend the FBI Citizens Academy"? The Mueller FBI actually *classified* the purged documents, making it extremely difficult even for prominent members of Congress to figure it all out.

Mueller's PC attitude and apparent blindness to the jihadi ideology showed not only in his purge of counterterrorism materials but also in the FBI's law enforcement operations during his tenure as FBI director, which stretched from 2001 to 2013. Team Mueller repeatedly ignored warnings about Boston Marathon bomber Tamerlan Tsarnaev. The dead brother attended the Islamic Society of Boston, a known terrorist recruitment mosque. Of course, the Obama White House restricted any FBI surveillance at mosques. Instead of maximizing the FBI's efficiency as the nation's premier domestic law enforcement agency, Mueller took the sensitive, inoffensive route in order to gain acceptance inside the mainstream media and Obama administration.

Mueller alibied that his agents had invested in "outreach" efforts at the mosque but admitted he was entirely unaware that the mosque was started by a prominent terrorist financier. The FBI director could have gleaned that intelligence had he allowed FBI agents to attend in-service training on "radical mosques that serve as incubators to terrorism." Training concerning mosques as places of radicalization is required by intelligence agencies worldwide that fight terrorism. But not at the FBI.

John Guandolo, the former FBI counterterrorism agent, criticized the FBI for yielding to pressure from Muslim groups in watering down its training of agents by limiting references to Islam and jihad, or holy war.

"I am not aware of any time in the FBI's history when FBI leadership was so incapable of performing their duties as they are today," Guandolo said. "In fact, all three of the Muslim organizations listed on the FBI's website as 'Outreach Partners' are Muslim Brotherhood organizations. The FBI's inability or lack of desire to aggressively pursue obvious major threats to the republic is stunning and frightening."

I understand that J. Edgar Hoover was an imperfect being, but most FBI retirees would smile at the image of several Muslims in their *shalwar kameez* and *thobes* meeting with the director and demanding, "Mr. Hoover, we find your FBI training materials offensive and racist. We *demand* to edit them."

The CIA is responsible for gathering intelligence on foreign soil and the FBI is responsible for countering foreign governments from gathering intelligence on *our* soil. So it's ironic that Muslim groups, suspected of terrorist connections, would be granted access and editing authority to our counterterrorism manuals. Imagine if the Ohio State football team provided their game plan to Michigan.

There's so much wrong with this unconditional surrender of the FBI's prerogative in determining training needs. President Obama may have ordered Mueller to facilitate the purge, but an independent FBI director would respectfully decline to grant any outside group access to our training manuals, let alone the authority to make redactions.

The short-term result of this censorship is that the FBI now has politically correct counterterrorism training manuals. Any long-term effect is either unknown or to be determined, but neither one is good.

The Hamas-linked CAIR is routinely presented by the mainstream media as a civil rights organization. Its consistent pattern of encouraging Muslims *not* to cooperate with law enforcement is never mentioned. Reporters citing CAIR as a positive source or authority almost always fail to mention that it is an unindicted coconspirator in a Hamas terror funding case—so named by the Justice Department. During that case, a captured internal document of the Muslim Brotherhood was released. It named CAIR's parent organization as the Islamic Association for Palestine, as one of its allied groups. The overall mission of Brotherhood groups in the United States is to eliminate and destroy Western civilization.

Recall that national security strategist Angelo Codevilla attributed much of the FBI's problem to careerism and an out-of-control bureaucracy. I've used the term "careerism" throughout the book, but what does it mean? Some words that are synonymous with careerism are cowardice, ball-less, obstructionist, and worthless.

As Codevilla said, "Bureaucrats…figure out on which side their bread is going to be buttered. They learn to think, feel, and do what advances their careers."

CHAPTER 31:

A Clash of Cultures

"You can't handle the truth!"
—*A Few Good Men*

Culture is defined as the customs and beliefs of a particular group. It can only occur through communication. An FBI agent absorbs the Bureau's culture in many ways over time. A part is gleaned from the written word, while the bulk occurs by observation and mentoring.

On July 6, 2016, when the FBI director announced his decision not to recommend charges against Hillary Clinton, it was clear that Mr. Comey was culturally clueless of the agency he led. The FBI is a fact-finding institution, and we never, as in *never*, make recommendations on guilt or innocence. That is the sole purview of the Department of Justice. We'd complete our investigation and provide the US Attorneys Office with documents and forensic and electronic evidence, but *never* a conclusion.

In the old television series *Dragnet*, Jack Webb played Joe Friday, a dour, monotonic Los Angeles detective. During interviews, Friday would always caution, "All we want are the facts, ma'am."

Comey made the self-serving decision to do something that no FBI director had ever done: He announced to the public that the FBI found no evidence of a crime. Then, as required, Comey sent the FBI report to Justice for the final or definitive decision to decline or prosecute. The FBI has *no* business in publicly announcing a prosecutorial opinion on any case.

By prematurely declaring a lack of evidence, Comey *forced* the Justice Department into agreeing. The director was mindful that he poisoned any jury pool should the Justice Department have decided to prosecute. And if that unlikely trial happened, Director Comey would have been the *only* witness necessary for a Hillary acquittal.

Clinton's attorney need ask only one question: "Director Comey, after your lengthy investigation, why did you determine Mrs. Clinton innocent of all charges that she stands accused of today?"

After the tarmac meeting, Attorney General Loretta Lynch took some heat with people calling for her recusal. She demurred and offered, "I'll allow the career prosecutors in my office to make a decision." If anyone was listening closely, this was not a recusal, though it sounded like one. A few days later, some media type mentioned the R word again, and Lynch repeated her "career prosecutors" mantra. The attorney general was *always* the legal safety net who provided cover for Hillary. The polls had Clinton leading by 90 percent, and Lynch had her eye on the Supreme Court.

Loretta Lynch attempted to distance herself from the email decision with the impartial career prosecutor argument. Bruce Ohr, Andrew Weissmann, and Zainab Ahmad were the career prosecutors referred to by Lynch. These guys were meeting in back rooms discussing how to nail President Trump for pissing Russian whores.

Ohr met with Weissmann and Ahmad *prior* to the 2016 election, making clear that Christopher Steele *despised* candidate Trump and the dossier was unverified, paid for by Clinton cash, and probably lies. Rosenstein appointed a special counsel in large part based on Steele's information. Weissmann and Ahmad are then named to the special counsel staff, knowing that the predicate for the entire investigation was a sham. These are the career prosecutors who Lynch felt were impartial.

Comey made a similar argument after his pardon of Clinton: "All the agents working on the case agree with me."

Maybe some agent offered a mild protest ("I think that Mrs. Clinton may have some criminal exposure, sir"), but you can bet that everyone jumped on board once Comey declared, "Well, I'm glad that we're all in agreement."

Every FBI agent has opinions on their cases. I would hand-deliver my prosecution report to the assistant United States attorney and verbally volunteer, "This asshole is guilty as hell." It never occurred to me to call a press conference to influence the public. Comey was duty-bound to meet with Attorney General Lynch, discuss his findings, and offer his opinion. Then if the AG agreed, she would call a press conference with Comey standing three feet *behind* the podium. The AG may ask the FBI director to comment, but his presence is strictly in a supporting role.

Comey's July 5 judge-and-jury one-act play proves that he had no clue of our culture. And by default, if he wasn't clueless then he was corrupt. Comey ignored evidence for political purposes. This one questionable incident in his judgment (email case) was followed by Comey leaking evidence, lying to Congress, and being an arrogant self-righteous defender of his mistakes. All three are bad and constitute a pattern of deception and corruption.

This culture clash leading to the FBI's fall from grace has been an ongoing spectacle. It seems to have no ending. The Bureau's leadership crisis begat loss of independence, which begat its politicization. Eric Holder or Loretta Lynch could've stopped the slide; instead they greased the skids.

The attorney general outranks the FBI director and is considered the top law enforcement official in the country. One may assume that the individual chosen is unbiased and independent. Not lately. Eric Holder carried water for President Obama, who had a disdain for law enforcement.

FBI agents are law enforcement officers who carry guns and badges and make felony arrests. I have been assigned to four task forces with local police, and my father was a Philadelphia police officer. Agents feel a deep affinity for their brother police officers since we work the mean streets together. It's a wonderful marriage since local cops have sources and the FBI has *resources*. In the post-9/11 era, it is imperative for the feds and local law enforcement to share intel, manpower, money, and equipment. The days of being territorial with oversize egos are over. We all share a common goal, which is to keep the public safe.

There is a certain amount of truth to the term "blue wall," which translates to police officers standing together when threatened from the outside.

And here's a not so well-kept secret: Both the FBI and local police consider politicians as outsiders with an agenda not based on any sense of justice but rather on reelection. This is not surprising to the public, but what may be shocking is that a majority of law enforcement officers during the Obama years felt that the attorneys general (Holder and Lynch) shared a deep prejudice *against* the law enforcement community. By extension, they consider the Department of Justice a political entity. The implications have resulted in cautious law enforcement and a public at risk.

According to the *Washington Times* one former G-man stated that frustrated agents quit the Bureau in the waning days of the Obama administration due to the acrimony between the FBI and Justice Department. Part of the problem was Mr. Holder pressuring the FBI to investigate local police agencies for civil rights violations.

As the *Times* reported, "The department opened more than 20 civil rights investigations into local police departments between 2009 and 2014, more than doubling the number of reviews from the previous five years." But they refused to prosecute an honor killing with substantial evidence for fear of pissing off Muslims. They evidently had no problem pissing off police officers who put their butts on the line every day to protect blacks, whites, *and* Muslims.

The *Washington Times* also cited a former Justice Department lawyer who felt that many people in law enforcement, including the FBI, were "demoralized by the probes, believing they were risking their lives without any support from Main Justice in Washington."

In 1988, I was assigned to work with the Cleveland police narcotics unit. I spent many long days with these coppers since drug work is never a nine-to-five affair. The police officers were professional, competent, and lacked any racial animus. There was never a time when they targeted a specific racial group. Sergeants Ray Gercar, Chas Lane, and Roy Warner and Detectives Tommy Shoulders, Dave PK, Danny Zaller, Paul Falzone, and Jackie S. targeted drug dealers.

It'd be ridiculous to claim that there *aren't* prejudiced law enforcement officers who target and kill African Americans, but my own experience backed by statistics indicate that they are a *small* fraction of the law enforcement community.

There is a long-standing debate concerning the criminal justice system. *"Does law enforcement target blacks, or do blacks commit a majority of crimes?"*

According to data compiled by the *Washington Post*, 50 percent of the victims of fatal police shootings are white, while 26 percent are black. The majority of these victims had a gun or "were armed or otherwise threatening the officer with potentially lethal force." **According to FBI data,** black criminals are more likely to kill cops than be killed by cops and 40 percent of cop killers are black. A police officer is 18.5 times more likely to be killed by a black person than a cop killing an unarmed black person.

The Obama administration, through Eric Holder, wielded amazing control over the formerly independent FBI. Both the president and the attorney general waged an anti-police campaign that contributed to the racial tensions in America. They had an obvious disdain for cops and labeled any incident involving a white police officer and a black citizen as police brutality. Both men routinely faced the cameras *prior* to any investigation and blamed law enforcement.

This influence reinforced the Bureau's loss of independence that Mueller set in motion. What were some of the outcomes when the FBI lost its independence? Two things are obvious, and they're both bad: Comey became an ideological puppet of the left, and the FBI was castrated.

J. Christian Adams served as an attorney in the Justice Department Civil Rights Division under Holder and stated that "Eric Holder waged an anti-police campaign that he believed in, and he was so successful in merging his ideology with the Department of Justice that some people there didn't even realize he was doing it."

On August 9, 2014, Michael Brown and Dorian Johnson left the Ferguson Market and Liquor Store in Ferguson, Missouri. Surveillance video shows Brown stealing some cigarillos and shoving the clerk. They walk down the middle of Canfield Drive, where officer Darren Wilson responds to the theft in his police car. He sees that Brown fits the description of a suspect in the convenience store theft. The events that next occur are corroborated by forensic evidence and a grand jury's conclusion. Brown, an African American, attacks Officer Wilson while attempting to grab his revolver. Wilson, who is white, shoots and kills Brown.

Prior to any investigation of the facts, both President Obama and Attorney General Holder infer that Brown is the victim of police brutality based on race. Subsequent police, FBI, and grand jury investigations determine that Officer Wilson acted appropriately in using deadly force. Any reasonable human being would accept their findings, and especially the top law enforcement officer in the land.

But not Eric Holder. Following Wilson's exoneration, AG Holder orders an investigation into the Ferguson Police Department since he disagreed with his own Justice Department's findings. He holds a press conference and details that Ferguson's police officers had engaged in police brutality, violated constitutional rights, and used financial extortion against the African American community. He later added that the Department of Justice could dismantle the entire police force to fix the structural problems, if necessary. This is a threat, in case you didn't catch it.

Another example of culture clash and leadership void previously discussed involves McCabe's table. Former FBI deputy director Andrew McCabe spent $70,000 in taxpayer dollars on a conference table. It's another instance of the vanity on the seventh floor of FBI HQ. This is not similar to some secretary of agriculture sprucing up his throne room. The FBI should have the best weapons, crime lab, and training academy, but not some wooden shrine for some bureaucrat to sit around and discuss how to frame the president.

McCabe's upgrade would've been forgotten had he simply apologized and called Home Depot for a $2,000 conference table. Leaders admit their mistakes, accept the consequences and move forward, always *forward*. But somehow the FBI tied this purchase to national security. These cowards pulled a sacred card from their deck simply to avoid embarrassment.

But their deceit didn't stop with the table. Senator Chuck Grassley revealed that there were numerous *other* redactions that made no sense, nor were they made to protect national security secrets.

If the FBI withheld the truth about a piece of wood how can we trust these HBOs when they they're testifying before Congress?

CHAPTER 32:

The "Un"-Just Department

"Magic Mirror on the wall. Who is the fairest one of all?"
—*Snow White and the Seven Dwarfs*

The pattern of preassigning guilt based on racism repeated itself during Loretta Lynch's tenure as attorney general. Any well-publicized incident involving white police officers in a confrontation with African Americans would be considered suspect by the president and attorney general. Her rush to judgment as the top Justice official denied due process to many innocent cops.

On July 16, 2009, Harvard University professor Henry Louis Gates Jr. was arrested at his Cambridge, Massachusetts, home by local police officer Sergeant James Crowley. The officer was responding to a 911 caller's report of men breaking and entering the residence. Gates was African American, and Crowley was white.

Gates found the front door to his home jammed shut and, with the help of his driver, tried to force it open. A local witness reported their activity to the police as a potential burglary in progress. When Sergeant

Crowley arrived, Gates explained the situation and the officer nodded and asked, "Can I see some ID?"

Gates became angry and refused to show any ID, claiming the request was racial profiling. This presented Crowley with a dilemma since his request seemed a logical remedy to the situation. If the license ID matched the address, then, "Good night, sir." But Gates chose to escalate the situation by refusing to provide his ID.

Crowley was faced with an impasse. Had the cop backed off his ID request and Gates *been* a burglar, then the cop shouldn't be a cop. Crowley eventually charged Gates with disorderly conduct. It all could have been avoided had Gates not been so thin-skinned.

A day after the incident and *before* any investigation, President Obama determined the cop was a racist: "I don't know, not having been there and not seeing all the facts, what role race played in that. But I think it's fair to say, number one, any of us would be pretty angry; number two, that the Cambridge police acted *stupidly* in arresting somebody when there was already proof that they were in their own home, and, number three, what I think we *know* separate and apart from this incident is that there's a long history in this country of African Americans and Latinos being stopped by law enforcement disproportionately."

Fact check: Gates wasn't being stopped by Crowley based on race. The police had been called, and Sergeant Crowley responded, minus knowledge of ethnicity.

The former president's inference seemed to be that a white police officer would've handled the incident differently had Gates been white.

The merits of the Garner case were discussed elsewhere in the book but it's a prime example of the recent divide between law enforcement and the public. There have been a rash of cases involving individuals who refuse to obey lawful and sometimes unlawful commands of law enforcement officers. I've made plenty of arrests, and problems usually occur *after* you announce, "FBI, you're under arrest." There are some folks who do *not* desire to be arrested. I've had guns pointed at me, attempts to slice my throat with a knife, and been punched squarely between my eyes. Sometimes an individual may not offer a violent reaction but will passively resist by squirming. Just for the record, it is almost impossible to place handcuffs on a moving target. The problem is that once a law enforcement officer declares their intent to arrest someone, the options narrow.

You probably could say, "Well, never mind. I didn't realize you had such strong feelings about it. Have a nice day."

But that would be the end of your law enforcement career. Suspects can save both sides a lot of heartburn by assuming the position and making their point later.

The Garner case, though tragic, had its due process involving investigations and reviews by the New York Police Department, the New York City District Attorney, the New York Field Office of the FBI, and the United States Attorney for the Southern District of New York. All declared that the police officers acted appropriately.

But racial politics raised its ugly head within the Justice Department when Attorney General Loretta Lynch ignored the New York cops, New York District Attorney, the New York FBI agents, *and* her own US Attorneys Office. She ordered the FBI to send agents from outside New York to reinvestigate the Garner case.

The fact that the FBI director allowed this to happen is a strong indication that the Bureau has merged with the Justice Department. Comey basically admitted that his agents who conducted the initial investigation either showed racial bias or were incompetent. A proper response would have been, "Mrs. Attorney General, that ain't happening." If Lynch then pressured Obama to order Comey to send in outside FBI agents, Comey should have resigned.

There are some miscellaneous factors contributing to the increasing tension between law enforcement and citizens. Mayors of many large urban areas are anti-police. They have ordered law enforcement to stand down and ignore the destruction of property, arson, and aggravated assault. They rationalize that the presence of law enforcement increases the rage of these anarchists. I always believed that cops were the group that saved the citizens from the barbarians at our gate.

Groups like Antifa wave the deep state flag of "the resistance." They paint an image of a futuristic sci-fi flick with the hooded good guys fighting the evil establishment. But these resisters with bandanas covering their face while attacking police officers and destroying property are basic cowards and thugs. Their protests are *not*, as liberals claim, constitutionally protected, since Antifa throws bricks at police officers while looting stores. It is anarchy, and though I would never suggest that we gun them down, I do believe that an ass kicking may be in order. A brick is a deadly weapon, and if you disagree, have a friend toss a four-pound jagged rock at your head from twenty yards. Your natural reaction would be to run or shoot them, yet the police exhibit amazing restraint in the face of such assaults.

My father was a Philadelphia police officer in the 1950s and '60s, and any object tossed his way would result in some "counseling," followed by an arrest. People of my generation would also protect their property and businesses. Those businesses provided food and shelter for their family, so if some Antifa geek got bloodied when he attempted to sledgehammer the window of some Italian sandwich shop, the justice system of old would admonish the idiot and ask, "What'd you expect?"

Today's justice system would arrest the shop owner for assault, and then they'd be sued by the poor, innocent Antifa victim.

Liberal mayors order police officers to stand down as anarchists break windows, block traffic, and burn cars. This is a morale killer. During the Baltimore riots, I watched Antifa goons throw bricks at Baltimore Police Department officers, who retreated. The visual of that night broke my heart.

Recall what Hans von Spakovsky of the Heritage Foundation said: "Holder and Lynch totally politicized the Justice Department. There was no compunction about interfering with a criminal investigation." But others say tensions are a result of *cultural* differences endemic to both organizations, with one side tending toward the hard-charging crime-stoppers and the other the more cautious legal wranglers.

Our official FBI handbook includes several pages on mission, but the credentials that we carry everyday sums it up with a simple directive: "Agents are charged with the duty of investigating violations of laws of the United States."

There is no mention about picking and choosing sides based on party, race, or ideology. If an FBI agent is shot, they'd bleed blue.

CHAPTER 33:

The Alexandria Factor

Seattle Police Department officers can no longer
use the word "suspect" in reports. Instead, they
must use the term "community member."

Can law enforcement prevent lone wolf attacks?

The term "lone wolf terrorist" has primarily been associated with radical Muslims. But the shooting of Congressman Steve Scalise in Alexandria, Virginia, has forever changed that narrow definition. James Hodgkinson isn't a Muslim and wasn't motivated by religion, but he *is* a lone wolf terrorist.

Individuals with classic symptoms such as psychosis exhibit identical behavior patterns as those who radicalize on ideologies. Dylann Roof, who killed nine African Americans at Bible study in Charleston, South Carolina, had a long struggle with mental health issues, and Major Nidal Malik Hasan, a Muslim Army psychiatrist, killed thirteen people at Fort Hood, Texas, in the name of Allah. Both Roof and Hasan gave plenty of indications that they were ticking bombs, though the public believed Roof was crazy whereas Hasan was radicalized by ideology. So, what's the common thread?

Hodgkinson, Roof, Hasan, and Boston bomber Tamerlan Tsarnaev were *all* driven by ideology and whipped up into a violent frenzy by like-minded folks. The press labeled Hodgkinson as mentally unstable but didn't paint Tamerlan with the same diagnostic brush. The Alexandria shooting has demonstrated that lone wolf terrorists come in different flavors. The fact that Hodgkinson had a political agenda does not place him in a separate category.

And while we're redefining *lone wolf* attacks, let's throw in the rash of school and other random shootings. Stephen Paddock killed fifty-nine people at a Vegas concert. Omar Mateen killed forty-nine and injured fifty-eight in Orlando nightclub. Christopher Sean Harper-Mercer shot and killed eight fellow students and a teacher at Umpqua Community College. Adam Lanza killed twenty first graders and six adults at Sandy Hook Elementary School in Newtown, Connecticut. Jiverly Voong killed thirteen people and wounded four others at an immigration services center, in Binghamton, New York. And Seung-hui Cho, a twenty-three-year-old Virginia Tech senior, opened fire on campus, killing thirty-two people.

The FBI's dependency on the Justice Department has slowed down the business of justice under the guise of oversight. When combined with needless political correctness, the results can be devastating.

Corey Johnson immersed himself in radical Islam and became addicted to online videos of beheadings, so his sister dimed him out. The FBI's Joint Terrorism Task Force became involved after European intelligence reported that Corey threatened, "By Allah, we will kill every single Infidel student at a local school." Over one hundred students at that English school quit attending, fearing a terrorist attack. Corey admitted to FBI agents that he supported Anwar al-Awlaki, a known terrorist and spiritual patron of lone wolf jihadists. This is clue number three.

The agents' hands were legally tied due to political correctness and an inability of Congress to pass sane laws regarding insanity. It was easier to punt on human time bombs who are providing every clue that they *will* detonate. All the FBI had in its terrorist toolbox was the unrealistic and ineffective approach of "redirection." This program is similar to holding a shiny object up to redirect a disturbed individual's attention from maiming people to volunteering at a nursing home. Law enforcement and school officials in Parkland, Florida, used redirection before seventeen innocent students and teachers were gunned down by another time bomb. They'll all eventually go boom; it just depends on the length of their fuse. Redirection is aimed at not offending anyone, so the program *might* work on some fourteen-year-old boy to correct a potty mouth.

Corey ignored the FBI and continued his Islamic indoctrination online. After nearly a year of delays, FBI agents had enough evidence to charge Corey for making terror threats over social media. But there was an administrative snag that delayed the arrest.

Corey was invited to a sleepover at his friend Kyle Bancroft's house. Around 4:00 a.m., he was reading the Quran to work up the courage to kill Kyle's mother, Elaine; his brother, Dane; and Dane's friend, Jovanni Brand. Corey repeatedly stabbed Jovanni in his bed and slit his throat, and when Elaine approached the boys' bedrooms, Corey stabbed her thirty-two times. Dane heard the screams and saved his mom, but both were hospitalized in critical condition.

Corey confessed to police that he stabbed the victims because of his Muslim faith. He watched videos of Muslim jihadists on his cell phone just prior to the attacks.

According to records released by the Jupiter, Florida, Police Department, local officials were notified by the FBI that charges would be filed against Corey for social media terrorist threats in the summer of 2017. But for whatever reason this didn't happen, and in the early morning hours of March 2018, the jihad stabbings at Palm Beach

Gardens *did* happen. My bet is that the Justice Department was reluctant to approve Corey's arrest.

The movie *Clockwork Orange* concerns a warped English kid, Alex, who rapes and terrorizes people. After his capture they attempt an experimental psychological conditioning technique. The "Ludovico technique" had about the same effect on Alex as "redirection" did on Corey. What Alex needed was castration with dull gardening shears. We need to admit that some individuals are evil and be more concerned about the feelings of victims and their families.

This type of attack will continue indefinitely unless we prevent rather than react to lone wolf attacks. Our mentality should no longer accept a low body count with the rationalization of "It could've been a lot worse." So, how does law enforcement identify the attacker prior to the bullets and bombs? The easy answer is that we'll have to hurt someone's feelings.

After every lone wolf attack, special interest groups, politicians, and the media blame law enforcement. They wonder why we didn't prevent the attack since the attacker was a known entity. They feign outrage that the subject wasn't under surveillance. It requires twelve agents per twenty-four-hour shift to surveil one suspect. America has thousands of terrorist suspects, so the math makes it impossible. But if a cop or FBI agent ever snatched up a lone wolf suspect minus an arrest warrant, the same groups would scream Fourth Amendment violations. If America truly wants to prevent lone wolf attacks, then something has to change. As you're reading this, lone wolf terrorists are planning to kill you, and your family. You'll *never* eliminate lone wolf attacks but you can *reduce* them significantly with a few politically incorrect measures that will never happen.

1. Profile. It's a dirty word to many but a very successful investigative technique.

2. Increase involuntary commitments to psychiatric units. This involves a ninety-six-hour period of observation and evaluation. Only very specific facts should trigger the commitment, such as irrational behavior coupled with a history of violence or verbal or written threats combined with assault, drug, or weapons convictions. Also, this individual should not be allowed to purchase or own a firearm.

3. Enforce laws that have penalties for "incitement to violence." Individuals who communicate real threats to groups or individuals and encourage others to join them in violent acts should be immediately questioned by police. There is a recent precedent case in the United States where Michelle Carter was convicted of manslaughter for encouraging her boyfriend to commit suicide via texts.

4. Make the watch list a stop list. There are a few hundred thousand people on our watch list. They land on the list by having suspected terrorist ties, but every day at our ports of entry, thousands of watch list designees are waived through customs with a "Have a nice day." And no one is watching them.

5. Eliminate the restrictions on mosque surveillance. President Obama has placed mosques off limits to law enforcement. Many lone wolf terrorists are radicalized at US mosques.

6. Develop human intelligence. Lone wolf terrorists do not operate in a vacuum. Every mass murderer listed above provided clues to their intentions on social media or to friends and family members. It's only after victims lay in the street that these potential sources admit that they "knew this would happen."

7. Allow law enforcement to follow suspects to encrypted sites. Law enforcement monitors open social media and follows individuals who are espousing violence, but a warrant is required to follow suspects to the dark web.

If America doesn't take aggressive action on lone wolf terrorism, then we'll eventually have checkpoints on our highways, barbed wire around our schools, and empty malls and sports stadiums.

The leaks of Eric Snowden, Chelsea Manning, and Reality Winner damaged national security. Although Snowden's and Manning's leaks occurred during the Obama presidency, there are several dynamics that tie these leaks to the deep state. The trio received top-secret clearances despite plenty of indicators that they were security risks. Why were they granted top-secret clearance? FBI agents no longer conduct the background security investigations on contract employees, and the result is often shoddy work. The background check for security clearances has been farmed out to *for-profit* corporations that are on the clock. Though many companies employ former law enforcement types, their contract renewal is based on turning over these cases quickly, but a proper background investigation for a top-secret clearance takes time and effort.

One example of how untrustworthy individuals are routinely handed the keys to our national security secrets is the social media postings of Reality Winner. Her employer was Pluribus International Corporation based in Alexandria, Virginia. The company is a government contractor, and as an employee Winner had a top-secret security clearance.

Two postings on Winner's Facebook page should have alerted her background investigator to a problem. The two postings were: "Why burn a flag…Donald Trump thinks crosses burn much better" and "On a positive note, this Tuesday [election of Trump], we became the United States of the Russian Federation."

Many individuals spout similar or more offensive speech, but they are civilians and not entrusted with US secrets.

Winner had an obvious hatred of President Trump fueled by ideology. Did she have a First Amendment right to speak her mind? Most definitely, but that didn't entitle her to a top-secret clearance. Most of the FBI agents in my era would have considered Winner a security risk.

CHAPTER 34

The Freeh Years: The "Bright" Line

"Oh, behave! Yeah! Yeah, baby, behave!"
—*Austin Powers: International Man of Mystery*

I like Louie Freeh. When I was presented with the Director's Award for Excellence, Louie welcomed my wife, Lori, and daughters, Gia and Dani, to FBI HQ. Our paths crossed many times starting in the 1980s when Louie was an assistant United States attorney in New York and I was an agent working organized crime. I'd occasionally drop evidence off and we'd shoot the bull for a few minutes. Joe Pistone, aka Donnie Brasco, and I actually caught up with Louie in Moscow while he was meeting with Vladimir Putin. Louie somehow knew we had arrived from Siberia, and he's a close personal friend of the Pistone family.

Director Freeh enacted new guidelines in the 1990s governing the conduct of *all* FBI employees, emphasizing higher standards of ethical behavior and allowing inquiries about sexual and other improper activity. He categorized it as the bright (ethical) line.

I understood and agreed with Louie's goal to regain our polish as the world's premier law enforcement agency. But that came with some unintended consequences.

The catchall phrase "improper behavior" is a land mine since it's not an absolute like "murder" or "espionage."

"I have determined that we have been too tolerant of certain types of behavior," Freeh said, adding that he wanted to "draw a bright line which should serve to put all employees on notice of my expectations." Freeh attempted to standardize and define objectionable behavior. This is a difficult thing to do with human beings.

The bright line was well intended but poorly defined and executed. It aimed at eliminating improper behavior but had unintended consequences such as decreasing esprit de corps and creating unnecessary paranoia by pressuring employees into becoming snitches. A report filed in this electronic era prevents second chances and ends careers for deserved people. The line prevents employees from handling problems at the lowest level possible through mentoring and peer pressure.

During my first week in Vietnam, my squad leader mustered a few of us and minus any words led us into the dark. We reached a point in the perimeter where a single Marine stood watch, and they proceeded to beat the snot out of him. I had no idea what the Marine did to deserve such an ass whipping. The group left, and I stayed behind with the guy, who had a bloody nose.

"What the fuck was that about?" I asked.

"I fell asleep on post last night."

I didn't have a reply, and after a minute the Marine looked at me and said, "I deserved that."

It took me a couple of days to figure out my presence, and it was a powerful message. One lesson learned was that you *never* fall asleep on post since the lives of the entire platoon depend on you. And secondly, this tough-love session was my initiation into the combat fraternity of brothers.

The Marine committed a mortal sin and would remember that beating for the remainder of his life. I know this because it's affected *me* till this day. Not only did *he* abstain from any future naps on duty, but the visual images of brothers beating a brother kept me *very* vigilant on post.

I later learned that the Marine had distinguished himself during several firefights and was a good man. Though the squad leader recognized that a very bright line had been breached, he felt no need to go on paper or report it to the brass.

"He fucked up and won't do it again."

Freeh's guidelines specifically addressed adultery and other sexual activity. Peter Strzok and Lisa Page were not yet with the Bureau but probably would've ignored this section of the guidelines anyway.

Freeh stressed that "*any* sexual conduct might be investigated and evaluated in connection with granting top-secret security clearances."

Bureaucratic translation: "Don't get caught." Freeh's guidelines stipulate that "the FBI will draw adverse conclusions if there is an attempt to conceal activities that might make the employee vulnerable to coercion, espionage or theft of documents."

Freeh's use of "attempt to conceal" is an unofficial term for the very official FBI violation of "lack of candor."

Bureaucratic translation: Lack of candor is *lying* and the most *frequent* offense of termination by the FBI. It's the old adage of "the cover-up is worse than the crime."

Agents *should* be shining examples of propriety, morals, and sound judgment, but that comes with a price. Louie attempted to duplicate the honor system of West Point and Annapolis, requiring agents to dime out coworkers for ethics violations. And like in golf, agents were expected to call penalty shots on themselves. Who can argue against a bright line regarding ethics, especially in law enforcement? But many absolutes can become blurred over time, and Louie's bright line was *not* well received by the brick agents.

Louie was correct that many behaviors like murder and theft require an immovable line in the sand. But when you allow others to use *their* moral compass as judge and jury, it is a recipe for disaster. For example, misuse of a Bureau car is a very common violation punishable by thirty days on the bricks and loss of salary. That's a big hit when the mortgage comes due. How about having a drink on duty? That used to be a pretty common occurrence and was often followed with misuse of a Bureau car. That's a bad combo for sure, but there is some gray area to consider.

Some of the behavior considered unethical has some collateral benefits. On my first Friday after joining the Pittsburgh Field Office as a brand-new agent, I was informed that I'd be joining a group at some downtown bar. It wasn't a request but rather a directive from a senior agent. Turns out that many of the Pittsburgh agents met every Friday afternoon for a few pops. It was a fantastic tradition that built esprit de corps and made us more effective as agents. Some of you reading this will disagree, but you'd be wrong. After one or two drinks, we'd get into our Bureau cars and go home. We were not intoxicated, but we twice crossed Freeh's bright line. Any bang for the buck in this Pittsburgh ritual? Many old-timers believe so, and there are other examples of the line blurring.

Some agents ran up to the line, some straddled it, and many went way over it. When FBI agents were able to mentor rookies, they regulated the bright line. There was no need to report some behavioral infraction to management since it was dealt with at the squad level.

If an agent had a fender bender with a Bureau car, rather than do a bunch of paperwork and possibly receive a letter of censure, agents took the car to an auto body "contact." The squad would all chip in some money to repair the damage, and life went on. *Contacts* are individuals who will help law enforcement officers, and they run the gamut from doctors to auto body shops. Every FBI division has contacts who offer discounts on jewelry, furniture, clothes, liquor, and other sundry items to cops and agents at reduced prices. There was actually a doctor in Memphis who had a side door that cops could use for a variety of medical treatments, ranging from penicillin shots for STDs to removing bullets from accidental discharges. Of course, FBI agents shouldn't take stuff at reduced prices since that courtesy invites some reciprocity. A free cup of coffee and hamburger may be viewed as a bribe, or it can lead to a source of information.

Another Bureau tradition that's been deemed unethical is taking office-wide collections for agents who've been suspended. The goal is to cover the approximate amount of the paycheck that was lost. An envelope was passed throughout the office and everyone gave willingly with the proviso of "there but for the grace of God goes me." Sometime in the 1990s, Bureau officials discontinued the practice, citing tax issues.

Golf is the only sport that depends on the participants calling fouls on themselves. Professional golfers will penalize themselves for infractions that offer them no advantage but do so knowing that they'll lose a few hundred thousand dollars.

Though admirable, it would not work in law enforcement. My partner Fred and I were conducting a surveillance when our subject picked up a hooker and went to a motel. It was a frigid winter night and two hours later it dawned on us that we were starved since we'd been tailing this OC (organized crime) mope all day. We tossed out some options such as breaking off or chancing a run for some fast food. We decided on a third option, which was to flatten two of the tires on the subject's car. Worked like a charm since he could never fix the flats or have someone pick him up in the twenty minutes we'd be gone.

FBI agents must have the public's confidence. They'd never plant evidence or lie on the witness stand, but would they consider flattening two tires as crossing some ethical line? Perhaps but I hope not.

The bright line guidelines also provide for suspension or dismissal for unauthorized disclosure of classified or sensitive FBI information.

Those circumstances should involve a firing squad, and there'd been a few dead bodies had Comey continued Freeh's bright line. Comey didn't throw the penalty flag on himself after he disclosed an investigative memo. The Comey era was a virtual sieve of leaked documents by FBI employees, led by James Comey himself.

A few months before enacting the guidelines, Freeh suspended James Fox, head of the FBI's New York Field Office, on grounds that he had commented about the 1993 World Trade Center bombing case on television in violation of a federal judge's gag order.

But Louie's bright line dimmed when his friend was involved in unethical behavior. There's no need to get into names but suffice it to say investigations recommended that his friend be suspended or fired. With those findings, combined with the bright line, one may assume that he'd be in real trouble. Everyone awaited Freeh's decision, and it was a surprise. The director suspended his friend for thirty days, *with* pay, and then *promoted* him. In an interview with *Newsweek,* Freeh conceded that "there was a flawed investigation, and I relied on that." He said he took "full responsibility" for the resulting damage to the FBI's image and admitted that he had promoted his friend because of their "long and close association."

The bottom line is that Louie's line was written in invisible ink.

I actually have no problem with Louie Freeh being loyal to a friend and would've done the same thing. But then again, I would not have drawn an ethical line in the sand in the first place.

CHAPTER 35

"Can I speak with an agent?"

"The government solution to a problem is
usually as bad as the problem."

Have you tried to contact an FBI office these days? You'll probably reach a recorded menu that provides a variety of options, none of which include speaking with an agent.

A few years ago I received a call from an old friend. Tom (not his real name) was a former police officer on active duty with the Marine Corps. His MOS (job) was intelligence, so Tom had several deployments to the Sandbox. A Marine Corps intelligence officer has their crap together, and Tom scored a great asset who provided reliable and actionable intelligence. After his fourth deployment, Tom retired and settled in the western United States.

We caught up with our lives before Tom said, "I need some help."

"Whatta you got?"

Tom explained that three years ago the terrorists discovered that his asset had cooperated with the Americans, placing himself along with his family in danger. Tom assisted his source through the dense paperwork required to gain refugee status. The asset and family had been living happily in the United States until recently.

Tom continued: "I got a call from him a few months ago. He told me he identified several al-Qaida at his local [US] mosque."

"I'm retired," I said. "You need to contact the FBI."

"My source called them twice, and I've made three attempts to give someone the information."

"How'd that go?"

A quick aside: The Obama White House assured America that tracking our phone calls and email would stop terrorism. I actually don't consider this an intrusion on my privacy since I'll trade some freedom for security. And yet, Obama prohibited snooping on mosques, where terrorists congregate. The government's sweeping surveillance of our most private communications *excludes* the jihad factories where homegrown terrorists are sometimes radicalized.

Since October 2011, mosques have been off-limits to FBI agents. No more surveillance or undercover sting operations without high-level approval from a special oversight body at the Justice Department, dubbed the Sensitive Operations Review Committee. Who makes up this body, and how do they decide requests? Nobody knows; the names of the chairman, members, and staff are kept secret. We *do* know the panel was set up under pressure from Islamist groups who complained about FBI stings at mosques. Just months before the panel's formation, the Council on American-Islamic Relations teamed up with the ACLU to sue the FBI for allegedly violating the civil rights of Muslims in Los Angeles by hiring an undercover agent to infiltrate and monitor mosques there.

Steven Emerson is head of the Investigative Project on Terrorism, considered the country's top data center on Islamic terror groups in the United States. Emerson considers the ISIS threat on American soil frightening. Oliver "Buck" Revell, the former head of FBI investigations and counterterrorism, said, "It is not an exaggeration to say that because of Democrat political correctness hamstringing our FBI agents, they could not combat the Islamists in our midst without Steven Emerson."

Before mosques were excluded from domestic spying by the Obama administration, the FBI launched dozens of successful sting operations against homegrown jihadists inside mosques. They also disrupted dozens of plots against the homeland, and had they been allowed to continue, perhaps the many victims of the Boston Marathon bombings would not have lost their lives and limbs. The FBI *never* canvassed Boston mosques until four days *after* the April 15 attacks, and it did not check out the radical Boston mosque where the Muslim bombers worshipped. The Bureau couldn't even contact mosque leaders for help in identifying them *after* their images were captured on closed-circuit TV cameras and cell phones.

One of the Muslim bombers made extremist outbursts during worship, yet because the mosque wasn't monitored, red flags were not raised inside the FBI about his increasing radicalization. This is particularly disturbing in light of recent independent surveys of American mosques, which vary on the number of mosques that preach violent jihad or distribute violent literature to worshippers. A 2008 WorldNetDaily undercover survey of more than a hundred American mosques and Islamic schools exposed widespread radicalism, finding that three in four (75 percent) Islamic centers are hotbeds of anti-Western extremism. Ron Kessler in a *NEWSMAX* article states that the FBI estimates only 10 percent of Imans preach jihad and extremism in a study of the 2,000 mosques in the United States. (Other studies vary with the low range of 10 percent and the high at 90 percent.)

My friend and former Marine intel officer explained, "I contacted FBI Headquarters, and then the office near me. They forwarded my calls to some central tip line. Same thing with my source."

"Let me guess, no return call."

"I'm wondering if you could make a call."

"No problem, Tom. It's my alma mater."

I fully believed that there would be no problems in *my* contacting an FBI office, identifying myself as a retired agent, and getting some action on a legitimate terrorist threat. When I was a rookie agent, retired guys were considered heroes. They'd occasionally call and request that we'd run a tag for their private investigation business.* We'd talk some shop about their time in the Bureau, and I always learned some investigative tidbit. But sometime in the early 1990s, retired agents became bothersome dinosaurs in the eyes of the FBI.

The old squad bays had a frat-like feeling, with agents screaming on phones or at each other with feet propped up on the desk while smoking a cigar. I've witnessed fistfights between agents, and profanity was common. Although that visual when judged by today's standards may seem unsettling, it somehow provided a positive environment in building esprit de corps.

Come the 1990s and the squad areas became a quiet sedentary row of cubicles. Interaction occurred primarily through emails, though agents may be sitting ten feet apart. One didn't dare raise their voice. One agent was suspended for arguing with his supervisor. That was considered a routine occurrence in my day. This loss of mentoring indirectly led to the Comey debacle. New agents no longer benefited from the years of experience older agents gained by dealing with criminals *and* bureaucrats.

Agents, long in the tooth, could no longer mentor the rookies for fear of offending them. Any complaint to the front office required SES types to open investigations and get to the bottom of one agent offering the advice of "get your fuckin' head outta your ass." The field offices use to resolve 99 percent of all problems minus FBI HQ meddling. But that was before everyone became a victim and the Bureau

---

*   Running a tag for a retired guy in today's FBI would get the agent indicted.

didn't have separate hotlines for misogyny, homophobia, sexual harassment, gender equality, and racial prejudice.

The only hotline that you can't seem to reach is the criminal hotline.

The new crop of agents has thinner skins and an assortment of coordinators to contact if they feel offended, abused, or harassed. It became easier for senior agents to keep their trap shut and count the days to retirement. This led to a dysfunctional FBI family, and the result was a lost generation of agents. And make no mistake that it also led to agents like Peter Strzok, Andy McCabe, and James Comey.

So I picked up my cell phone and dialed the FBI office with jurisdiction over the alleged al-Qaida mosque. I pressed six for the Joint Terrorism Task Force and a recording asked to leave a message. I basically stated, "My name is John Ligato. I'm a retired FBI agent, and I have some reliable information on terrorist activities in your division. My number is…"

Two days later I repeated my message, and two days after that I was pissed. I understand that an FBI office receives hundreds of calls and must prioritize them, but there were three red flags that made my call special: I was a retired FBI agent, I used the buzzword "reliable," and the topic was the Bureau's number one priority—terrorism.

The FBI's recorded menu limits contact with a human except for the executive office. It's time to talk with the big boss and ask, "What the fuck is going on?!" I understand that there's little chance that anyone in the general public could cold-call an FBI office and speak with the SAC (Special Agent in Charge). They are rightfully protected by a palace guard of assistants who will take a message and then reply, "Someone will get back to you." But I'm not the general public.

When I finally was able to break through to a human being, a pleasant female voice asked, "Can I help you?"

"Yes, ma'am. I am a retired FBI agent, and I have reliable information of possible terrorist activities in your division."

"I'll connect you with the JTTF…"

"Wait! I've left several messages with them already."

"Okay, give me the information and someone will get back to you."

No one did, so I contacted the office again a week later and spoke with a switchboard operator who had no authority but at least was human. I decided to plead my case with him. I go through my spiel of being a retired agent, terrorism, etc., and actually whine, "This is *really* important."

The guy immediately challenges me with, "How do I know you're a retired agent?"

I have no answer and say, "Look, pal, I want you to connect me with the JTTF or the SAC right now."

"That's not an option. Stand by."

I'm connected to the same tip line where Tom and his source had already left messages. I make three pleas to speak with a real live FBI agent but am told on all three occasions, "That's not an option." Sounds like a script to me. It's now game on, and I have a secret weapon.

Retired assistant director Tony Daniels is my good bud and fellow Slippery Rock State College alumni. We catch up and I explain my problem, fully expecting Tony to say, "I'll handle it." But what he actually says is, "John, they won't return my calls."

It'd been twenty years since Tony retired, and the new group of SES types had never met AD Daniels. Tony operated a major investigative agency in DC and explained that over the last decade he lost access to the FBI contacts built over three decades. He explained, "I've tried to pass on cases we've worked for possible prosecution, and it's like I never worked for the B."

"But," Tony offered, "I'm having dinner tomorrow with a recently retired assistant director, so send me the information."

I sent it off and two days later the SAC of the office where the mosque is located calls and begins thanking me for passing on the info. There was no mention of the six-month delay or my inability to speak with a real live FBI agent.

After a moment of polite chit chat, I ask, "What the heck is going on with the FBI?"

The resulting conversation was both convoluted and painful, but the SAC did say, "This information is critical since we've suspected that particular mosque but couldn't get near it."

Of course, they couldn't because the FBI *can* physically surveil Burger King, Joel Osteen, Billy Joel, the Mormon Tabernacle Choir, synagogues, and the Catholic Church, but *not* mosques. The Catholics would especially welcome a squad of covert FBI agents due to the likely increase in the collection plate.

This whole snafu is another example of the structural defect in the FBI's armor that led to the Comey Gang. Although this specific incident may have merely delayed a case, there have been more disastrous results with the new Bureau.

CHAPTER 36:

"I Believe He's Gonna Shoot Up a School"

"The English think incompetence is the same thing as sincerity."
—Quentin Crisp

The public has difficulty communicating directly with an actual FBI crime fighter. In the good old days, John Q. Citizen could report a bank robbery in progress and the FBI would come running. Agents were assigned "complaint duty," and this seemingly boring task generated informants and solved crimes. Local people contacting local agents who understood local problems. If warranted, agents would personally meet with the caller, allowing them the opportunity to evaluate their reliability. Dial your local FBI office today to report a crime and a pleasant recorded voice will say, "If this is an emergency dial 911, but if you wish to provide information stay on the line." Remain on the line and you will be transferred to the FBI tip line located in West Virginia or DC.

The prompt to dial 911 is an admission that the Bureau no longer responds directly to crimes. I understand that police departments are the best first responders to emergencies, but there are exceptions. Years ago, I had an informant contact me who was threatened by a subject in my case. The bad guys had figured out that he was a snitch, and that makes for a dangerous situation. It was happening in real time, and I was reluctant to contact the local police due to the sensitive nature of the players. I was able to respond in time to prevent any violence. My point is that FBI agents need to be able to saddle up and quickly respond to legitimate threats, but we've become this burdensome, lethargic bureaucracy.

The FBI tip line is a crapshoot since some clerk is taking complaints and dependent on an agent to prioritize the information. This system often results in irritation, but recent failures have allowed dangerous criminals to fly under the radar.

A woman in Parkland, Florida, called an FBI tip line to describe a young man she knew with an arsenal of knives and guns who was "going to explode" and said she feared him "getting into a school and just shooting the place up."

She stated, "I do believe something's going to happen," according to a transcript from the tip line. Something did when nineteen-year-old Nikolas Cruz killed seventeen people after he stormed his former school, Marjory Stoneman Douglas High School, with an AR-15-style gun.

The FBI admitted that it had failed to act on the tip and follow protocols to assess the threat. Under FBI protocols, that information should have been assessed as a potential threat to life and forwarded to its Miami Field Office for further investigation.

But would those seventeen individuals have been saved had the Miami office received the tip prior to the shootings? Broward County Sheriff Scott Israel said in a press conference that his office had received approximately *twenty* calls about Cruz. He said the calls for service were "assorted," with some coming from callers in other states. His deputies did not necessarily go out and respond to each of the calls. Israel said that acting on the tip the FBI received would not necessarily have averted the shooting.

Unfortunately, Israel is correct. If agents *had* visited Cruz, their hands would have been tied. There's not enough manpower to surveil the Nikolas Cruzes of the world, and you can't just snatch up crazy people. The politicians can't have it both ways by failing to provide legislation to prevent attacks and then criticizing law enforcement once people are lying in pools of blood.

"We are still investigating the facts," FBI director Christopher Wray said in a statement soon after the shootings. "I am committed to getting to the bottom of what happened in this particular matter, as well as reviewing our processes for responding to information that we receive from the public. It's up to all Americans to be vigilant, and when members of the public contact us with concerns, we must act properly and quickly.

"We have spoken with victims and families, and deeply regret the additional pain this causes all those affected by this horrific tragedy," Wray added. "All of the men and women of the FBI are dedicated to keeping the American people safe and are relentlessly committed to improving all that we do and how we do it."

Florida governor Rick Scott called for Wray to resign over the matter. That is an extreme measure since Wray was new on the job and in charge of a massive bureaucracy. It will take time for the new director to reboot the Bureau.

"Seventeen innocent people are dead and acknowledging a mistake isn't going to cut it," Scott said in a statement. "We constantly promote *'see something, say something,'* and a courageous person did just that to the FBI. But the FBI failed to act. 'See something, say something' is an incredibly important tool, and people must have confidence in the follow-through from law enforcement."

The Justice Department was also critical of the FBI's handling of the tip. "It is now clear that the warning signs were there and tips to the FBI were missed," former attorney general Jeff Sessions said in a statement. "We see the tragic consequences of those failures." Sessions ordered Deputy Attorney General Rod Rosenstein to review how the Justice Department and FBI process and respond to indications of potential violence. The Bureau has made the attempt to *tighten up* their protocols for reviewing and prioritizing tips.

But the FBI's usual response to the aftermath of any major screw-up is to investigate what went wrong, apologize, find a soldier to fall on their sword, and mandate remedial training for the troops. How's that working?

CHAPTER 37:

Do Muslims Present a Law Enforcement Threat?

"Speak the truth, even if it is bitter."
—Islamic quote

Caving to Muslim pressure to edit FBI training manuals is a symptom of the political correctness inside the Bureau. Demands from Muslim pressure groups are likely to continue given the FBI's role in national counterterrorism. It's seems part of an overall effort to expand Islam worldwide but does that goal represent any concern to law enforcement? Most *major* changes begin with *minor* concessions. A shoreline doesn't erode overnight but over centuries.

Many Muslims immigrating to Europe and North America make demands that their new nation concede chunks of their culture to accommodate the new arrivals. There's a subtle distinction between *requesting* that a Muslim dish be *added* to a school menu than to *demand* that pork be *eliminated* from school menus. Muslims have insisted workers be given time from their jobs to pray, and that prayer rugs be placed in *every* Canadian subway station.

Sgt. Cesilia Valdovinos, a member the US Army's 704th Brigade Support Battalion who converted to Islam alleges her command sergeant major, pulled her out of rank and made her remove her hijab. Valdovinos asserted, "My religious preference is only to unveil in front of my husband in the comfort of my own home." Valdovinos further claimed she was removed from her post as a "culinary arts specialist" because of her *religious* preference to *not* handle pork. She filed a Military Equal Opportunity Office (MEO) complaint that was reportedly found to be "unsubstantiated." Valdovinos now intends to take legal action against the US Army.

The instances of Muslim demands at school and work increase each year. For example, three hundred Muslims walked off the job at a JBS Swift & Company meatpacking facility in Grand Island, Nebraska. They marched on city hall, complaining that they were denied time to pray at sunset during the month of Ramadan. Two days later, the company agreed to accommodate the demands. At what point does a Bob Mueller or the head of JBS Swift say, "No!"

Prior to 9/11, the FBI was woefully unprepared for foreign terrorist acts on American soil. We lacked Arabic linguists, intelligence, and the willingness to target radical mosques and organizations. The World Trade Tower attack revealed these weaknesses, but the eight years of the Obama presidency was mainly an attempt to appease rather than investigate radical Islamists.

Obama and Attorney General Holder placed administrative roadblocks in front of the FBI, and the result is another ticking time bomb. Is the FBI ready to battle homegrown terrorists now that the caliphate in Syria no longer exists?

Following the 9/11 attacks, the FBI attempted to hire Arabic linguists to aid in the war on terrorism. As discussed previously, in 2002 FBI linguist, Gamal Abdel-Hafiz, refused to interpret a secret recording of a Muslim suspect. He said, "A Muslim doesn't record another Muslim." Hafiz was promoted.

Let me get the obvious out of the way: Not all Muslims are terrorists *or* support terrorism. But do some Muslims represent a credible threat to America? The answer has *nothing* to do with religion but rather *assimilation*. A concerning number of Muslims who immigrate to America make minimal attempts to weave themselves into the fabric of our society.

I adopted two infants from Korea and am the grandson of Italian immigrants, so why would I want to close the door to any other ethnic group? The short answer is that immigration minus assimilation equals segregation. Think about it.

Let me *repeat*: Not all Muslims are terrorists or support terrorism. Some mullahs (spiritual leaders) teach the outright annihilation of Israel and America. This could be a deal breaker to those of us who may feel threatened living a few doors down from a mosque. That any American imam would refer to America as *the Great Satan* is cause for alarm.

The counterargument that the Bible teaches violence and death for nonbelievers is true, but current-day Catholics are not signing up for a modern-day Crusades or screaming, "Jesus is the Lord" seconds before mowing down innocent civilians with a car or an AK-47. There are the occasional murders perpetrated by Catholics based on their religious beliefs, primarily at abortion clinics, but they are few and far between.

One argument used by Muslims to justify their accommodation demands is that America was not founded on Judeo-Christian values. But it was.

The Declaration of Independence, the Treaty of Paris in 1783, and the Constitution are three documents that dispute that claim. The Declaration has many references to God. The Treaty of Paris was the document that ended the American Revolution and granted the United States independence from Great Britain. In a real sense, the United States formally became a nation on September 3, 1783. The preamble to this treaty states it is based upon the "Holy and Undivided Trinity." The concept of the Holy Trinity is *unique* to Christianity. The

Constitution honors the Christian Sabbath—when it was completed on September 17, 1787, the delegates signed it in the "Year of our Lord." This is a direct reference to Christianity.

Muslim demands on American institutions demonstrate their unwillingness to assimilate. Muslim families in Montgomery County, Maryland, demanded that the end of Ramadan (Eid al-Fitr) be added to the list of religious holidays, just like Christmas or Rosh Hashanah. But instead of adjusting the calendar, the school board caved to pressure and made their holiday schedule "religion neutral." Christmas is now "Winter break," and there is no such thing as "Easter break."

Many Muslims come from countries where Christians are persecuted and treated with disdain. Nine of the ten countries with the worst records for persecution of Christians have populations that are at least 50 percent Muslim.

When European immigrants migrated to the United States, there is no evidence that they demanded schools change their menus to accommodate their dietary needs. My mother didn't picket St. Thomas Aquinas school demanding the nuns serve me pizza and lasagna.

In 2011, French president Nicolas Sarkozy told his country that multiculturalism, Europe's grand experiment in expanded immigration, had failed in France. Sarkozy citied the growing segregation of segments of a Muslim population that is the largest in Europe. He criticized Muslims for pushing a cultural clash with France by insisting on veiled women and by praying "in an ostentatious way in the street."

France has also lost a portion of its public school system. A newspaper referenced a secret intelligence report under the headline "The Muslim Communalism Defies School System and Is Seeking to Gain Ground in the French Education System." The report cites *"chronic absenteeism"* of 90 percent during Muslim holidays not recognized by the state. It concluded that Muslim allegiance is to their own religious groups rather than to the society at large. French Prime Minister Manuel Valls warned of "separate Islamic societies." He used the words "isolation" and "wasteland" to describe certain Muslim districts and residents.

The government of Holland announced steps to increase counterterrorism surveillance of Muslim neighborhoods. In addition, they will slow down the overt messaging of radical Islam teachings in their schools.

Again, immigration *minus* assimilation equals segregation. The goal of the ethnic groups who immigrated to the United States before and after the Industrial Revolution was assimilation. Why else would one leave their native land and search for a better life? My grandparents learned the language and embraced the culture, and their children joined the American military. My father proudly served in Europe with the US Army during World War II and fought against Mussolini's Italian troops. Dad viewed himself first and foremost as an American. He loved his Italian heritage but never confused his loyalties. Dad never attempted to convert anyone to Catholicism or impose Italian law in South Philly.

Breitbart.com reported on a poll by the The Center for Security Policy that shows 51 percent of US Muslims want Sharia Law and 25 percent of those polled agreed that *"violence against Americans here in the United States can be justified as part of the global jihad."*

Though polls are only as valid as the pollsters, there exists enough statistical evidence to suggest that Muslims are less likely to assimilate at the rate of our European ancestors.

Muslims who migrated to Europe have been slow to celebrate the holidays and recognize the history and traditions of their new home. Some have no intention of assimilating. Many Americans falsely believe that the United States could never experience the European immigration model of Muslim segregation.

But President Obama settled 54,514 Somalia refugees in America during his presidency. Of that number almost 12 percent were sent to Minnesota, hence the election of Congresswoman Ilhan Omar. If US voting districts are inundated with any homogenous ethnic group, they will gain representation in government. That diversity normally constitutes a positive outcome in a democracy but only if the new arrivals assimilate.

Nahren Anweya is the Director of Special Projects for the Middle Eastern Women's Coalition. She spoke of visiting Omar's Congressional district, *"You won't even think you're in America."* If that trend continues in America, we will eventually create two Americas. Should the number of Muslim immigrants become significant, then immigration minus assimilation becomes invasion. This is both a local *and* federal law enforcement issue.

Representative Omar's Fifth Congressional District in Minnesota is an example of a ticking cultural and legal time bomb. The time will come when Muslims control some city councils and county commissions and push a sharia agenda. When that occurs, you'll have the equivalent of sanctuary Muslim cities with blurred lines of democracy and laws. England already has Sharia courts but they don't wield any real power. It's more of a resolution court for disputes among Muslims. Sharia law does not legally exist in any European country, but the trend of these *unofficial* courts is troubling.

Large pockets of segregated Muslim communities are a recipe for anarchy, and we need only observe Europe to see our own future.

Front Page Magazine published an article by Daniel Greenfield, a Shillman Journalism Fellow at the Freedom Center and New York writer focusing on radical Islam. He wrote that, "The city of Cologne, Germany recently took in 10,000 mostly Muslim refugees (adding to the) 120,000 Muslims already in the city making them more than 10 percent of the population. It has been estimated that Cologne will (eventually) become a majority Muslim city. On New Year's Eve 2016, the crowd outside the Cologne Cathedral was dominated by young Muslim men who threw fireworks at police and sexually assaulted women and girls trapped in the crowd. A crowd of 1,000 men, hundreds of them Muslim refugees prowled, assaulted and robbed any woman they could find."

Police arrested eight men, all carrying asylum papers. They were part of the refugees previously welcomed by the people of Cologne. Mayor Henriette Reker, who had vigorously advocated for the refugee immigration, was forced to declare it a crisis. Greenfield's article described a man who was unable to protect his wife and teenage daughter from the mob. A seventeen-year-old girl described being brutally violated and seeing other girls in the police station in the same condition.

CBS correspondent Clarissa Ward interviewed Abu Rumaysah, a member of *Sharia Patrol* in London. "I want to see Sharia in Europe, and I want to see it in America as well." Abu patrols the streets of London with other Muslim men harassing *Western* women and men who dare to drink alcohol, gamble, or dress inappropriately. "*You may not dress like that in Muslim area!*" the Sharia patrols shout, calling a woman in a short skirt "a prostitute."

Swedish police admit to *contested* zones since the 2013 Stockholm ghetto riots in which hundreds of cars and buildings were burned, the *Investors Business Daily* reports. "The police confirm that there are now vehicle checkpoints operated by Muslim gangs on the borders of these zones."

"A more precise name for these zones," says Middle Eastern expert Daniel Pipes, "would be Dar al-Islam—the House of Islam or the place where Islam rules."

The arrival of millions of asylum seekers is a chunk of the problem. Thousands of individuals are coached to claim danger in their home country. These claims are almost impossible to verify.

Using the Pew Research Center's most recent population estimates, here are some facts about the size and makeup of the Muslim population in Europe.

Statistics indicate that France and Germany have the largest Muslim populations in Europe. As of mid-2016 Muslims consisted of 8.8 percent of the French population and 6.1 percent of Germany. Muslims make up 25 percent of Cyprus which is part of the European Union.

The FBI will be very much involved if the segregation trend continues in the United States. Large pockets of unassimilated Muslims in cities is a recipe for disaster. Permitting Muslim groups to redact Bureau counterterrorism training documents is a symptom of this progressive disease. The fact that these ad hoc editors had terrorist ties added insult to injury.

For the United States to survive united and in harmony, there can only be one nation, one flag, and one people—Americans.

CHAPTER 38:

The Salem Witch Hunt

"You're on double secret probation."
—*Animal House*

The FBI rarely initiates a case based on gossip or anonymous sources. Our informants must be flesh and blood and provide reliable information. FBI supervisors will put an agent on the clock to either find evidence or close the case. A preliminary inquiry lasts ninety days and can only be extended by new facts and circumstances and not unproven allegations.

But special counsels have no time restraints and can go on for years before putting a scalp on the board. They routinely go fishing outside the scope of their original mandate. Robert Mueller had cast a massive criminal net in addition to investigating Russian interference with our 2016 election. This is inevitable with special counsels, and victims include an assortment of dead and injured fish, ranging from guppies to whales. Mr. Mueller revealed his biased hand by the mere act of selecting the targets of his investigation. He made no attempt to view Russian collusion as a nonpartisan sport by exclusively targeting conservative republicans.

In his order appointing Mueller special counsel, Rod Rosenstein wrote that his responsibility was to ensure a "full and thorough investigation of the Russian government's efforts to interfere in the 2016 election." But Mueller ignored all the red flags concerning Podesta and Hillary Clinton while concentrating totally on Trump.

Other players within the Russian-obstruction loop included Loretta Lynch, Bill and Hillary Clinton, Barack Obama, James Clapper, and the Comey Gang.

Peter Schweizer is the author of the book *Clinton Cash: The Untold Story of How and Why Foreign Governments and Businesses Helped Make Bill and Hillary Rich*, and he knows where the bodies are buried concerning the complex relationship between Clinton ally John Podesta and Russia. Schweizer feels that Podesta may have violated federal law when he failed to disclose his stock holdings in a Kremlin-funded company. In 2011, Podesta joined the board of a very small energy company called Joule Unlimited, based out of Massachusetts. The *Daily Caller* reported that about two months after he joined the board, a Russian entity called Rusnano put a billion rubles—which is about $35 million—into Podesta's company.

Rusnano is *not* a private company; it's directly funded by the Kremlin. In fact, the Russian science minister called Rusnano Putin's child. So, you have the Russian government investing in one of John Podesta's businesses in 2011 while he was an advisor to Hillary Clinton at the State Department. In 2013, Podesta became a special counselor to President Obama at the White House, which required him to fill out financial disclosure forms. According to the *Daily Caller,* Podesta's financial forms failed to disclose seventy-five thousand shares of stock that he had in Joule Unlimited. This is likely illegal. Podesta doesn't seem all too concerned about a loud rap on his door at 0500.

There is a subtle irony in the special counsel's investigation. Though some laws such as obstruction are interpretive, others are crystal clear. Hillary's guilt is apparent from the facts and in the plain language of the federal statute. It's called a prima facie case: "clear on the basis of known facts." And the individual who waived his legal magic wand proclaiming Hillary stupid but innocent was none other than James Comey. The circle of life.

The alleged obstruction conversation between President Trump and James Comey will never be known. Voice inflection, background, personal style, ethnicity, and even hearing loss can change the entire meaning and intention of a sentence. And, as anyone who is in a relationship will attest, people interpret words differently. This makes it legally and morally impossible to determine guilt in obstruction cases.

Mueller had a problem. After a two-year investigation there was no evidence of Trump colluding with the Russians. He completed his special counsel mission and handed the four-hundred-plus pages to Attorney General Bar who announced, "no collusion and no obstruction."

On the surface, Mueller's report seemed like a complete exoneration of the president, but it was actually an act of a vindictive man. The special counsel couldn't let Trump skate knowing that would result in his re-election in 2020. So he molded his words into a guided missile and placed it in the hands of the Democratic Party. "While this report does not conclude that the president committed a crime, it also does *not* exonerate him."

He left the back door open to obstruction knowing that the final two years of the Trump presidency would be impeachment gridlock.

By their nature, investigators have a predatory mind-set. They often make assumptions of guilt simply because *someone* had to do it. They view a lack of arrests, indictments, or convictions as a personal failure. When you add ideology and emotions to the mix, the victim becomes impartiality. Robert Mueller could *not* be impartial as a special counsel since he was conflicted from the start.

James Comey strongly inferred that the president attempted to obstruct justice, but Mr. Trump said, "It ain't so." James Comey and Robert Mueller are friends, and after Donald Trump fired Comey, the former FBI director leaked investigative memos and cried *obstruction*. This placed Mueller in the untenable position of deciding if his protégé was a liar and leaker.

The obvious danger with a prosecutor who lacks impartiality is in the interpretation of laws. The obstruction law makes it a crime to threaten, intimidate, or retaliate against participants in a criminal or civil proceeding. Some laws are not open to interpretation, but obstruction of justice is highly interpretive, and two attorneys can view identical facts and come to different conclusions. The special counsel report planted a legal IED set to explode in the Democrats' interpretation of obstruction.

The Mueller probe was intended to be limited in scope to Russian attempts to influence our election through collusion. But Deputy Attorney General Rod Rosenstein allowed Mueller to go rogue and unchained him to investigate financial crimes, concentrating on President Trump's family and friends.

The convictions of Manafort, Flynn, Papadopoulos, and any other individual caught in the Mueller web should be tossed. Mueller should've recused himself, but it's too late, which makes the special counsel findings forever tainted. It was predicated on lies that caused a chain reaction and ended in indictments, wasted tax dollars, and political energy that was needed elsewhere. Had the FBI and Robert Mueller not known that the Steele dossier was gossip, then they acted in good faith, but this was not the case. The FBI and members of Mueller's team were briefed by Bruce Ohr that the information used in the FISA warrant was BS, yet they certified it as fact anyway. Talk about the fruit of the poisonous tree.

There's no disputing that Russia utilized its intelligence capabilities to screw with America. That's what a foreign entity does. Russia pretends to be a democracy, but it's a dictatorship that despises American values. And as you are reading this, American intel officers are attempting to somehow screw with the operation of the Russian government. That's what we do. If America is *not* conducting covert intel operations against Russia, China, and North Korea, then we are derelict in our duties.

If Russia attempting to influence our 2016 election assaults your ethical sinuses, then so should America's attempt to influence an Israeli election.

In 2016, a congressional investigation concluded that the State Department paid hundreds of thousands of dollars in taxpayer grants to an Israeli group. It was no secret that Israeli prime minister Benjamin Netanyahu and President Obama had a mutual distaste for each other. This prompted the US president to spend $350,000 in tax dollars to oust the Israeli prime minister. The money went to an organization called OneVoice, which used it to build a voter database and train political activists to get rid of Netanyahu. They even kicked back some money to a political consulting firm with ties to Obama's campaign. A US Senate subcommittee confirmed that OneVoice mentioned its intent in an email to a State Department official in Jerusalem.

And if you're interested, the Easter Bunny died.

The FBI's Shift to the Left (A Look at Recruitment/Mentoring)

"Liberalism is the wolf on the sled dog team."
—Susan Stamper Brown

Many recent FBI hires tend to be more suited for academia rather than meeting some snitch named Scrotum at a warehouse at midnight. I've seen agents assigned to the violent crimes squad that shouldn't be dealing with violent criminals. I'm not advocating that we exclusively recruit MMA fighters or US Army Rangers. A diverse workforce in terms of ethnicity, gender, and subject matter expertise is critical to accomplishing the FBI mission in 2020 and beyond.

Is it possible to tinker with the FBI selection process to skew the hiring of liberals or conservatives? Candidates must be at least twenty-three years old but no older than thirty-seven at the time of appointment. Other requirements include US citizenship, a four-year degree from an accredited college, a valid US driver's license, and at least three years of professional work experience.

Sounds simple enough, but probably 25,000-plus people apply each year for only 500 to 750 agent positions. The Bureau has its pick of the employment litter, and they somehow cull the herd based on objective criteria. Most of it, anyway. The cognitive and psychological test is standardized, but the interview comprises 60 percent of the total score. The overwhelming majority of applicants have master's, law, PhD, MBA, or Ed.M. degrees, and one agent I met had a veterinarian medical degree. These individuals have no difficulty passing the preamble tests.

Jonathan Gilliam, a former US Navy SEAL, wanted to be an FBI agent, and prior to being interviewed he received some advice. Two FBI agents separately advised Gilliam to "go in and think like a liberal. Do not go in and take that test thinking like a SEAL."

"Do that," they cautioned, "and you'll fail."

Gilliam took their advice. "And that's what I did, and I passed."

Though the interview questions may be standardized, they provide enough clues to determine your leanings. There's also the chitchat that occurs before and after the interviews. The FBI should examine its recruiting criteria and make sure that ten liberals don't land in one place and attempt to overthrow the government. That's what happened with the Midyear investigative team, aka the Comey Gang.

Bill Gertz is a senior editor at the *Washington Free Beacon* and national security columnist for the *Washington Times*. He discussed the Bureau's movement from conservative to liberal values. It occurred simultaneously with Mueller's blending of the FBI with the Justice Department. A coincidence? I think not.

Gertz wrote that under President Barack Obama, "The FBI suffered a string of failures that critics blame on the FBI being pressured by liberal, politically correct policies that emphasized multiculturalism of its workforce over competence and results."

We can probably consider Mueller's concession to Muslim political groups CAIR and ISNA tinkering with the FBI's training manuals a failure. In fact, the one recurring theme during the Obama-

Holder control of the Justice Department was the conscious effort to water down terrorist attacks. Obama was running for re-election and declared lone wolf attacks on American soil a thing of the past. It was a false claim, and the FBI was a willing participant to reinforce the narrative that the administration had defeated terrorism.

The FBI's shift to the left on Obama's watch was evident when, contrary to the evidence, Bureau officials initially put out word that various lone wolf attacks had no link to terrorism.

Gertz wrote, "Similarly, when North Korea conducted a major cyber attack against Sony Pictures Entertainment in 2014, the FBI agent heading the probe at first said there was no foreign involvement in the hack."

In another case of note, after a supporter of Senator Bernie Sanders shot a Republican congressman and four other people in Alexandria, Virginia, the FBI sought to minimize the politics of the incident. The agent running the investigation, Tim S., told reporters the shooting was "spontaneous," despite evidence the shooter had a list of targeted members of Congress. Giving the killer the benefit of the doubt really strains common sense.

Why would our government paint a false narrative regarding terrorist threats to America? Perhaps they didn't wish to panic the public, but that theory doesn't wash since they are all too ready to immediately point their partisan fingers at any right-wing nut who shoots up a synagogue.

There is a certain irony in the FBI's recent turn to the left, steered by the Comey Gang but jump-started by Mueller. Ideology suddenly became a factor in investigative decisions. The checks and balances that apply to the field do not apply to headquarters. If an FBI supervisor opens a case in Memphis, he'll assign a case agent to investigate. New cases are designated as "initial inquiries," and the clock is ticking. After ninety days the case agent must demonstrate some progress, and if there is none the agent can either request an extension, close the case, or designate it in the limbo of "pending inactive."

The seventh floor at FBI headquarters can basically ignore the checks and balances required of the field. Much like the special counsel, they can dig indefinitely, using the most intrusive investigative techniques until they find *something*. Due to the government's unlimited resources, this constitutes a slam dunk.

The FISA warrant is an example of their abuse of power. The standard for the government to listen to a citizen's private conversations is extremely high. A judge granting a Title III must assure themselves that the government has attempted *every other* investigative technique since monitoring someone's private talks is considered a *last* resort. But the Comey Gang had no real oversight. They were the top of the bureaucratic heap and conspiring with the political Justice Department to short-circuit the intent of the law. Sally Yates, James Comey, Loretta Lynch, Andy McCabe, Bill Priestap, Peter Strzok, and the others who endorsed, approved, authored, and authorized the FISA application were all in the same ideological bed.

The FBI needs to recruit individuals with some real-world experience and common sense. People who had been punched in the nose at least once *before* the FBI Academy. That's not to say that we require knuckle-dragging dinosaurs, but the pendulum has swung too far away from *agents* like Joe Pistone. Joe had the formal education combined with the experiences growing up in melting pot of Patterson, New Jersey.

Though the Bureau requires a minimum of three years' professional experience for special agent jobs many recent hires lack *real-world* experience. Five years in some office cubicle or the womb of an academic setting does not necessarily prepare one for a law enforcement career. What constitutes real life experience? Maye a year or two in Africa working for the Peace Corps, waiting on tables at some diner, coaching youth sports, working construction, or being deployed to the sand box with the Army.

These *real*-life interactions round out the candidate making them better prepared to deal with informants and match wits with criminals who may lack formal education but have PhD's in common sense and instinct. There was an agent chosen for an undercover assignment with the Italian Mafia. The guy was full-blooded Italian with Sicilian ancestry right out of central casting for a wise guy role. His only problem was that he grew up in rural Kansas and knew nothing about the Italian culture. After a month, two wise guys got together and announced, *"Something ain't right about that guy."* Although they couldn't articulate the specifics, their instincts were spot on and they refused to interact the undercover.

The public is not aware that all FBI agents *must* retire at the age of fifty-seven. The rationale may have something to do with the aging process affecting your ability to subdue a two-hundred-pound psycho. This requirement may have made sense a few decades ago, but the majority of fifty-seven-year-old FBI agents haven't lost a step and could still bench press a two-hundred-pound bad guy. The unintended result of this arbitrary age requirement is its effect on mentoring and the loss of subject matter experts. Entire generations of new FBI agents are deprived of the veterans' institutional knowledge.

This is a simple fix. Agents that can pass the physical fitness test, qualify at firearms, and are rated "Outstanding" on their job performance get to stay.

In the span of sixteen years, liberal directors Robert Mueller and James Comey transformed the FBI from an illustrious crime-fighting organization to a politically correct retribution machine that was answerable to no one.

Comey no longer attempts to hide his disdain for conservatism. He lied about the Steele dossier when denying knowledge of who paid for it. If he wasn't lying, then he was incompetent since he signed three of the FISA applications on Carter Page without verifying the reliability of the source or the information.

I doubt that there are any statistics on the breakdown of liberals versus conservatives within the FBI. I served for several decades and can't recall a single conversation that would indicate an agent's political bent. Squad bay conversations centered on family, cases, sports, firearms, and office gossip. There probably were some political conversations, but none that caused any lasting heartburn. I'm guessing that agents of my era were more conservative since many of us were veterans and cops.

Is there a danger recruiting agents from only one side of the pond? Director Wray should review the application process. Who knows what he'll find.

Available voter registration information shows that thirteen of the seventeen members of Mueller's team had registered as Democrats, while four had no affiliation or their affiliation could not be found. Mueller made the identical mistake that Comey made when staffing the director's office with like-minded folks.

A different viewpoint can be very helpful.

In a 2017 analysis for the *Washington Free Beacon*, Bill Gertz wrote, "Once a bastion of conservative anti-communism under long-time director J. Edgar Hoover, the FBI has become one of the more liberal political agencies of government, and some critics say appears increasingly to operate outside normal constitutional controls."

The FBI is a paramilitary organization with a chain of command and a degree of danger. In my estimation, former military personnel make the best law enforcement officers. The transition from the military to law enforcement is seamless. Veterans aren't clock watchers and will cover your butt, because that's how they're wired. That's very comforting when you're busting through some door executing a search warrant.

Which I was about to do right after posting the new agent. Frank had recently transitioned directly from the Marine Corps to the FBI. He still had that new-agent smell to him.

"You got the back door."

The rookie nods and asks, "What are my orders?"

"Anyone comes out that's not wearing one of these blue raid jackets, you detain them."

The former Marine nods again, but there's another question lurking in his gourd, so I clarify: "This is *not* a practical problem at the FBI Academy. If they're armed and point a gun your way, then shoot 'em. If they're just escaping and get past you, then wave good-bye and we'll round them up later. But *don't* leave your post."

"I'm good to go."

Executing a narcotics search warrant is a dangerous proposition. There are a few things that *really* piss off drug dealers. Their short list consists of cops and snitches but especially rip-offs. When screams of "FBI" or "Police" precede the splintering of the front door, bad guys must make split-second decisions on how to protect their product. If it's cops, the options include toilet flushing, secret hiding places, and a rare shoot-out. But if it's a basic rip-off, they'll shoot it out almost every time.

Knock-and-announce is a legal requirement when executing search warrants, but it's often ignored when dealing with drug dealers. The entry team busts the door off its hinges, *then* screams "FBI" and spreads out, clearing rooms. The good news is that nobody's home, but we do seize some cocaine and I head back to the office to process the evidence.

About an hour later it dawns on me that Frank is missing. I'd been busy with the paperwork and didn't count heads as we left. I ask a few agents who'd been on the raid, "Anyone see Frank?"

Killer recalls, "He was standing near the back door of the house when I left."

I radio Frank on his handie-talkie and ask, "What's your 20?"

"I'm still at the back door like you told me."

It turns out that no one relieved the former Marine from his post. Some of you reading this may find this behavior odd, perhaps lacking initiative or common sense, but as Colonel Jessup stated in *A Few Good Men,* "You want me on that wall. You need me on that wall!" Well, it was Frank's turn on the wall.

I was recruited into the FBI by a former nun. J. Edgar Hoover was barely cold when his successor, L. Patrick Gray, opened the door for female agents. On July 17, 1972, Joanne Pierce Misko and Susan Roley Malone were sworn in as FBI Special Agents.

Joanne was a former nun and Susan, a former Marine, making this duo a diverse beginning for lady agents. As an individual who attended Catholic school for twelve years and later joined the Marines, these two trailblazers seemed perfectly recruited.

FBI agents of the 1970s and 1980s included many veterans and police officers. Almost every squad had military veterans and the FBI I knew was totally color-blind. If wounded, we'd all bleed blue. The most frequent word I heard upon joining the B was "family." Agents were transferred to strange locations where their only support system was the FBI family. A transfer from Helena, Montana, to New York City can be a shock to the system and seem like a foreign country. But the arrivals were met by agents and spouses who guided them to the best physicians, schools, neighborhoods, grocery stores, and babysitters. Their welcome included sweat equity and food while the household took shape. I keep hearing that those days are gone with an "every man for himself" attitude.

How do new agents learn the customs, traditions, and unwritten rules of the Federal Bureau of Investigation? Trial and error seem like a dangerous option, but the one practice that has maintained the FBI standards of excellence is *mentoring.* You won't find any written mentoring guidelines, but it's an indispensable tool.

Mentoring is a ritual where senior agents school new agents on the do's and don'ts. Two circumstances have basically eliminated this crucial survival skill. The first is the reconfiguration of office space, and the second change is that the later generations of agents are easily offended. The old FBI office spaces were large open squad bays with four desks abutted to each other. Senior agents would listen to new agents' phone calls, quiz them later, and offer such advice as "Don't ever tell an AUSA your snitch's business," or "You fucked up that 302; *never* include an opinion."

Mentoring worked, and it took many different forms.

A week after I graduated from the FBI Academy, I was sitting at my desk in the Pittsburgh Field Office when the PA system loudly announces, "*Bank robbery!*" They rattled off the name and location of the bank along with a description of the suspects. I notice agents writing stuff down, then gather their coats, guns, and keys and hurry out the door. The posse is heading toward their horses to chase the bank robbers, but I'm unsure of my duties. New agents had a thirty-day probation period back then, and today was day eight, so I sit like some inanimate lawn ornament. When the pack had gone, a squad secretary approaches me and says, "John, you *may* want to go to cover the bank robbery."

I head out the door, take the elevator down to the street, and run two blocks to the garage where I mount my stead. It's an old, rusted swayed-back Chrysler with a million miles, no air conditioning, and a Motorola police radio the size of a jukebox. As I pull out of the garage, it dawns on me that I have no idea of the bank's location. The radio is busting with the nonstop chatter of *real* agents and though I may be an FNG, I am not stupid enough to interrupt with a transmission of, "Where's the bank?"

I'm rolling down Forbes Avenue when I spot a pay phone, jump out, and call the switchboard. Armed with the bank's location, I hit the gas and attempt to catch up with the pack but am stuck in traffic. I gaze at the passenger seat and notice a blue dome emergency light, then look for the siren toggle. *Bam, shazam!* I hit the siren and feel like a real-life cop just like my dad, the Philadelphia police officer. The blue light is a portable magnetic dome that you plug into the cigarette lighter and place on the roof of the car.

Two things happen in quick succession, both bad. The blue dome falls off the roof and crashes onto Forbes Avenue, which is closely followed by the plug, which hits my chin as it joins the dome. I later discover that my car roof was vinyl, which unfortunately is *not* magnetic.

I somehow reach the bank and run up the steps, halting at the yellow evidence tape. The gash on my chin is leaking blood on my white-on-white shirt. My brain is in civilian mode, but I'd watched enough police shows to understand that *no one,* but cops, cross the yellow tape lest they contaminate a crime scene.

Standing at the top of the steps and chomping on a cigar is the FBI bank robbery coordinator, Special Agent Ralph Young. He is a large man sporting a modified fedora and a rep for being rottweiler mean to rookie agents. Ralph just stares at me as I stand frozen inches from the yellow evidence tape.

He finally asks, "You a fuckin' agent?" Which is a rhetorical question since Mr. Young has observed me roaming the office for the past week.

"Yes, sir."

"Well, go clean yourself up, then get your ass inside the bank and act like a fuckin' agent. Interview someone!"

So that's what I did, but it isn't the last chapter of Ralph's tutorial on new agents in need of remedial training.

The next day Ralph Young invites me to his desk, where he alternately berates me while also providing the critical do's and don'ts not covered at the FBI Academy. It's a fascinating insight into the unwritten rules of surviving both the criminals *and* the bureaucrats. I take the ass-chewing in stride and at its conclusion, Ralph smiles and offers me a cigar.

That type of critical mentoring could never happen in today's Bureau. Ralph would've been suspended for the mere act of raising his voice, let alone cussing at another agent.

The victim of this latter-day political correctness would have been me.

CHAPTER 40

A Drive-by Gang Audit

"What the hell is a *smidgeon*?"

President Obama declares, there's "not even a *smidgeon* of corruption, I would say."

FBI agents are courageous and ready to do battle with the likes of "Machine Gun" Kelly and mobster John Gotti, but they'll turn to jelly upon receiving an audit letter from the Internal Revenue Service. The IRS is like a sausage-grinding machine that slowly but inevitably grinds meat into rubbery string. They paper you to death like the Chinese water torture of unending dripping documents on your head. An official document in a mailbox with an IRS logo produces instant panic.

Lois Gail Lerner is an attorney and former director of the Exempt Organizations Unit of the Internal Revenue Service. In 2013, she became the central figure in the IRS targeting of conservative groups. Lerner accomplished her mission by either denying them tax-exempt status outright or delaying that status until they could no longer take effective part in upcoming elections. She eventually resigned over the controversy.

Lois Lerner appeared before the House Committee on Oversight but refused to testify, instead offering a statement, saying in part: "I have not done anything wrong, I have not broken any laws, I have not violated any IRS rules or regulations, and I have not provided false information to this or any other congressional committee."

She uttered these words after taking an oath to tell the truth, yet Lerner's first three disclaimers were lies. After declaring herself innocent, she invoked her Fifth Amendment right not to incriminate herself, but she'd already accomplished that in her brief opening statement.

The House voted to hold Lerner in contempt of Congress, but the FBI said it found no evidence to support criminal charges, or none that were pursued by the Obama Justice Department. I am guessing that the more accurate course of this nonaction was Justice's *own* complicity in the IRS scandal.

The Obama administration attempted to clear itself of wrongdoing in a 2015 investigation that claimed to find "substantial evidence of mismanagement, poor judgment and institutional inertia" but "no evidence that any IRS official acted based on political, discriminatory, corrupt, or other inappropriate motives that would support a criminal prosecution."

Lerner retired and is living in her Bethesda, Maryland, home with her attorney husband, collecting a nice taxpayer-funded pension. I'm still not clear what "institutional inertia" means, but it appears to have something to do with lazy government workers.

A few years later, the government watchdog group Cause of Action Institute discovered that in October 2010 Lerner transferred 1.5 million pages of confidential tax documents from the IRS to Obama's Department of Justice. This action almost certainly broke the law and cast a new light on the Justice Department's decision not to prosecute Lerner.

If you follow the crumbs, the Obama administration used the powerful IRS to harass nonprofit conservative groups that the administration considered their political enemies. Obama surrogates publicly skewered the conservative Tea Party, painting them with a KKK brush.

Evidence of Lerner's alleged criminal activity include the transfer of the nonprofits' Schedule B forms, which are attachments that require the names and addresses of organization donors. Disclosing the conservative organizations' donors sent a clear message by placing them in the Department of Justice's crosshairs, thus making them gun shy to contribute further to conservative causes. The Justice Department had no legal right or authority to access these files minus a criminal investigation, which wasn't the case.

This is the sort of stuff of enemies lists, which was among the activities included in the articles of impeachment drafted against Richard Nixon that hastened his resignation in August 1974.

During the 2014 Super Bowl, Fox News correspondent Bill O'Reilly interviewed President Obama at halftime. Part of that interview concerned the IRS scandal.

> **O'Reilly:** You're saying no corruption? [Regarding the IRS]
> **Obama:** No.
> **O'Reilly:** None?
> **Obama:** No. There were some…there were some
> bone-headed decisions…
> **O'Reilly:** Bone-headed decisions…
> **Obama:** …out of…out of a local office…
> **O'Reilly:** But no mass corruption?
> **Obama:** Not even mass corruption, not even a smidgeon of cor-
> ruption, I would say.

At the time President Obama offered the "smidgeon" comment, his legal advisor had received communication that IRS headquarters was involved in targeting conservatives. A short time after this interview, a federal judge ordered the release of additional emails that indicated Obama was lying. His staff received documents that proved that Lois Lerner had met with DOJ's Election Crimes Division a month *before* the 2010 elections.

But when conservative watchdog groups demanded the additional IRS documents, the Department of Justice aggressively resisted releasing them, citing, "taxpayer privacy" and "deliberative privilege."

Deliberative privilege is bureaucratic mumbo jumbo for "We don't want to tell you." The only thing missing is "Nanna nanna boo boo."

Of course, the Justice Department wasn't about to share documents that made them complicit in what amounts to criminal activity. But the question is, did Lois Lerner meet with the Department of Justice and plot a conspiracy against conservative groups?

The answer is yes. DOJ's Richard Pilger, Director of Election Fraud, *admitted* that DOJ officials met Lerner in October of 2010. In fact, documents from a Freedom of Information Act lawsuit against the IRS show that Lerner asked the DOJ whether tax-exempt entities could be *criminally* prosecuted. Your government just upped the ante from harassment to incarceration for the crime of being conservative in a liberal administration. This occurred two years *before* the IRS conceded there was inappropriate targeting.

At the time of the 2014 Super Bowl interview, Obama's Justice Department under Eric Holder possessed documents and conducted meetings with Lerner that disputed the president's claim of "boneheaded decisions" out of a "*local*" (Cincinnati) office.

Lerner worked in DC, the Justice Department and Holder worked in DC, and the president's residence was the District of Columbia. But that constitutes only circumstantial evidence, so the question becomes, why didn't the Justice Department report Lerner's targeting of conservative groups? They knew but did nothing. Perhaps it's because the conservative groups granted nonprofit status may rally conservative voters and knock Obama out of office.

Lois Lerner had the president's talking points since she continually blamed "low-level" IRS employees in the Cincinnati office. A few years later, Lerner testified in a civil suit against the IRS by conservative groups but convinced the judge to seal her testimony due to threats on her life.

The *Cincinnati Enquirer* and the IRS employees she blamed have been fighting unsuccessfully to make her version of events public. Lerner and Obama's outright lies require the disinfectant of light, and the "low-level" employees need a public apology.

AG Holder was likely briefed regarding Lerner's meetings with the Justice Department employees, and the chances Obama was kept in the dark on a political issue are slim to none. They were good buds, and Holder often acted as a political arm of the Oval Office.

Though there is significant *circumstantial* evidence of a crime, the Lerner case lacks direct evidence. Short of an admission by the guilty parties, the court would require witnesses or documents.

There just happened to be *lots* of documents. The House Oversight Committee issued a press release revealing that the IRS sent a 1.1 million-page database containing taxpayer information of tax-exempt organizations to the FBI in October 2010, several weeks *before* the midterm elections. The FBI should not be receiving unsolicited confidential taxpayer information from the IRS unless they are involved in an active criminal investigation. The Justice Department said "it was informed by IRS officials that it [the database] contains legally *protected* taxpayer information that should *not* have ever been sent to the FBI and it now plans to return the full database to the IRS."

Translation: We got caught. Lerner never logically explained why she sent taxpayer information to the Justice Department unless she suspected criminal activity. And if she did articulate that suspicion, then why predominately conservative groups?

In addition, FBI documents indicated that top IRS officials in Washington, including Lois Lerner and Holly Paz, knew that the agency was specifically targeting Tea Party and other conservative organizations two full years *before* disclosing it to Congress and the public. *Knowing* is a component of criminal activity. The Latin term is "mens rea," which is a person's awareness of the fact that his or her conduct is criminal.

Lerner was director of the IRS Exempt Organizations Unit and Paz was the IRS acting director of Rulings and Agreements. A dynamic liberal duo who weaponized the IRS to target opposing views.

IRS agents' investigative interviews confirm that in 2013, "Senior IRS officials *knew* that [IRS] agents were targeting conservative groups for special scrutiny as early as 2011." Unsurprisingly, the Obama Justice Department and FBI "investigation" into the IRS scandal resulted in *no* criminal charges. The FBI director was Bob Mueller, the AG was Holder, and the president was Obama. At this point in our history, the FBI was a political agency.

A class-action lawsuit by the aggrieved groups was settled in Ohio and DC, with the IRS *admitting* to the illegal behaviors. The government ordered a $3.5 million settlement to be paid out.

On May 2, 2013, the Internal Revenue Service apologized for subjecting Tea Party groups to additional scrutiny during the 2012 election but denied any political motive. Don't hurt your brain in attempting to follow this IRS disclaimer.

Why did the government apologize and pay millions of dollars for an admission of targeting political groups if it was *not* motivated by politics? It certainly wasn't a computer error that targeted these conservative groups but a high-level government bureaucrat. Perhaps the government is playing word games as to what constitutes politics.

The "doesn't anyone go to jail anymore" chapter has an addendum. The entire IRS saga supports that premise since the Comey Gang and the Holder-Lynch Department of Justice worked in concert to pick and choose who was prosecuted based on ideology. Had the FBI been an independent entity in 2010–2011, Lois Lerner would have been indicted. No one expected President Obama or Eric Holder to do time, but there *was* a crime committed and admitted to by the IRS.

But according to President Obama, there was no mass corruption, "not even a *smidgeon* of corruption."

CHAPTER 41

Collusion Between the FBI and Clinton

> "Why, you speak treason!"
> "Fluently."
> —*The Adventures of Robin Hood*

As a retired FBI agent, it was painful to watch Peter Strzok testify before Congress. He wreaked of arrogance, and many of my fellow retirees wanted to reach into the television and choke that condescending smirk off his face. Strzok is a prime example of why FBI agents should maintain a very low profile. His television testimony singlehandedly transformed our image of steely-eyed silent heroes to pompous bullies.

Comey gave immunity to five Hillary Clinton State Department aides and IT experts. Those aides included Cheryl Mills, Clinton's former chief of staff, along with two State Department staffers, John Bentel and Heather Samuelson, in addition to Clinton's IT aide, Bryan Pagliano, and Paul Combetta, an employee at Platte River Networks, the firm hired to manage her server after she left the State Department.

Combetta googled Reddit for technical advice on how to strip a VIP (*very* VIP) email address from archives. He acknowledged that the archives were stored on a server that he had "full access to." Combetta's online moniker was "Stonetear" and the "VIP" was Hillary. When the poop hit the server, Combetta used the computer program Bleach Bit to destroy Clinton's records. This would normally not present a problem except for the order from Congress to preserve them.

Just for the record, this is obstruction of justice, and had it been ABC (anybody but Clinton), FBI agents would've cuffed them.

As an FBI agent, there are times when you'll offer immunity to the smaller guppies to catch the whale. But they are limited and conditional on the guppies providing information leading to the whale's capture. If you have evidence of a crime on the smaller fish, then you call the shots. Immunity is the last resort and not the best investigative technique. (That would be a Proffer, which was previously discussed.) Immunity is only given if you are 99 percent certain that the person has information of criminal activity and, more importantly, is willing to share it.

Comey may have broken the unofficial immunity record on Hillary's email case.

Comey inexplicably limited the FBI's ability to review Clinton's email archives from Platte River Networks that were created *after* June 1, 2014, and *before* February 1, 2015. The limitations in the immunity agreements with Ms. Mills and Ms. Samuelson also kept the FBI from looking at emails after Secretary Clinton left office. This is the exact period in which any communication concerning the destruction or concealment of federal records would have taken place. Why would he do so?

Title 18, Section 1519 of the federal code covers the destruction, alteration, or falsification of records in federal investigations and bankruptcies. A portion of the statue states:

> Whoever knowingly alters, destroys, mutilates, conceals,
> covers up…any record…with the intent to impede,

obstruct, or influence the investigation…shall be fined
under this title [or] imprisoned not more than 20 years.

Hillary destroyed thirty thousand emails *after* receiving a
Congressional subpoena to preserve her electronic communications.
She testified under oath, *and* with a straight face, that the disappeared
emails were all personal in nature concerning wedding plans and yoga
routines. Except that James Comey found classified material after
retrieving some of the deleted emails. So, James "*Impartial*" Comey
offered absolution for *four* federal violations: storing classified material
on an insecure server, destruction of public records, obstruction, and
perjury.

In March 2015, Hillary's legal advisors Cheryl Mills and David
Kendall had a conference call with Paul Combetta of Platte River
Networks. This is the location of Clinton's server, but Comey's limitations and immunities prevented the FBI from reviewing its records.
Combetta was initially untruthful until he received an immunity
agreement and by his third interview with the FBI admitted that *after*
the March 2015 call he used the Bleach Bit to destroy any remaining
copies of Clinton's emails. Bleach Bit is a software program designed to
prevent *forensic* recovery.

What immediately comes to mind is that Mr. Combetta may be
guilty of Title 18, Section 1001 for lying to the FBI, obstruction of justice, destruction of evidence, and contempt of Congress. I don't know
where the guy is now, but it's *not* the gray-bar hotel.

It's been documented that Obama knew about Clinton's clandestine email server and participated in email exchanges with his secretary
of state.

Mr. Comey's final statement on July 6 acknowledged "there is evidence of potential violations of the statutes regarding the handling of
classified information." But he nonetheless cleared Secretary Clinton
and ignored evidence of possible obstruction that resulted from the

destruction of emails known to be under subpoena by the House of Representatives. This courtesy did not, however, extend to conservatives or Trump allies.

Mueller and Comey operate under the scorched earth policy. Mueller indicted Manafort and Cohen to gain their cooperation. They are sleazy white-collar criminals and would've gotten pinched somewhere down the road. The problem is that Mueller misused the criminal justice system. If he wanted to make some white-collar arrests, he could have walked into any DC lobbyist firm and seized their books.

Jamming up someone to roll on bigger fish is done all the time. The first words out of any narcotics cop after every arrest are, "Who's your supplier?"

So why does this entire special counsel thing stink? Maybe it was the SWAT teams breaking doors down to arrest several geriatric nonviolent white-collar guys, or maybe it was the fact that Andrew Weissmann knew that the entire investigation was bullshit from day one, or perhaps it was the fact that Mueller needlessly destroyed many, many lives.

Comey began drafting an exoneration statement prior to interviewing the main subject (Hillary) in the case. This has never been the customary sequence of events with any law enforcement agency. Several FBI officials came to Comey's defense, stating that declaring someone innocent in the middle of the investigation is a normal practice.

But Matthew Miller, a former spokesperson for the Justice Department, tweeted, "The decision is never made until the end, even when there's a 99 percent chance it is only going to go one way."

Chris Swecker, who retired from the FBI in 2006 as assistant director for the criminal investigative division and acting executive assistant director for law enforcement services, told *Newsweek*, "That is just not how things operate…It's built in our DNA not to prejudge investigations, particularly from the top. To me, this is so far out of bounds it's not even in the stadium."

We may not be able to read the mind of James Comey, but we can judge his actions. The FBI director and his family had demonstrated sympathies toward the Clintons while suspecting President Trump of obstruction. He approved a FISA warrant that included unverified information about urinating Russian hookers and leaked official memos to the press.

Why did Bob Mueller hire Strzok and Page? The two were madly texting anti-Trump sentiments and were instrumental in the FISA warrant that begot the special counsel. It was only *after* Inspector General Horowitz exposed Strzok and Page's animus toward the president that Mueller canned them.

The FBI chief legal counsel was James Baker, who is very close to former FBI director James Comey. The two men were colleagues at the Justice Department and then at Bridgewater Associates, an investment management firm. After Comey's appointment to the FBI, he asked Baker to be his chief general counsel.

Just hours after FBI deputy director Andrew McCabe delivered private testimony to the House Intelligence Committee, new FBI director Christopher Wray announced that Baker would be leaving his post. At first no one was paying attention to FBI chief legal counsel James Baker. It was only after Baker was removed from his FBI role that things added up.

There was a core group of FBI and Justice staff determined to permanently send Trump packing back to Mar-a-Lago. It included Strzok, Page, Comey, McCabe, Baker, Ohr, Rosenstein, Lynch, Yates, and some others hiding in the DC weeds. This core group initially attempted to prevent the Trump presidency, and after that failed, they went the way of Russian collusion.

The Russia collusion investigation may have been just another way the players within the original scheme could keep a lid on the events in 2016 and still retain the insurance policy. The backstory to the FISA warrant is the key to exposing the entire sham. *That* warrant required illegal actions by the FBI and the DOJ upper management and leadership.

In December of 2018, former FBI director James Comey approached microphones following two days of contentious testimony before House lawmakers.

"The FBI's reputation has taken a big hit because the president with his acolytes has lied about it constantly," Comey lectured the assembled reporters following the final closed-door session with the House Judiciary and Oversight and Government Reform committees.

Comey solemnly concluded: "At some point, someone has to stand up and face the fear of their base, fear of mean tweets, stand up for the values of this country and not slink away into retirement but stand up and speak the truth."

This book is an attempt to do just that, Mr. Comey.